Oh My Goddess!

ああっ女神さまっ　The Queen of Vengeance

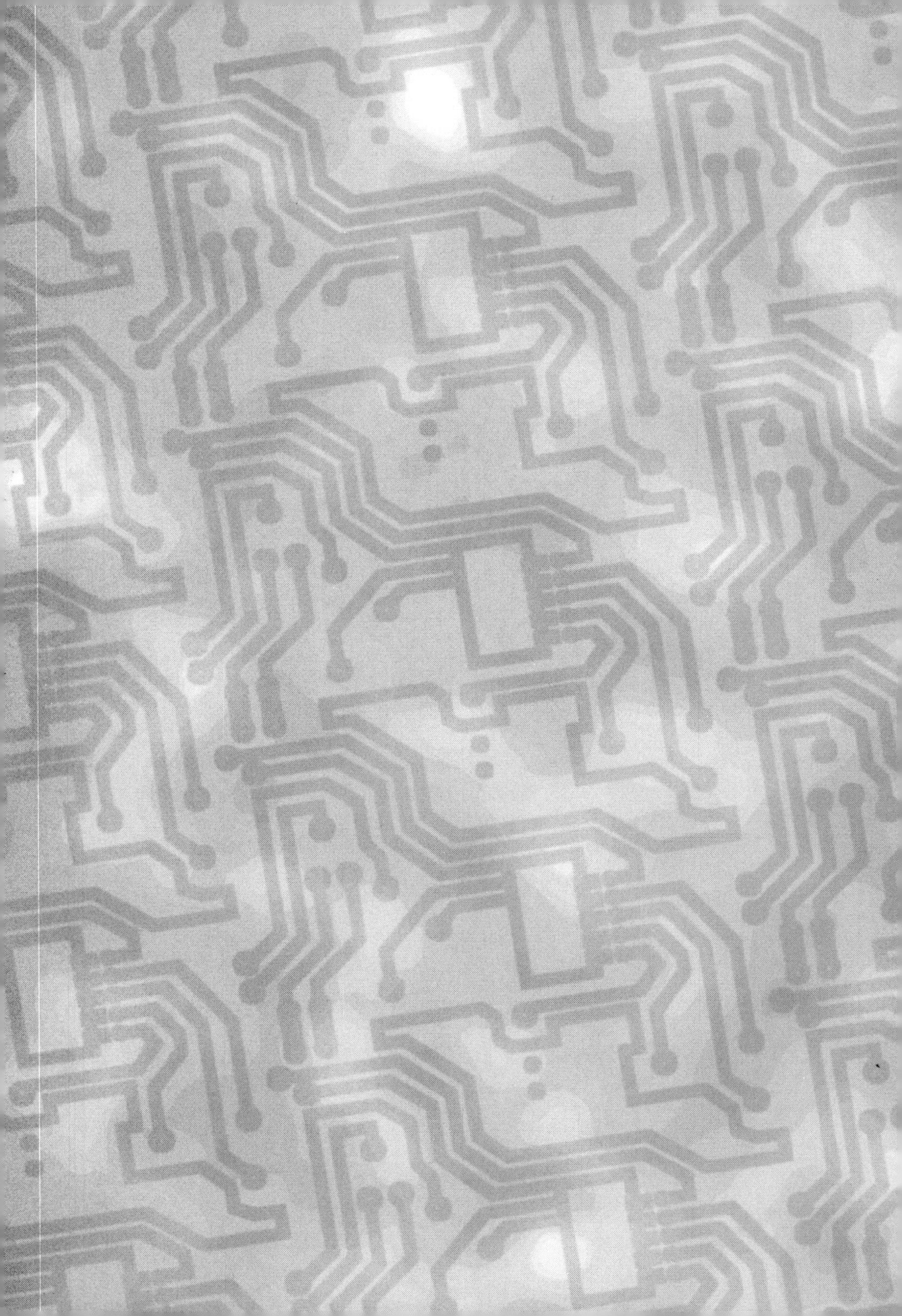

Oh My Goddess!

ああっ女神さまっ **The Queen of Vengeance**

STORY AND ART BY

Kosuke Fujishima

TRANSLATION BY

Dana Lewis & Toren Smith

LETTERING AND TOUCH-UP BY

Susie Lee & PC Orz

DARK HORSE COMICS®

PUBLISHER
Mike Richardson

SERIES EDITOR
Dave Chipps

COLLECTION EDITOR
Chris Warner

COLLECTION DESIGNERS
Amy Arendts & Julie Eggers Gassaway

ART DIRECTOR
Mark Cox

English-language version produced by Studio Proteus
for Dark Horse Comics, Inc.

OH MY GODDESS! Volume VII: The Queen of Vengeance

This book collects issues one through five of the Dark Horse comic-book series *Oh My Goddess! Part IV.*

Published by
Dark Horse Comics, Inc.
10956 SE Main Street
Milwaukie, OR 97222

www.darkhorse.com

To find a comics shop in your area, call the Comic Shop
Locator Service toll-free at 1-888-266-4226

First edition: November 1999
ISBN: 1-56971-431-2

3 5 7 9 10 8 6 4
Printed in Canada

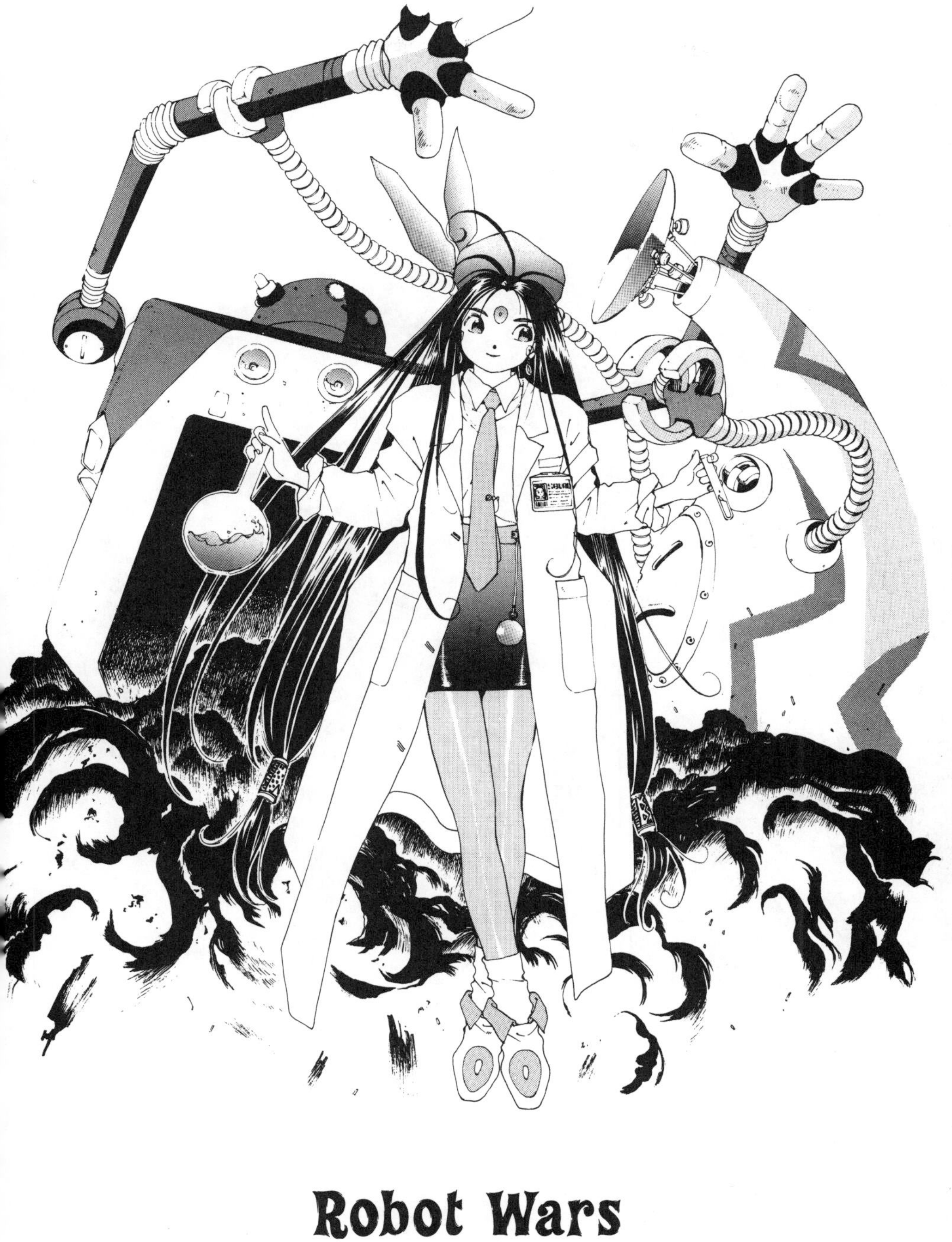

Robot Wars

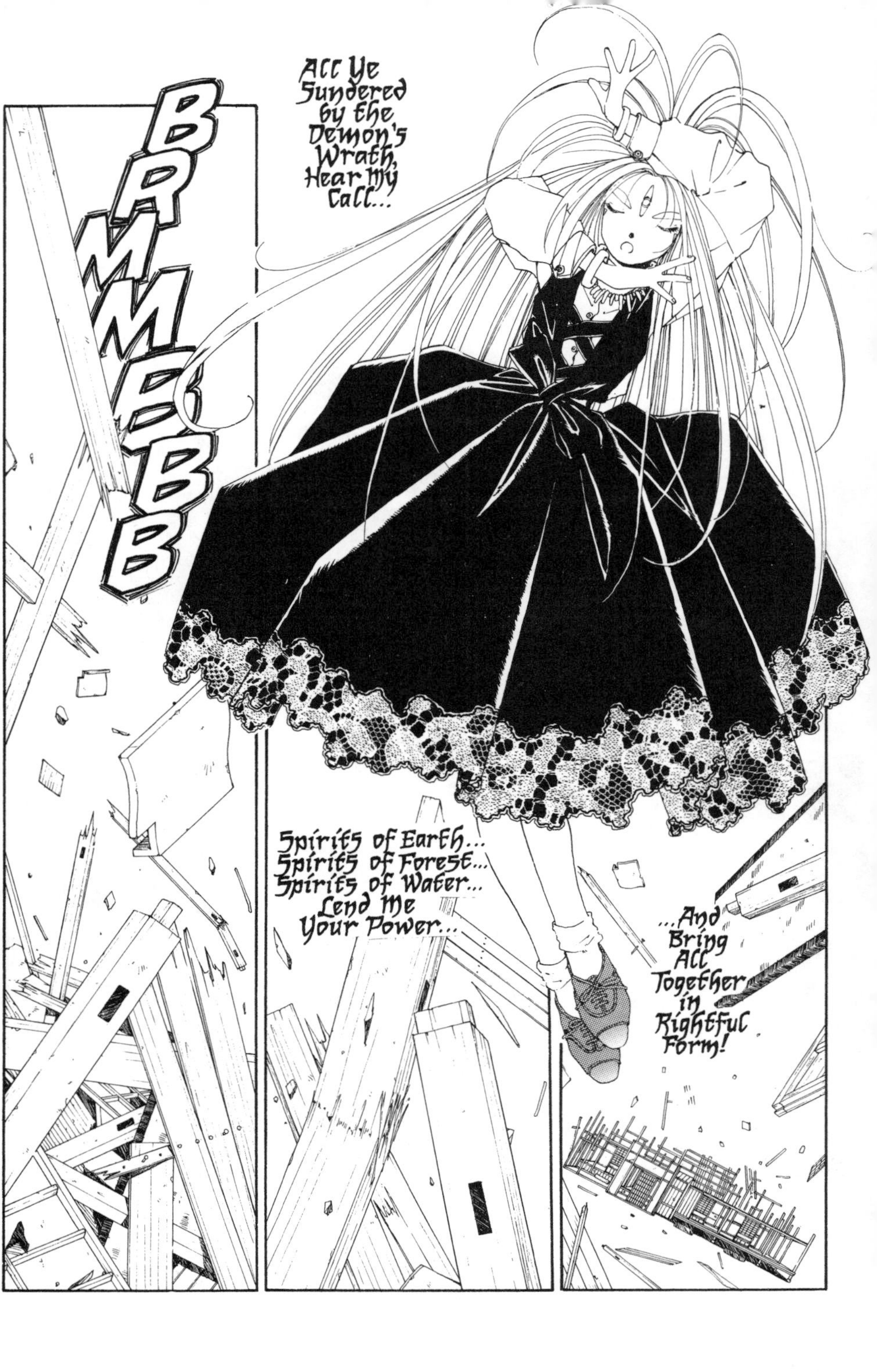
All Ye Sundered by the Demon's Wrath, Hear My Call...
BRMMEBB
Spirits of Earth... Spirits of Forest... Spirits of Water... Lend Me Your Power...
...And Bring All Together in Rightful Form!

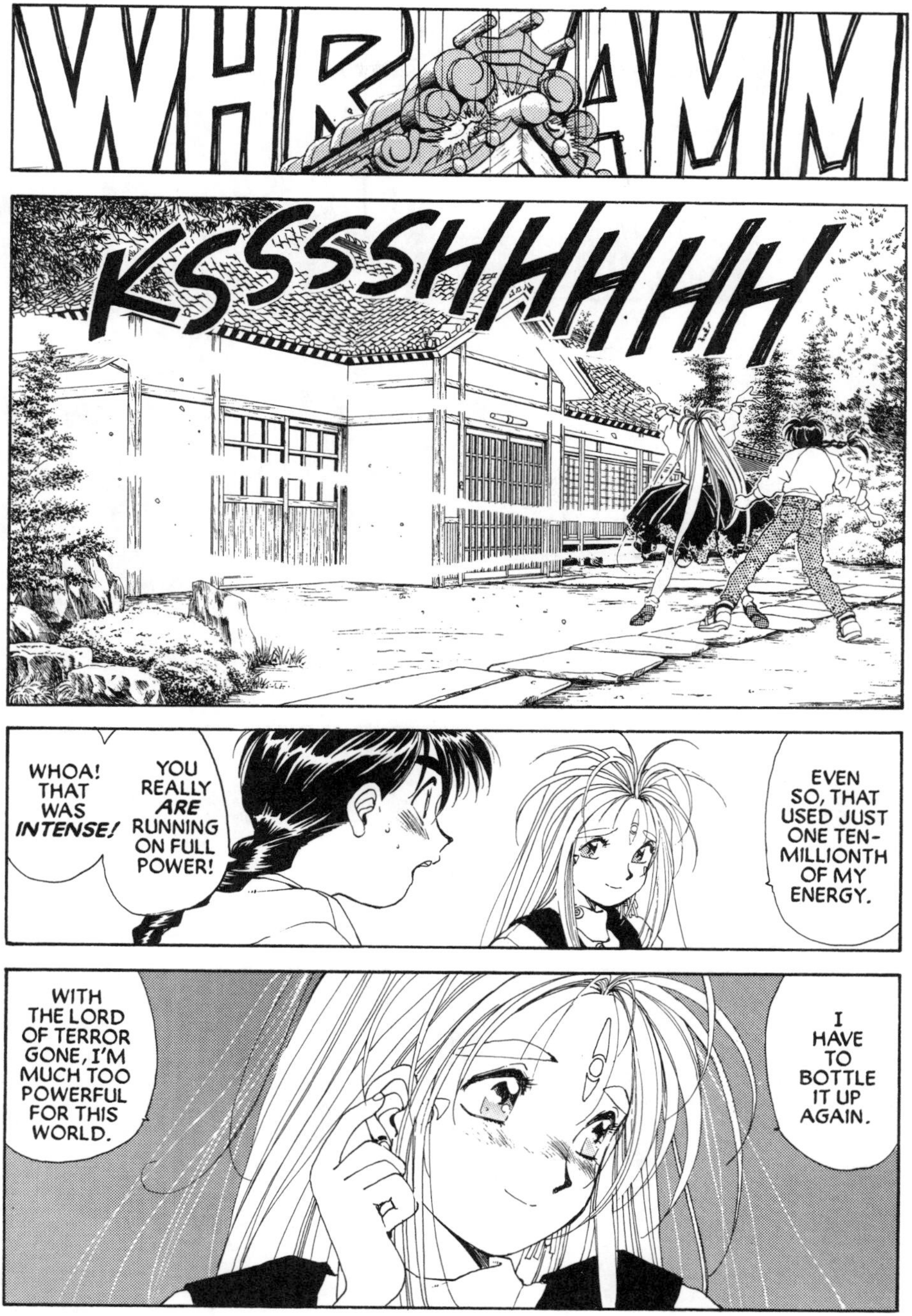
WHRAMM
KSSSSHHHHH
WHOA! THAT WAS INTENSE!
YOU REALLY ARE RUNNING ON FULL POWER!
EVEN SO, THAT USED JUST ONE TEN-MILLIONTH OF MY ENERGY.
WITH THE LORD OF TERROR GONE, I'M MUCH TOO POWERFUL FOR THIS WORLD.
I HAVE TO BOTTLE IT UP AGAIN.

HEY, *KEIICHI!* I'VE WHIPPED UP A NICE, NEW BEDROOM JUST FOR YOU TWO LOVEBIRDS!

UMM, BELLDANDY? CAN I ASK ONE LAST FAVOR BEFORE YOU...

THERE!

THAT'S BETTER... NOW EVERYTHING'S THE WAY IT WAS BEFORE.

SHEESH... THAT'S THE THANKS YOU GET!

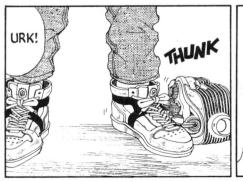

URK!

THUNK

ALAS, POOR *BMW!* I KNEW IT WELL...

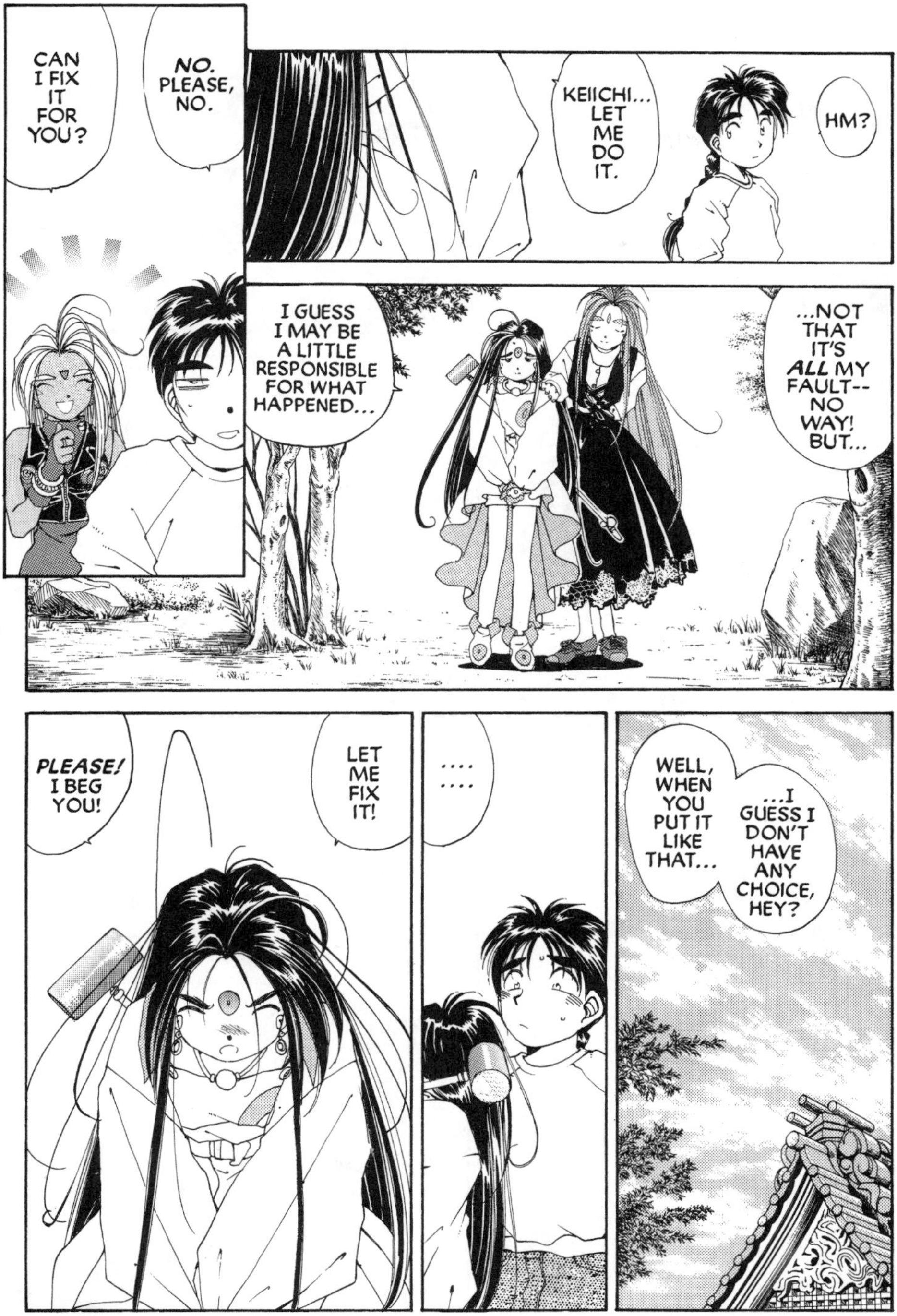
CAN I FIX IT FOR YOU?
NO. PLEASE, NO.
KEIICHI... LET ME DO IT.
HM?
I GUESS I MAY BE A LITTLE RESPONSIBLE FOR WHAT HAPPENED...
...NOT THAT IT'S ALL MY FAULT-- NO WAY! BUT...
PLEASE! I BEG YOU!
LET ME FIX IT!
....
WELL, WHEN YOU PUT IT LIKE THAT...
...I GUESS I DON'T HAVE ANY CHOICE, HEY?

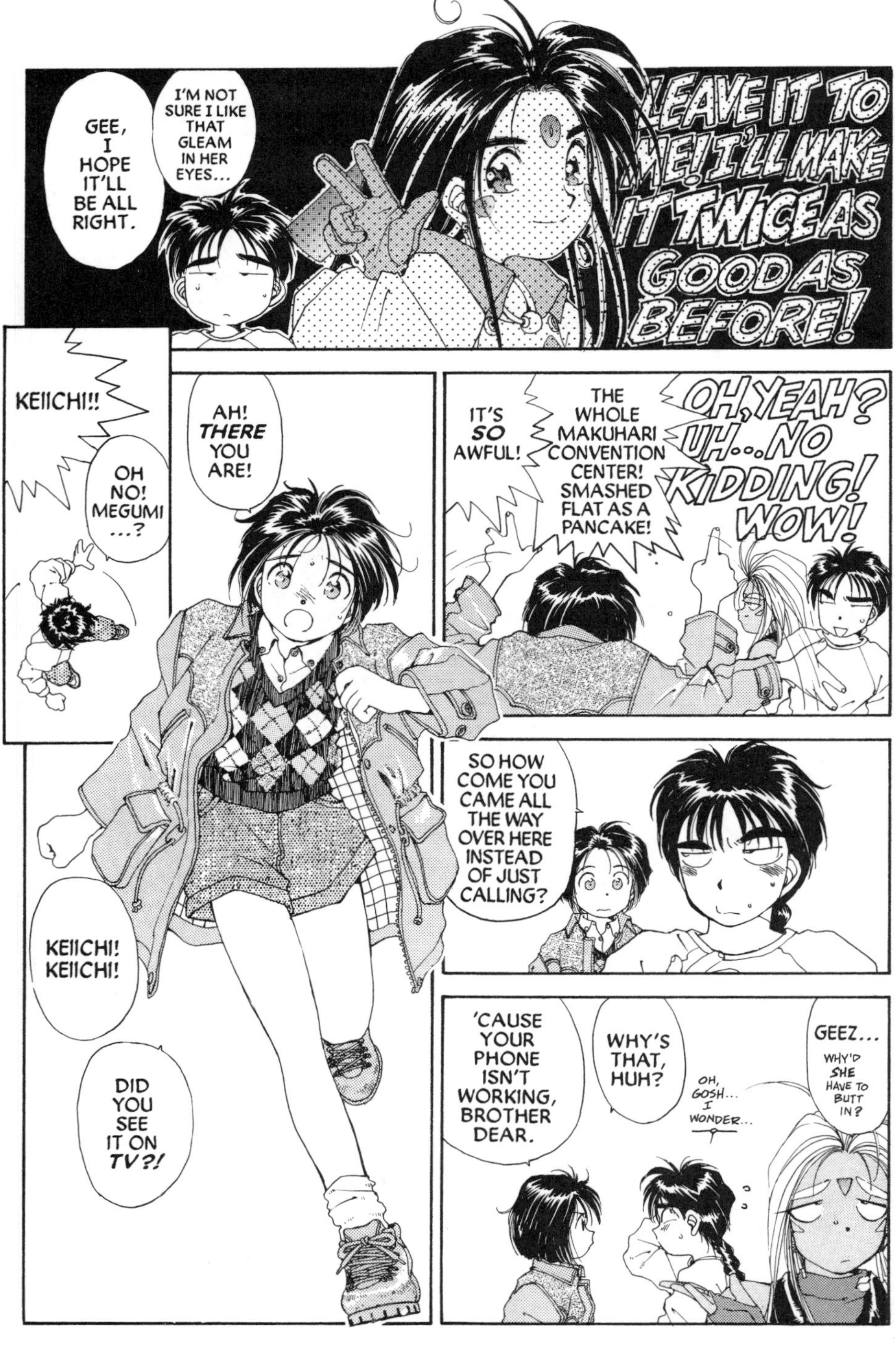

GEE, I HOPE IT'LL BE ALL RIGHT.
I'M NOT SURE I LIKE THAT GLEAM IN HER EYES...
LEAVE IT TO ME! I'LL MAKE IT TWICE AS GOOD AS BEFORE!
KEIICHI!!
OH NO! MEGUMI...?
AH! THERE YOU ARE!
KEIICHI! KEIICHI!
DID YOU SEE IT ON TV?!
IT'S SO AWFUL!
THE WHOLE MAKUHARI CONVENTION CENTER! SMASHED FLAT AS A PANCAKE!
OH, YEAH? UH...NO KIDDING! WOW!
SO HOW COME YOU CAME ALL THE WAY OVER HERE INSTEAD OF JUST CALLING?
'CAUSE YOUR PHONE ISN'T WORKING, BROTHER DEAR.
WHY'S THAT, HUH?
OH, GOSH... I WONDER...
GEEZ... WHY'D SHE HAVE TO BUTT IN?

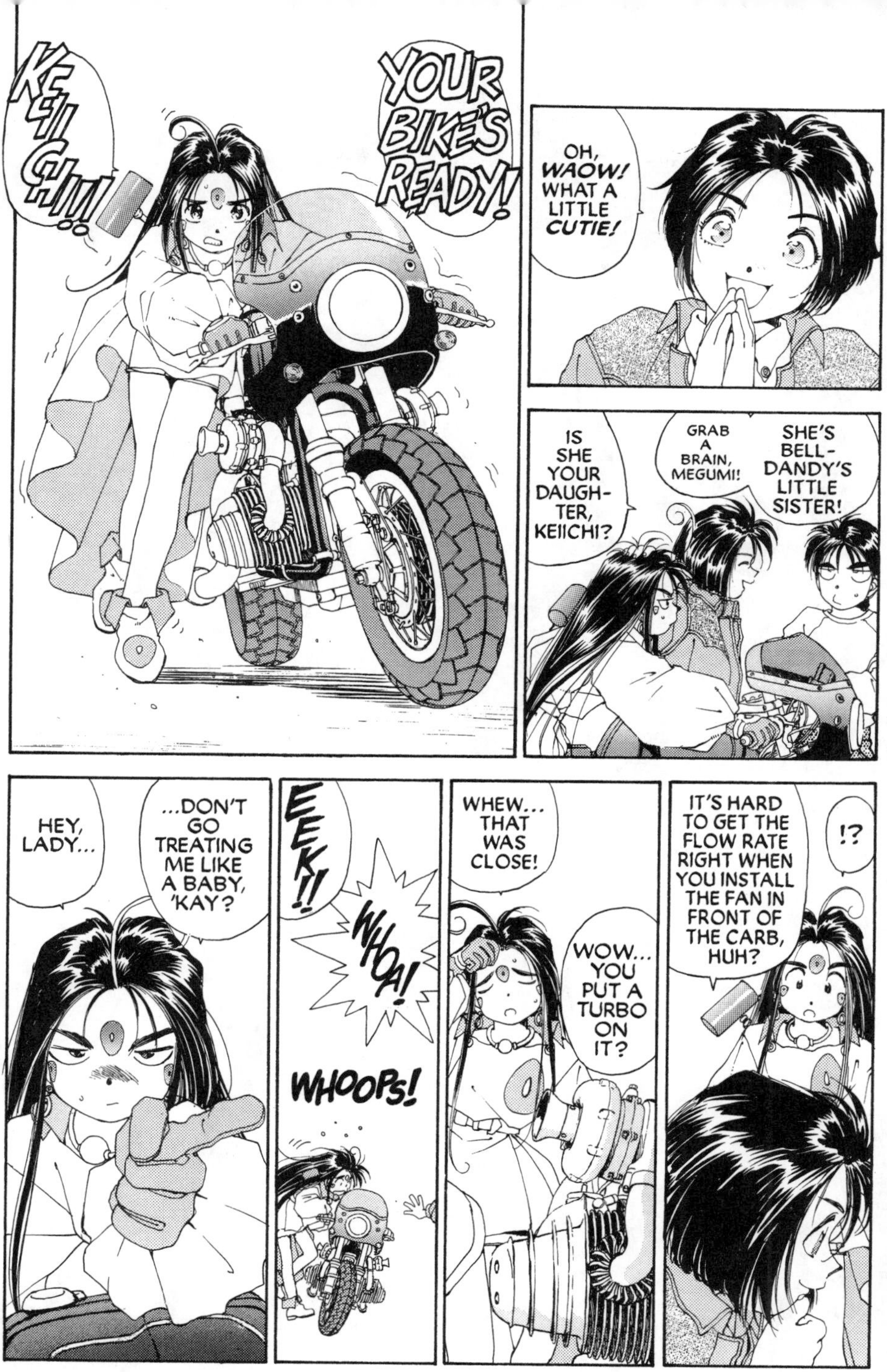
KEIICHI!!
YOUR BIKE'S READY!
OH, WAOW! WHAT A LITTLE CUTIE!
IS SHE YOUR DAUGHTER, KEIICHI?
GRAB A BRAIN, MEGUMI!
SHE'S BELL-DANDY'S LITTLE SISTER!
HEY, LADY...
...DON'T GO TREATING ME LIKE A BABY, 'KAY?
EEK!!
WHOA!
WHOOPS!
WHEW... THAT WAS CLOSE!
WOW... YOU PUT A TURBO ON IT?
IT'S HARD TO GET THE FLOW RATE RIGHT WHEN YOU INSTALL THE FAN IN FRONT OF THE CARB, HUH?
!?

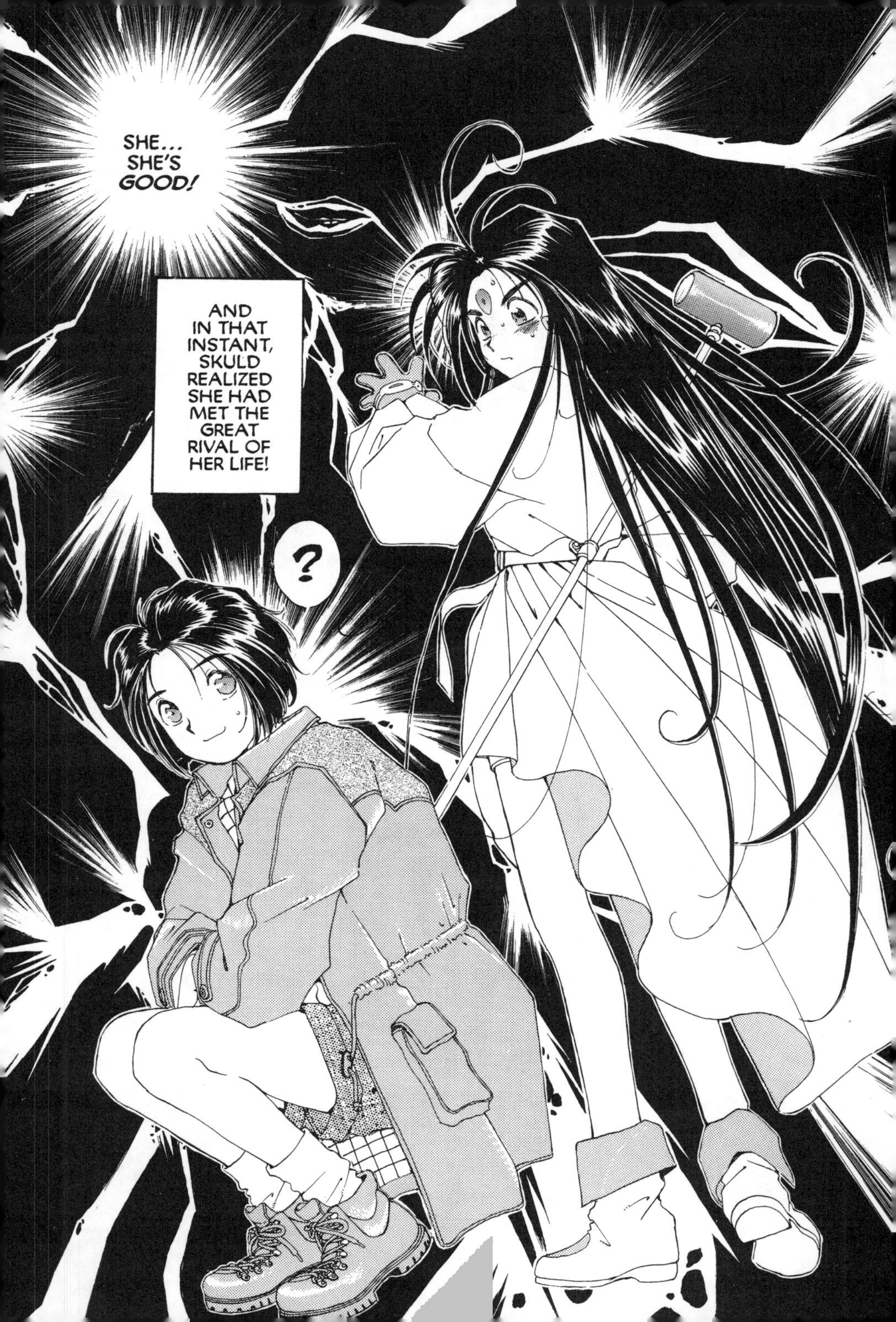
SHE... SHE'S *GOOD!*
AND IN THAT INSTANT, SKULD REALIZED SHE HAD MET THE GREAT RIVAL OF HER LIFE!
?

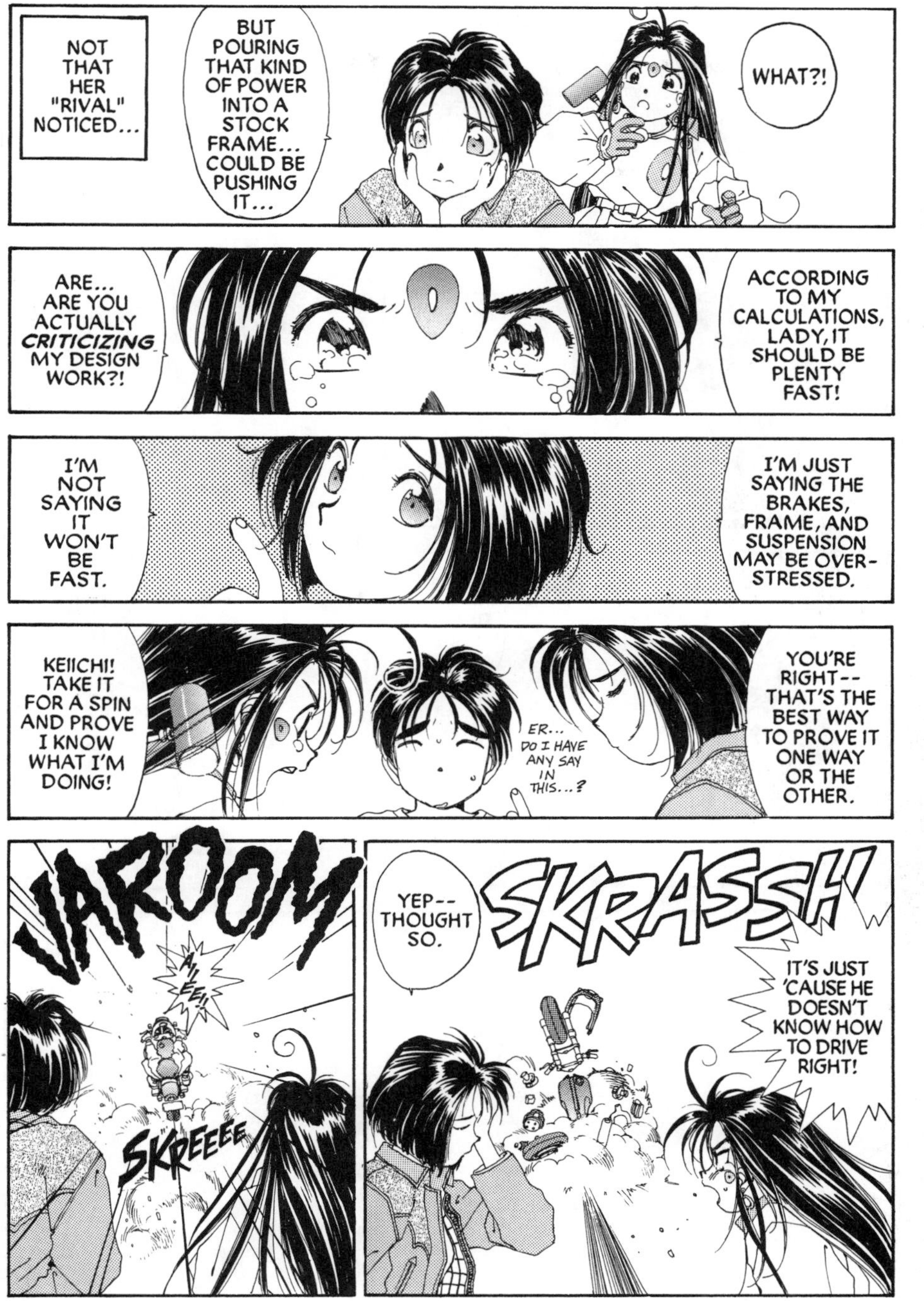
NOT THAT HER "RIVAL" NOTICED...
BUT POURING THAT KIND OF POWER INTO A STOCK FRAME... COULD BE PUSHING IT...
WHAT?!
ARE... ARE YOU ACTUALLY *CRITICIZING* MY DESIGN WORK?!
ACCORDING TO MY CALCULATIONS, LADY, IT SHOULD BE PLENTY FAST!
I'M NOT SAYING IT WON'T BE FAST.
I'M JUST SAYING THE BRAKES, FRAME, AND SUSPENSION MAY BE OVER-STRESSED.
KEIICHI! TAKE IT FOR A SPIN AND PROVE I KNOW WHAT I'M DOING!
ER... DO I HAVE ANY SAY IN THIS...?
YOU'RE RIGHT--THAT'S THE BEST WAY TO PROVE IT ONE WAY OR THE OTHER.
VAROOM
AIEE!!
SKREEEEE
YEP--THOUGHT SO.
SKRASSH
IT'S JUST 'CAUSE HE DOESN'T KNOW HOW TO DRIVE RIGHT!

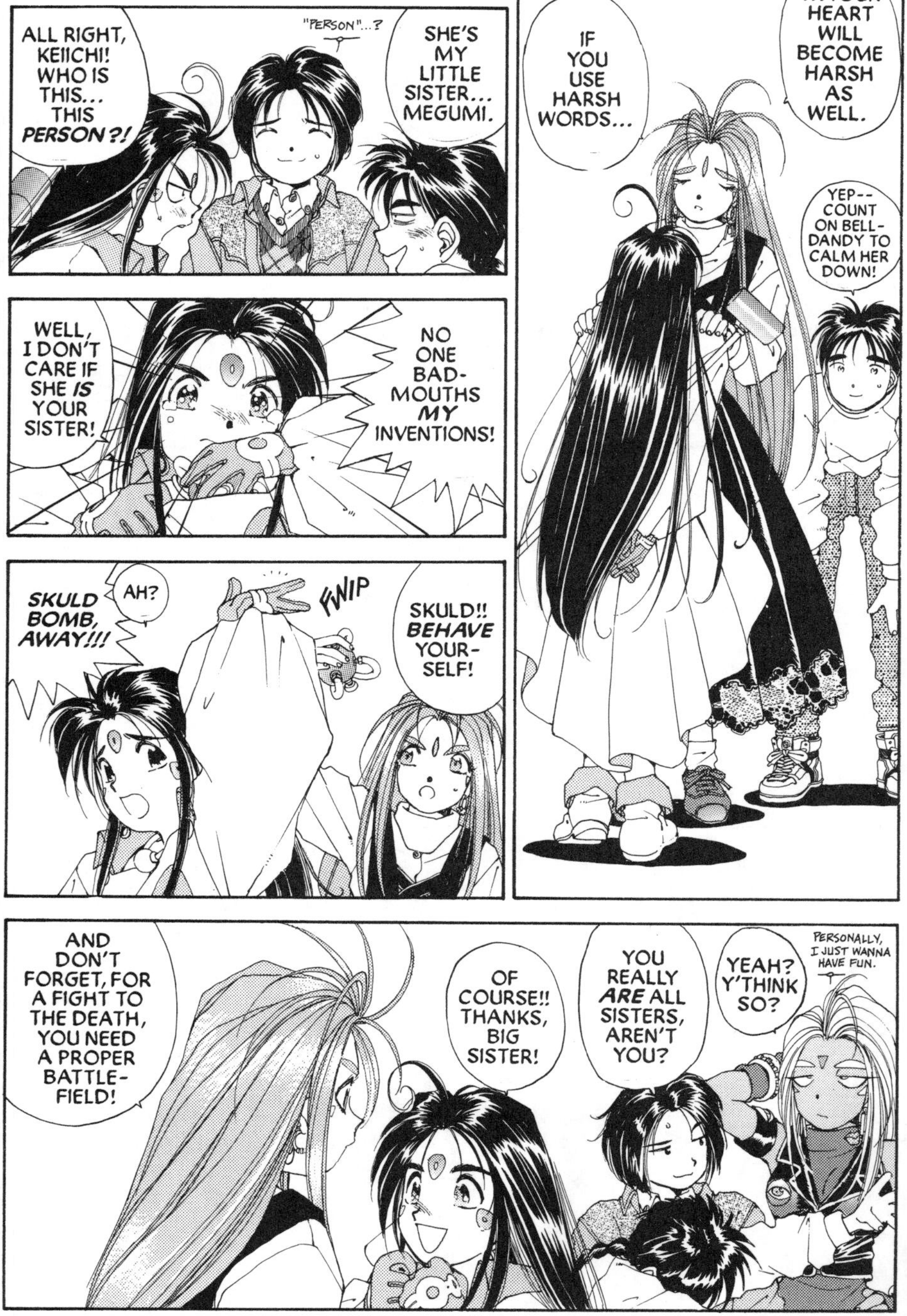

ALL RIGHT, KEIICHI! WHO IS THIS... THIS PERSON?!
"PERSON"...?
SHE'S MY LITTLE SISTER... MEGUMI.
WELL, I DON'T CARE IF SHE IS YOUR SISTER!
NO ONE BAD-MOUTHS MY INVENTIONS!
SKULD BOMB, AWAY!!!
AH?
FWIP
SKULD!! BEHAVE YOUR-SELF!
IF YOU USE HARSH WORDS...
...YOUR HEART WILL BECOME HARSH AS WELL.
YEP-- COUNT ON BELL-DANDY TO CALM HER DOWN!
AND DON'T FORGET, FOR A FIGHT TO THE DEATH, YOU NEED A PROPER BATTLE-FIELD!
OF COURSE!! THANKS, BIG SISTER!
YOU REALLY ARE ALL SISTERS, AREN'T YOU?
YEAH? Y'THINK SO?
PERSONALLY, I JUST WANNA HAVE FUN.

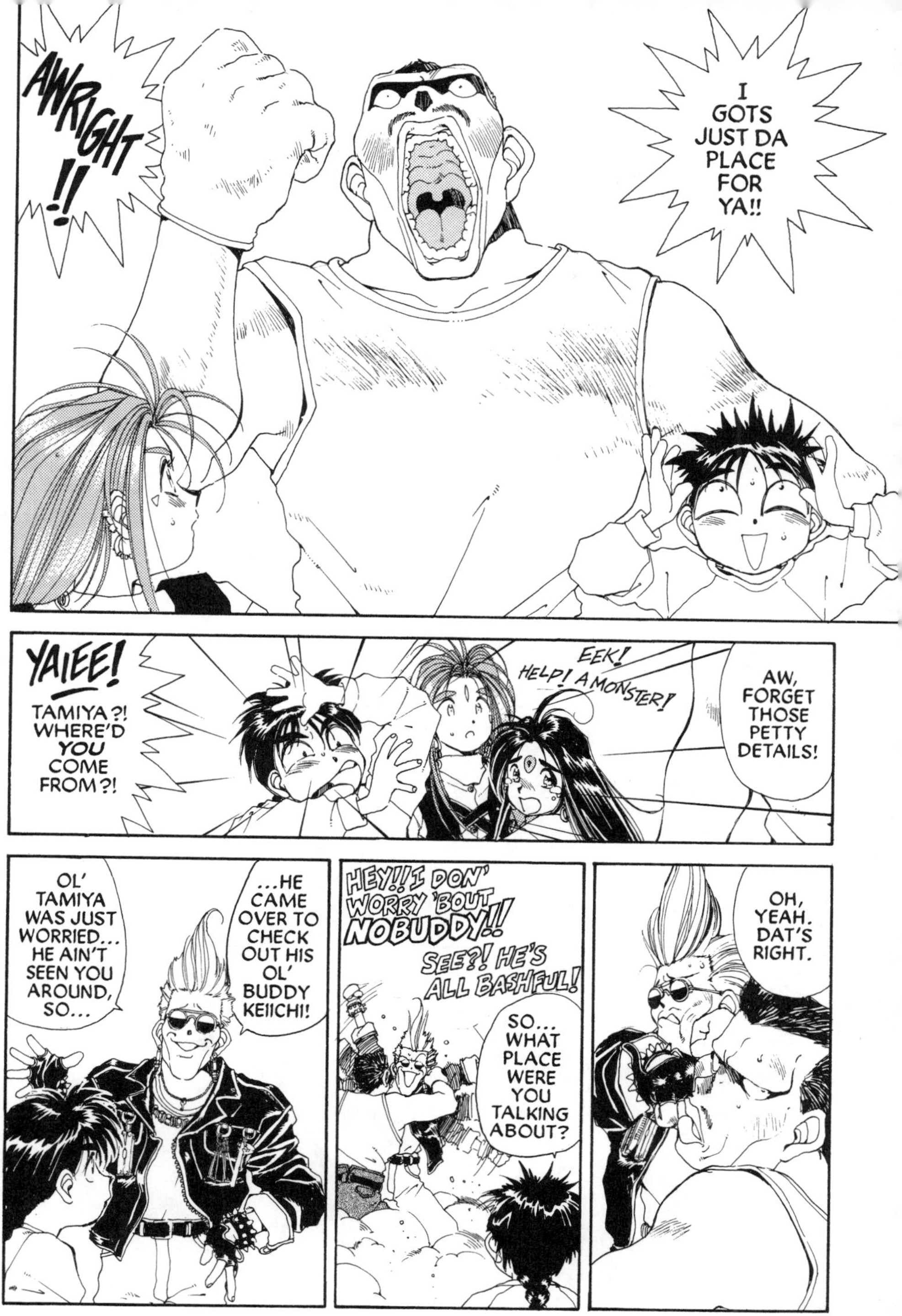
AWRIGHT!!
I GOTS JUST DA PLACE FOR YA!!
YAIEE!
TAMIYA?! WHERE'D YOU COME FROM?!
EEK! HELP! A MONSTER!
AW, FORGET THOSE PETTY DETAILS!
OL' TAMIYA WAS JUST WORRIED... HE AIN'T SEEN YOU AROUND, SO...
...HE CAME OVER TO CHECK OUT HIS OL' BUDDY KEIICHI!
HEY!! I DON' WORRY 'BOUT NOBUDDY!!
SEE?! HE'S ALL BASHFUL!
SO... WHAT PLACE WERE YOU TALKING ABOUT?
OH, YEAH. DAT'S RIGHT.

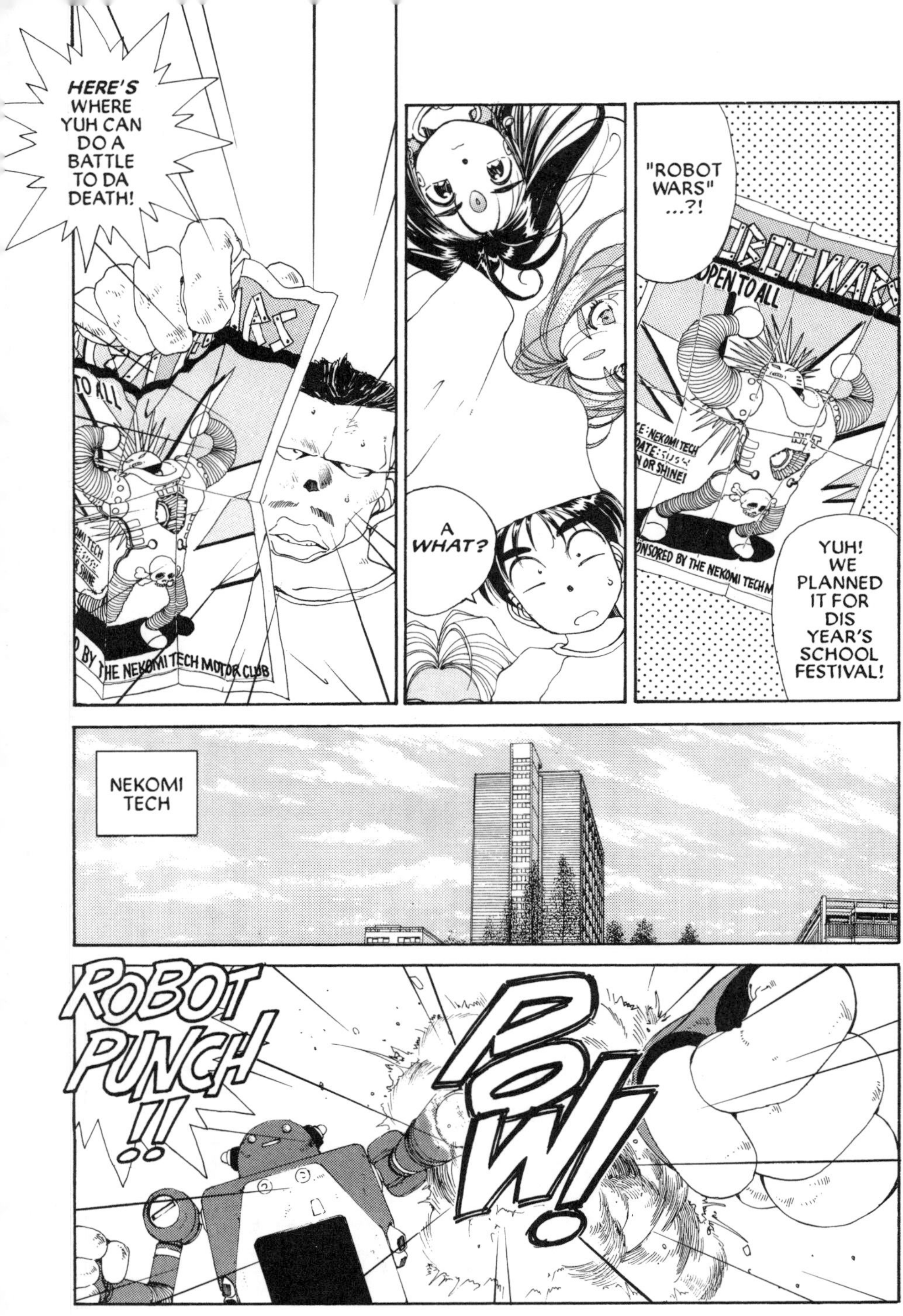
HERE'S WHERE YUH CAN DO A BATTLE TO DA DEATH!
THE NEKOMI TECH MOTOR CLUB
A WHAT?
"ROBOT WARS" ...?!
OPEN TO ALL
YUH! WE PLANNED IT FOR DIS YEAR'S SCHOOL FESTIVAL!
NEKOMI TECH
ROBOT PUNCH!!
POW!

X-ONE BLACK-HOLE BEAM!!! *E-ZAK*

CYGNUS X-1

NYARRGH!!

VREEEE

OR THAT'S WHAT I *THOUGHT* IT WAS.

WRONG?

BIG TIME!!

KRANG WHAM SQUEE

OKAY... HERE'S DUH RING LAYOUT.

DOSE EMPTY DRUMS IN DUH MIDDLE IS DA TARGET, SEE?

DUH ROBOTS FIGHTS TUH GRAB DEM DRUMS, AND DA ONE WITH DA MOSTEST WINS!

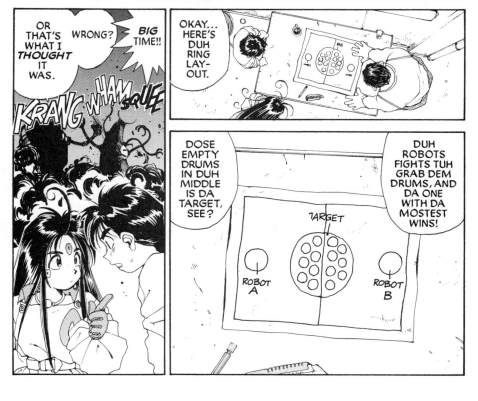

TARGET

ROBOT A

ROBOT B

WE PROVIDES DA MATERIALS!

YOU PROVIDES DA PEOPLE!

AN' YOU CAN MESS WIT DA UDDER GUY'S ROBOT ALL YUH WANT!

WHEWW... WHAT A RELIEF. IT'S A PRETTY NORMAL IDEA, FOR *THOSE* GUYS. EVEN IF THEY **ARE** KINDA WORKED UP ABOUT IT...

YER MATERIALS IS OVER DERE!

WHA-?!

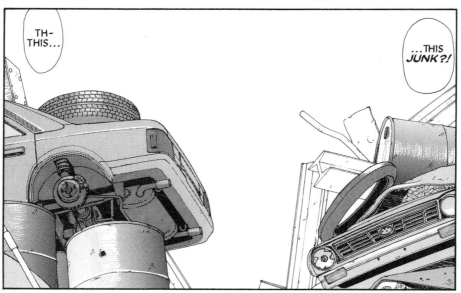

TH-THIS...

...THIS *JUNK?!*

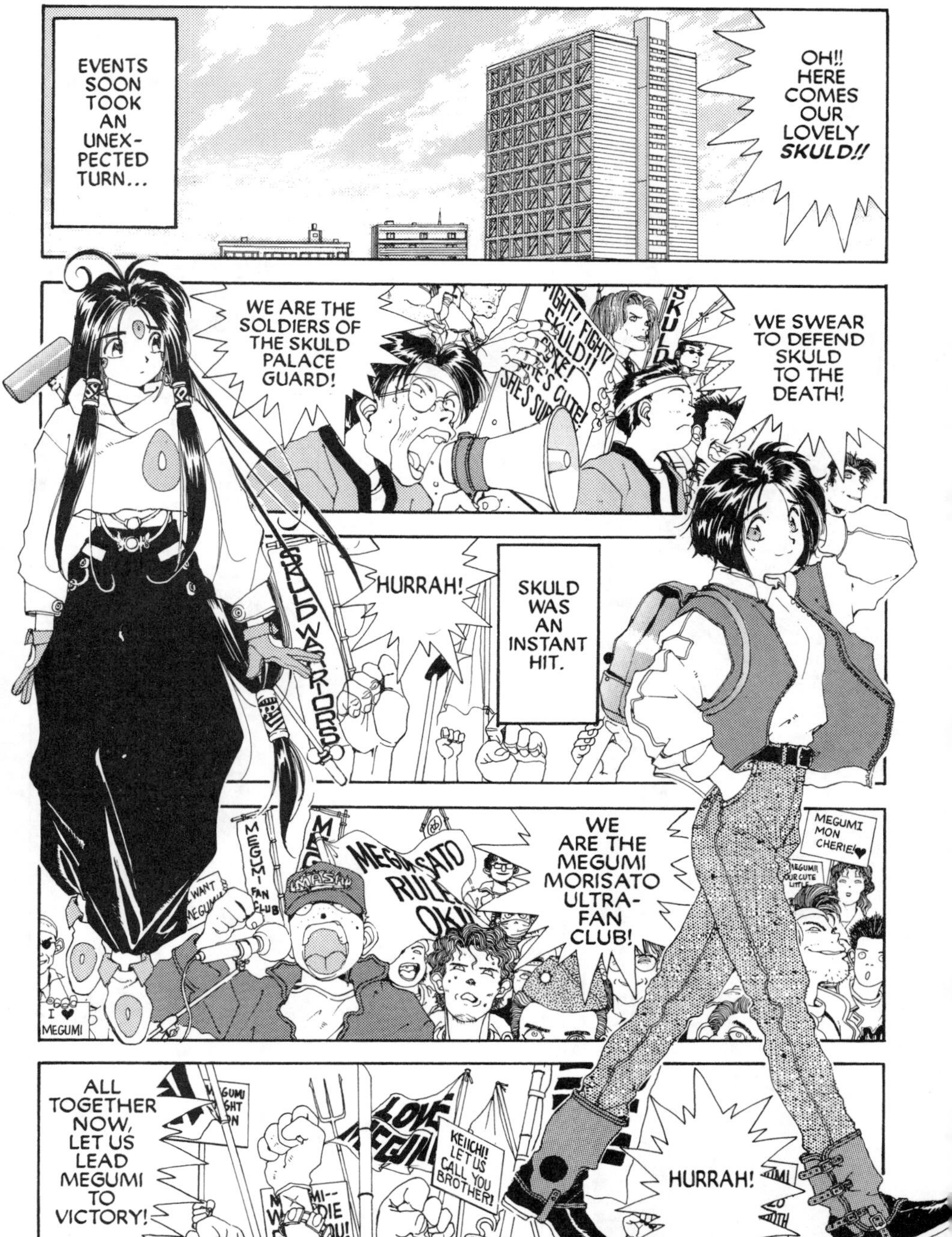

EVENTS SOON TOOK AN UNEXPECTED TURN...
OH!! HERE COMES OUR LOVELY *SKULD!!*
WE ARE THE SOLDIERS OF THE SKULD PALACE GUARD!
WE SWEAR TO DEFEND SKULD TO THE DEATH!
SKULD WARRIORS
HURRAH!
SKULD WAS AN INSTANT HIT.
MEGUMI FAN CLUB
WE ARE THE MEGUMI MORISATO ULTRA-FAN CLUB!
MEGUMI MON CHERIE!♥
I ♥ MEGUMI
ALL TOGETHER NOW, LET US LEAD MEGUMI TO VICTORY!
KEIICHI! LET US CALL YOU BROTHER!
HURRAH!

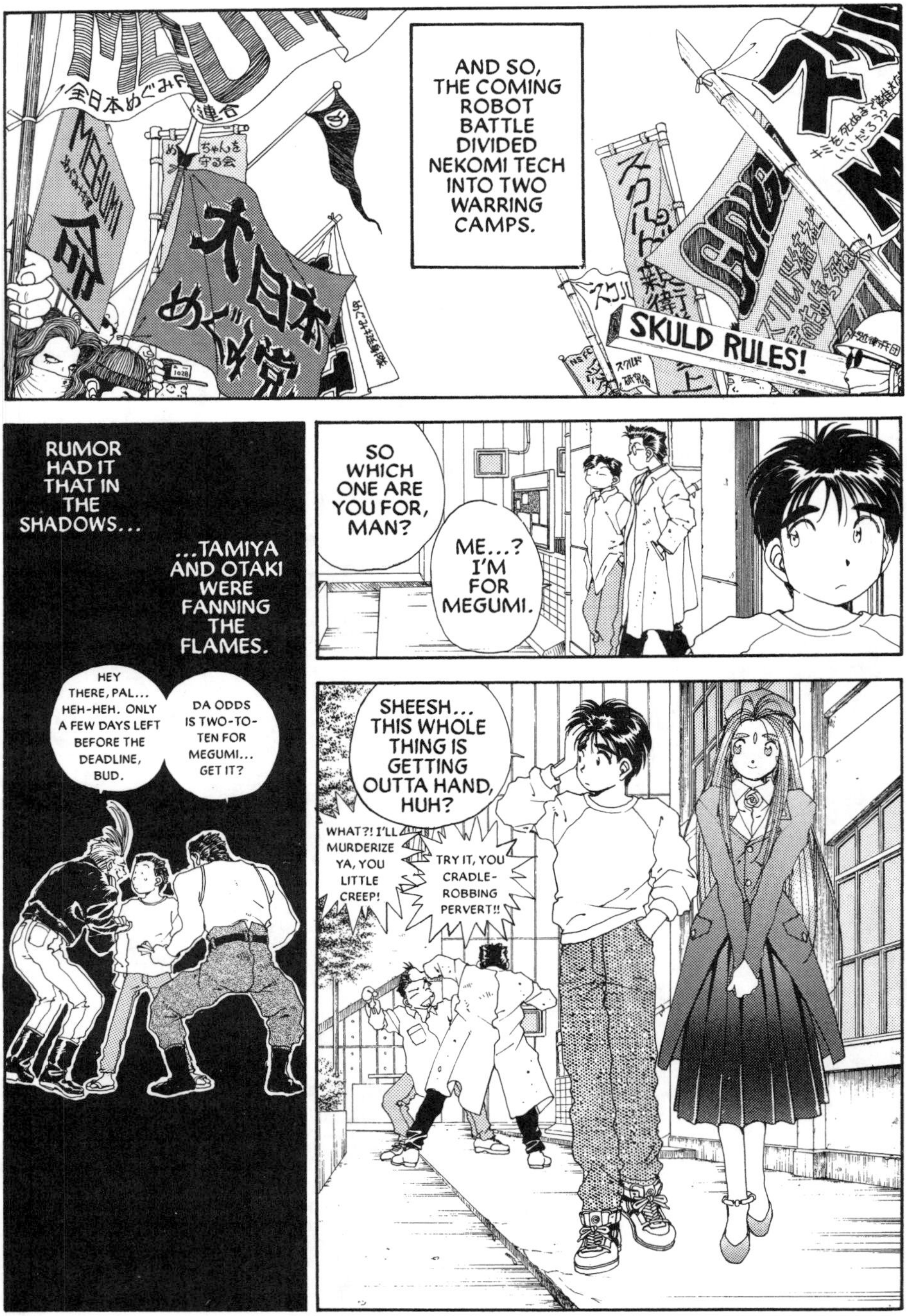
AND SO, THE COMING ROBOT BATTLE DIVIDED NEKOMI TECH INTO TWO WARRING CAMPS.
SKULD RULES!
RUMOR HAD IT THAT IN THE SHADOWS...
...TAMIYA AND OTAKI WERE FANNING THE FLAMES.
HEY THERE, PAL... HEH-HEH. ONLY A FEW DAYS LEFT BEFORE THE DEADLINE, BUD.
DA ODDS IS TWO-TO-TEN FOR MEGUMI... GET IT?
SO WHICH ONE ARE YOU FOR, MAN?
ME...? I'M FOR MEGUMI.
SHEESH... THIS WHOLE THING IS GETTING OUTTA HAND, HUH?
WHAT?! I'LL MURDERIZE YA, YOU LITTLE CREEP!
TRY IT, YOU CRADLE-ROBBING PERVERT!!

SKULD'S SUCH A STUBBORN CHILD...

...BUT I'M SURE SHE SEES A LITTLE BIT OF HERSELF IN MEGUMI.

AND AT THE SAME TIME, SOMETHING COMPLETELY DIFFERENT, TOO.

I HOPE SHE CAN FIND BOTH IN HER LIFE.

DON'T WORRY, KEIICHI. IN THE END THEY'LL BE GOOD FRIENDS.

WELL, I'M GLAD *SOMEONE'S* OPTIMISTIC.

HEY, DID YOU GUYS HEAR?

SKULD'S BUILDING HER MACHINE *ALL BY HERSELF!*

NO WAY?! CAN SHE REALLY PULL IT OFF?!

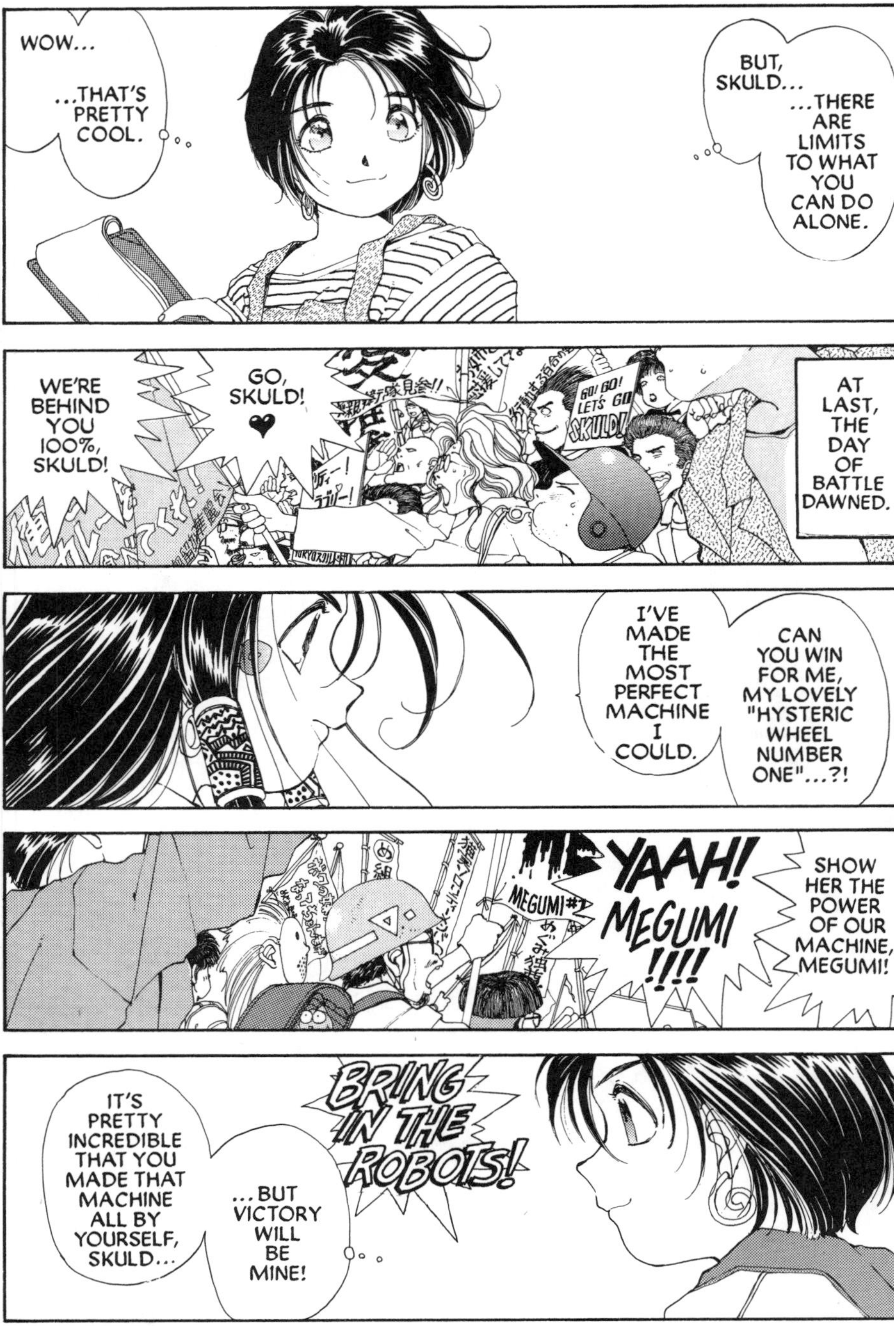
WOW...
...THAT'S PRETTY COOL.
BUT, SKULD...
...THERE ARE LIMITS TO WHAT YOU CAN DO ALONE.
WE'RE BEHIND YOU 100%, SKULD!
GO, SKULD! ♥
GO! GO! LET'S GO SKULD!
AT LAST, THE DAY OF BATTLE DAWNED.
I'VE MADE THE MOST PERFECT MACHINE I COULD.
CAN YOU WIN FOR ME, MY LOVELY "HYSTERIC WHEEL NUMBER ONE"...?!
YAAH! MEGUMI!!!!
SHOW HER THE POWER OF OUR MACHINE, MEGUMI!
IT'S PRETTY INCREDIBLE THAT YOU MADE THAT MACHINE ALL BY YOURSELF, SKULD...
...BUT VICTORY WILL BE MINE!
BRING IN THE ROBOTS!

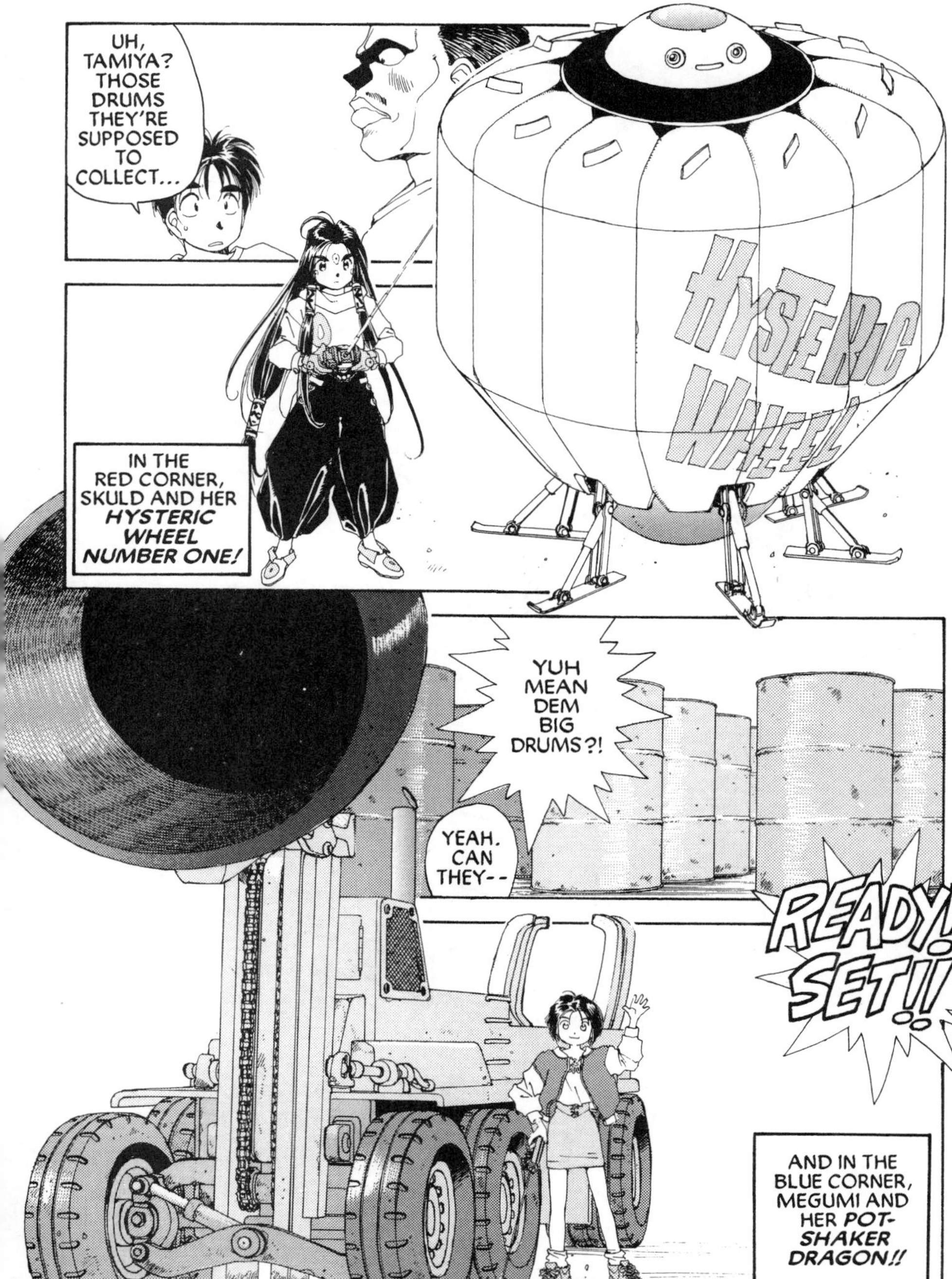
UH, TAMIYA? THOSE DRUMS THEY'RE SUPPOSED TO COLLECT...
HYSTERIC WHEEL
IN THE RED CORNER, SKULD AND HER *HYSTERIC WHEEL NUMBER ONE!*
YUH MEAN DEM BIG DRUMS?!
YEAH. CAN THEY--
READY! SET!!
AND IN THE BLUE CORNER, MEGUMI AND HER *POT-SHAKER DRAGON!!*

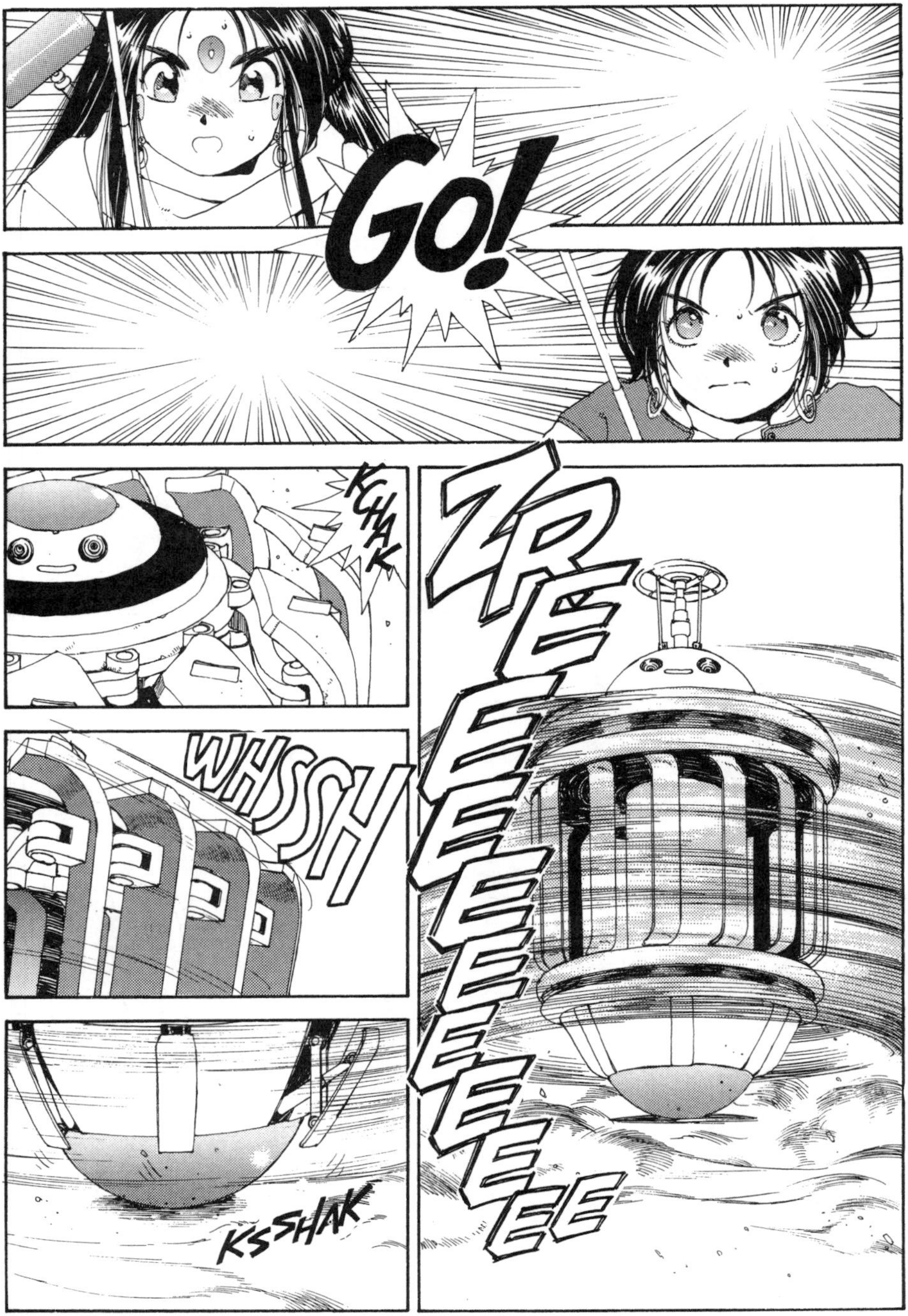
GO!
KCHAK
WHSSH
ZREEEEEEEEEEEEE
KSSHAK

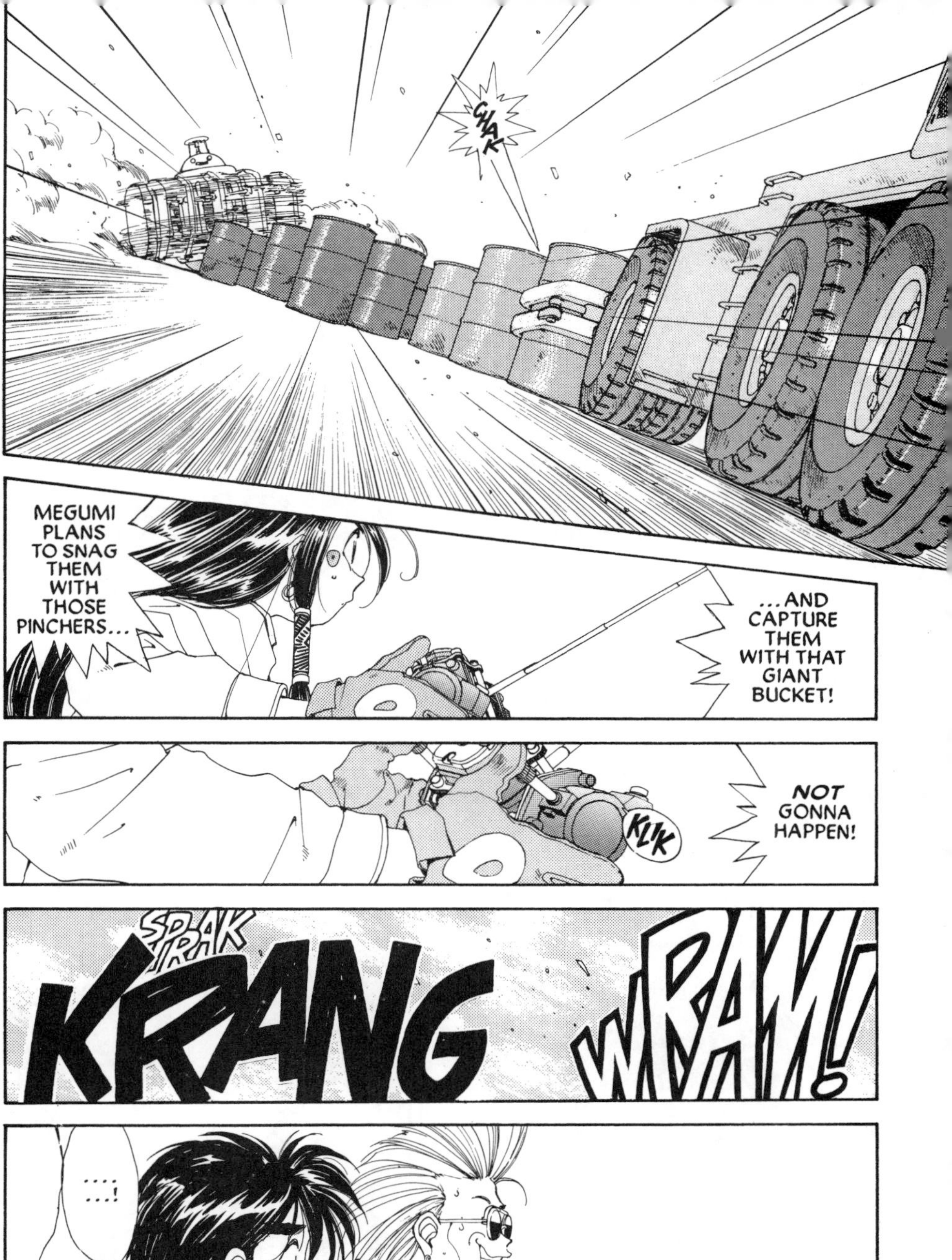
CHAK
MEGUMI PLANS TO SNAG THEM WITH THOSE PINCHERS...
...AND CAPTURE THEM WITH THAT GIANT BUCKET!
KLIK
NOT GONNA HAPPEN!
SPAK JRAK
KRANG
WRAM!
...
...!

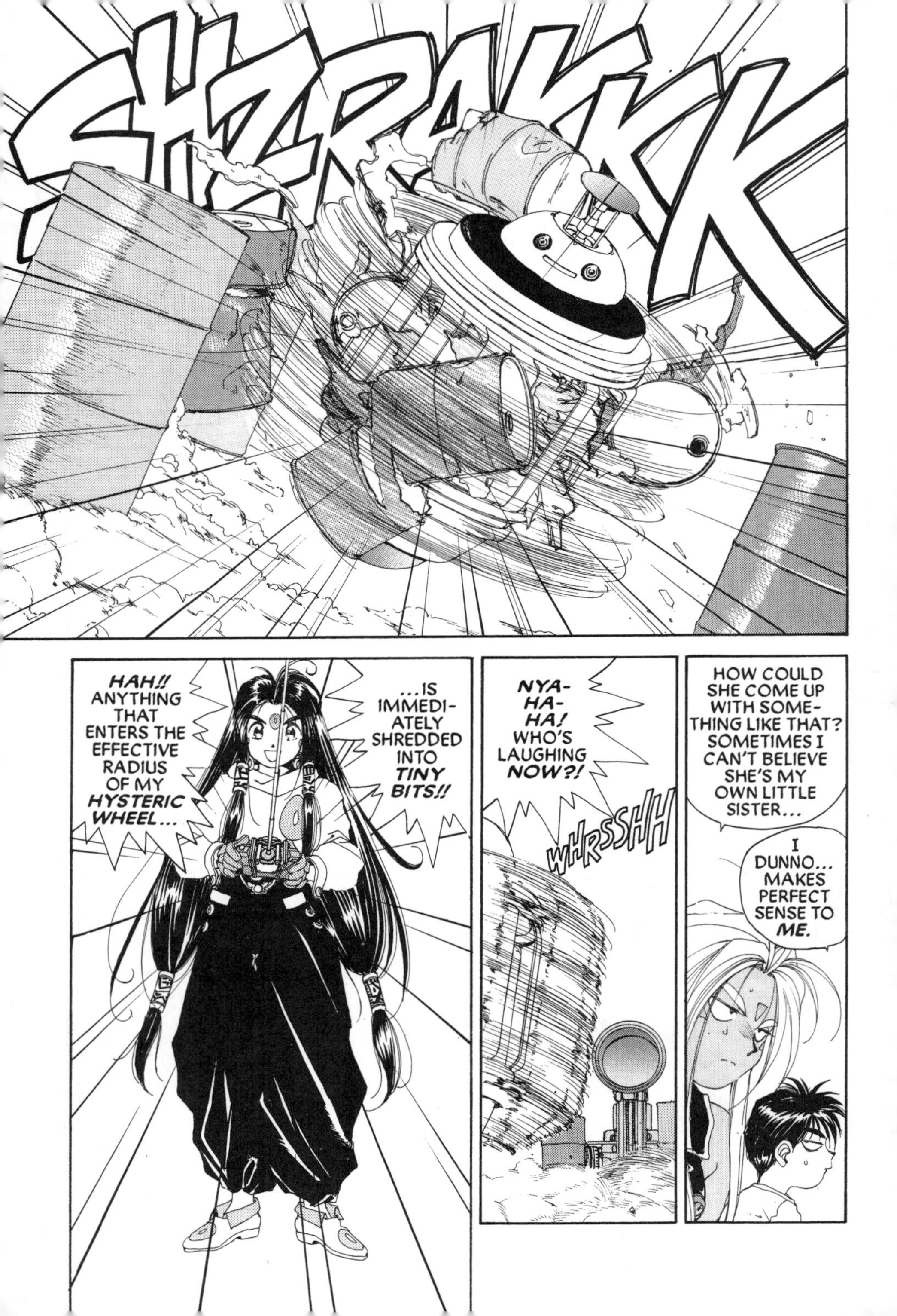
SHZRAKKK
HAH!! ANYTHING THAT ENTERS THE EFFECTIVE RADIUS OF MY HYSTERIC WHEEL...
...IS IMMEDIATELY SHREDDED INTO TINY BITS!!
NYA-HA-HA! WHO'S LAUGHING NOW?!
WHRSSHH
HOW COULD SHE COME UP WITH SOMETHING LIKE THAT? SOMETIMES I CAN'T BELIEVE SHE'S MY OWN LITTLE SISTER...
I DUNNO... MAKES PERFECT SENSE TO ME.

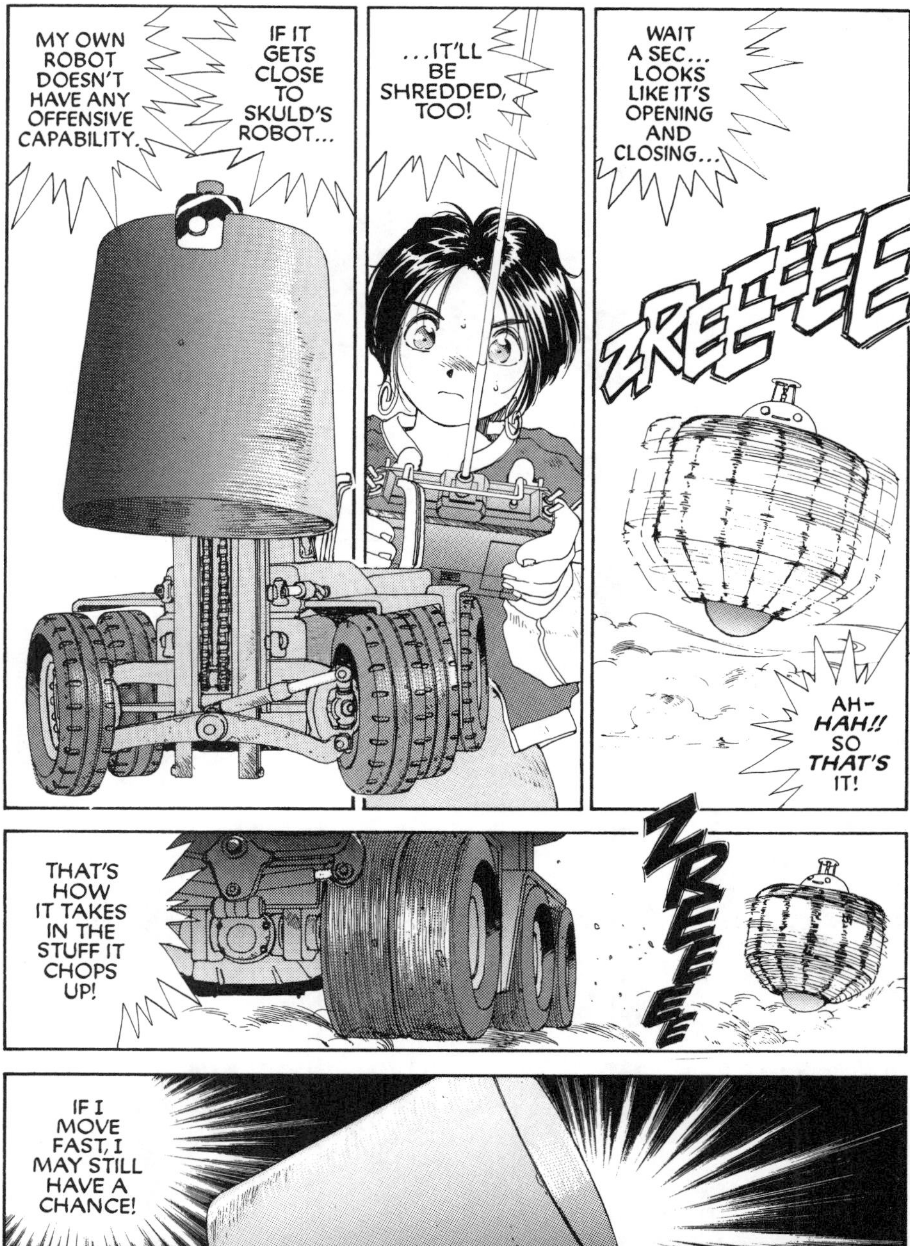
MY OWN ROBOT DOESN'T HAVE ANY OFFENSIVE CAPABILITY.
IF IT GETS CLOSE TO SKULD'S ROBOT...
...IT'LL BE SHREDDED, TOO!
WAIT A SEC... LOOKS LIKE IT'S OPENING AND CLOSING...
ZREEEEEE
AH-HAH!! SO THAT'S IT!
THAT'S HOW IT TAKES IN THE STUFF IT CHOPS UP!
ZREEEEE
IF I MOVE FAST, I MAY STILL HAVE A CHANCE!

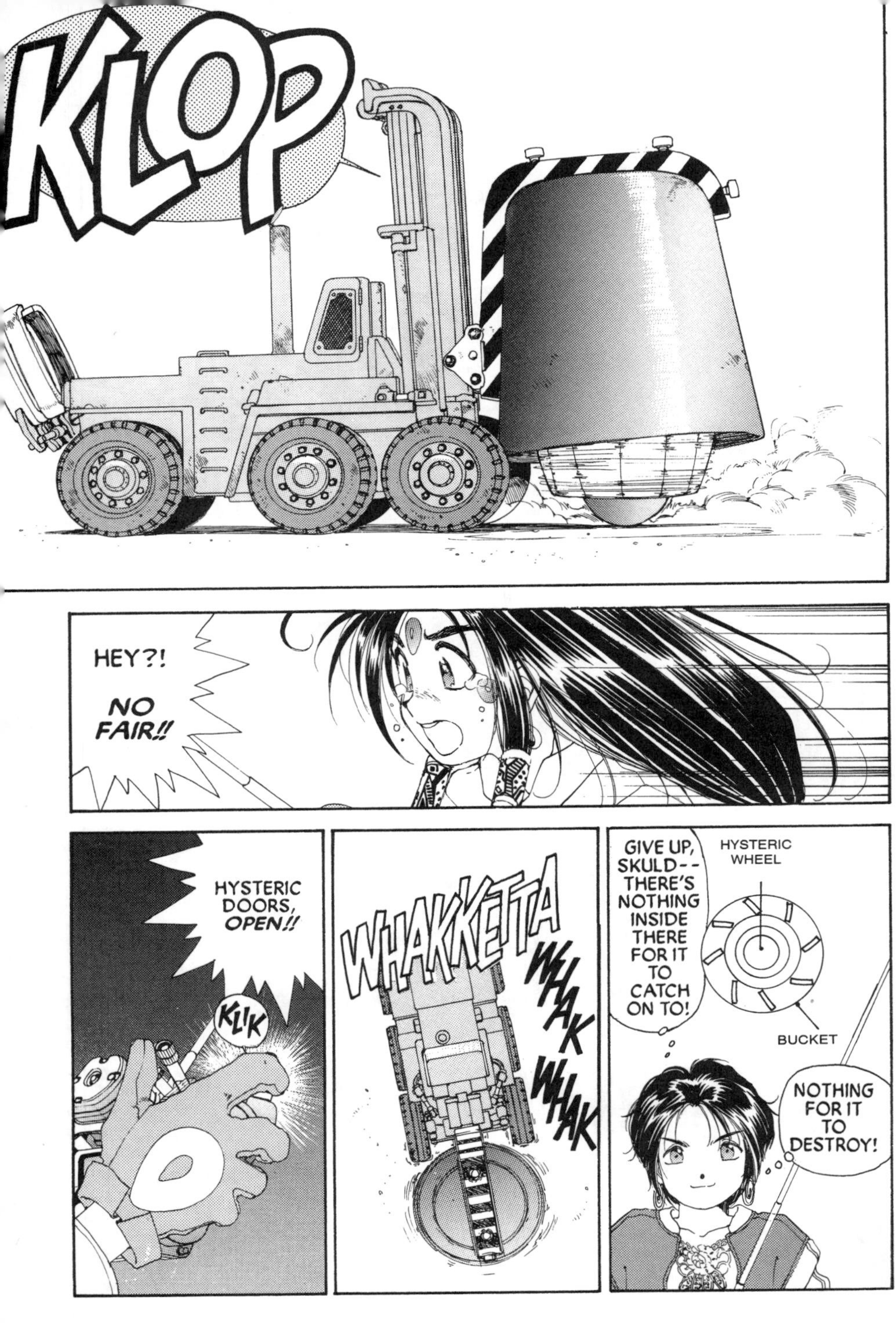
KLOP
HEY?!
NO FAIR!!
HYSTERIC DOORS, OPEN!!
KLIK
WHAKKETTA
WHAK WHAK WHAK
GIVE UP, SKULD-- THERE'S NOTHING INSIDE THERE FOR IT TO CATCH ON TO!
HYSTERIC WHEEL
BUCKET
NOTHING FOR IT TO DESTROY!

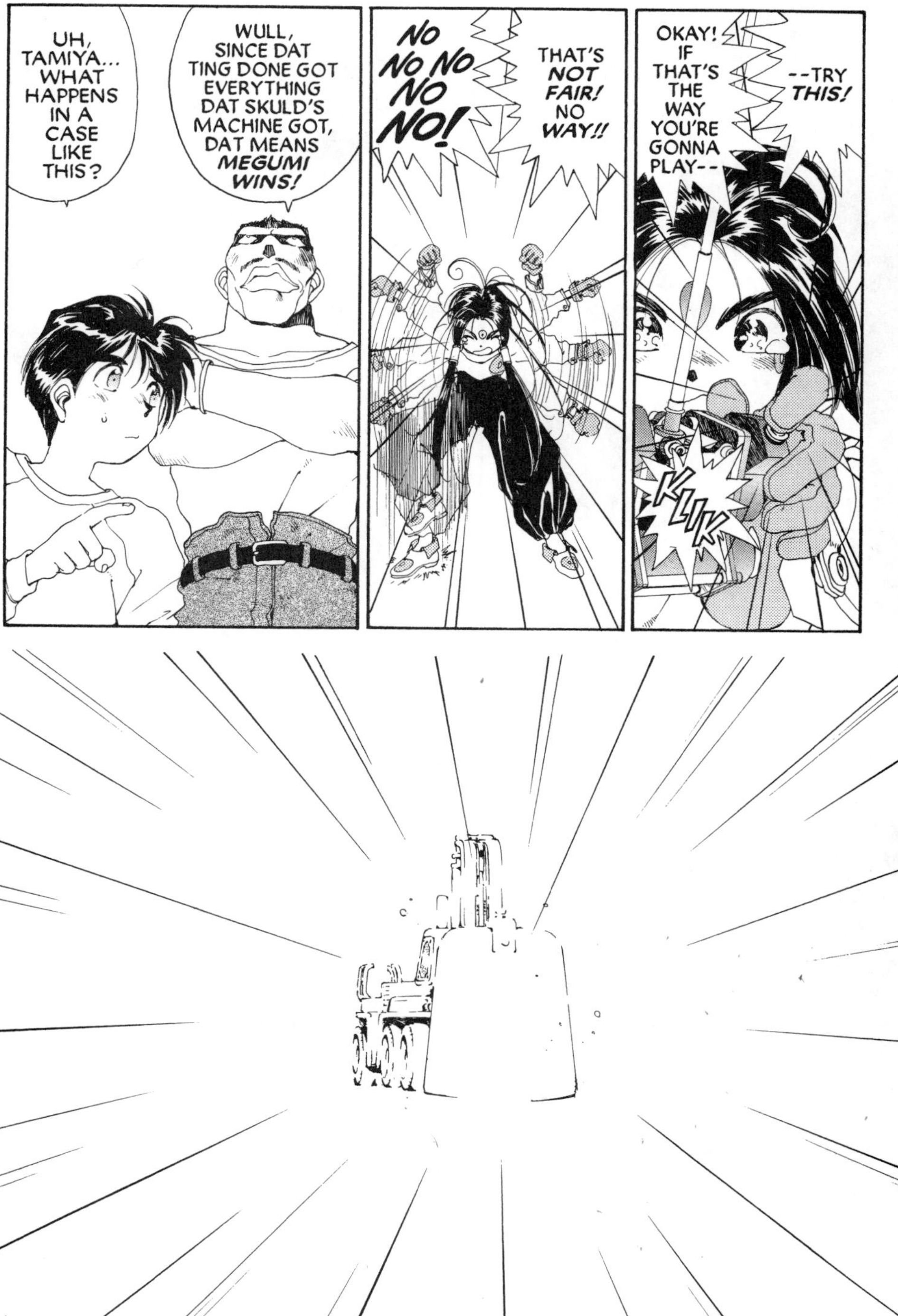
UH, TAMIYA... WHAT HAPPENS IN A CASE LIKE THIS?
WULL, SINCE DAT TING DONE GOT EVERYTHING DAT SKULD'S MACHINE GOT, DAT MEANS MEGUMI WINS!
NO NO NO NO NO NO!
THAT'S NOT FAIR! NO WAY!!
OKAY! IF THAT'S THE WAY YOU'RE GONNA PLAY--
--TRY THIS!
KLIK

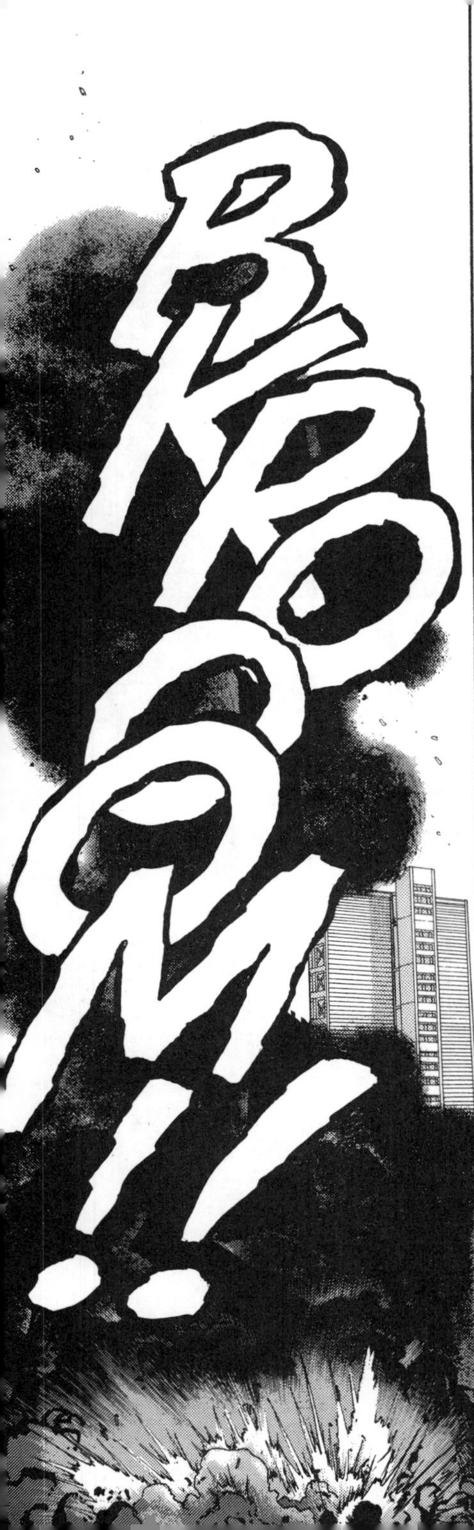
BROOOM!!

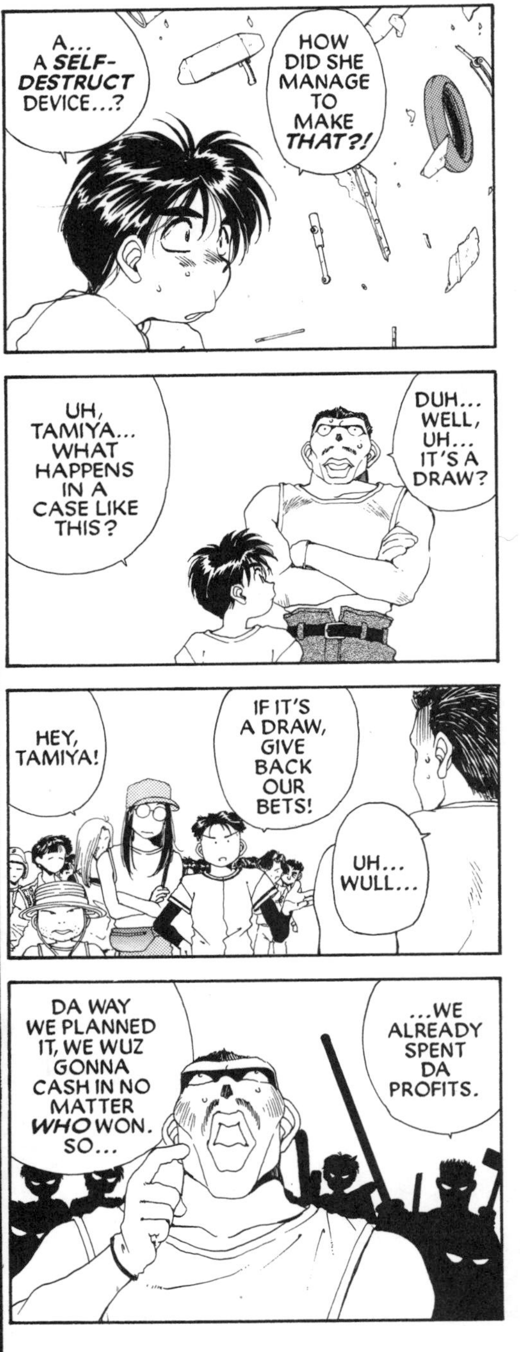
A... A SELF-DESTRUCT DEVICE...?
HOW DID SHE MANAGE TO MAKE THAT?!
UH, TAMIYA... WHAT HAPPENS IN A CASE LIKE THIS?
DUH... WELL, UH... IT'S A DRAW?
HEY, TAMIYA!
IF IT'S A DRAW, GIVE BACK OUR BETS!
UH... WULL...
DA WAY WE PLANNED IT, WE WUZ GONNA CASH IN NO MATTER WHO WON. SO...
...WE ALREADY SPENT DA PROFITS.

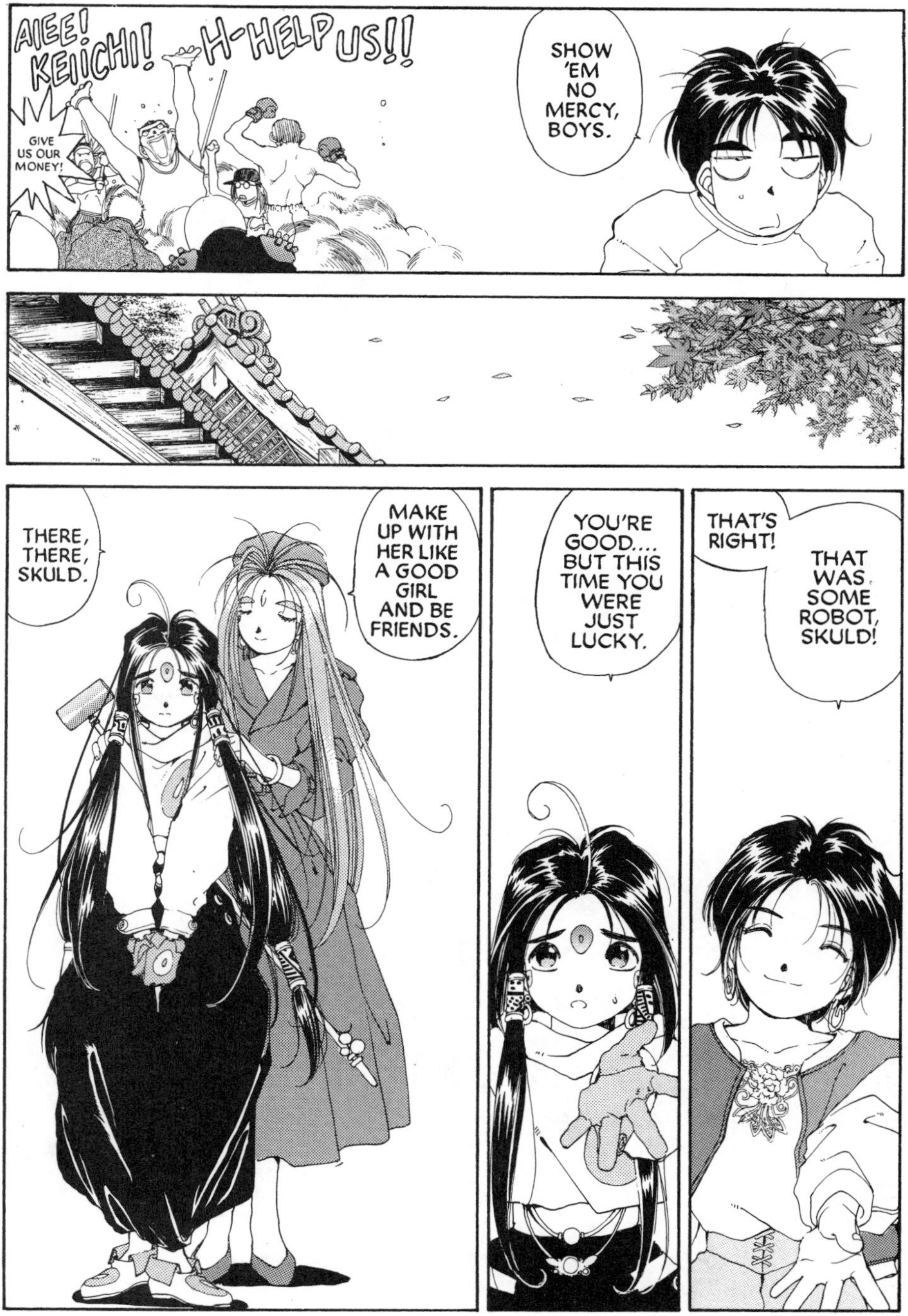
AIEE! KEIICHI!
H-HELP US!!
GIVE US OUR MONEY!
SHOW 'EM NO MERCY, BOYS.
THERE, THERE, SKULD.
MAKE UP WITH HER LIKE A GOOD GIRL AND BE FRIENDS.
YOU'RE GOOD.... BUT THIS TIME YOU WERE JUST LUCKY.
THAT'S RIGHT!
THAT WAS SOME ROBOT, SKULD!

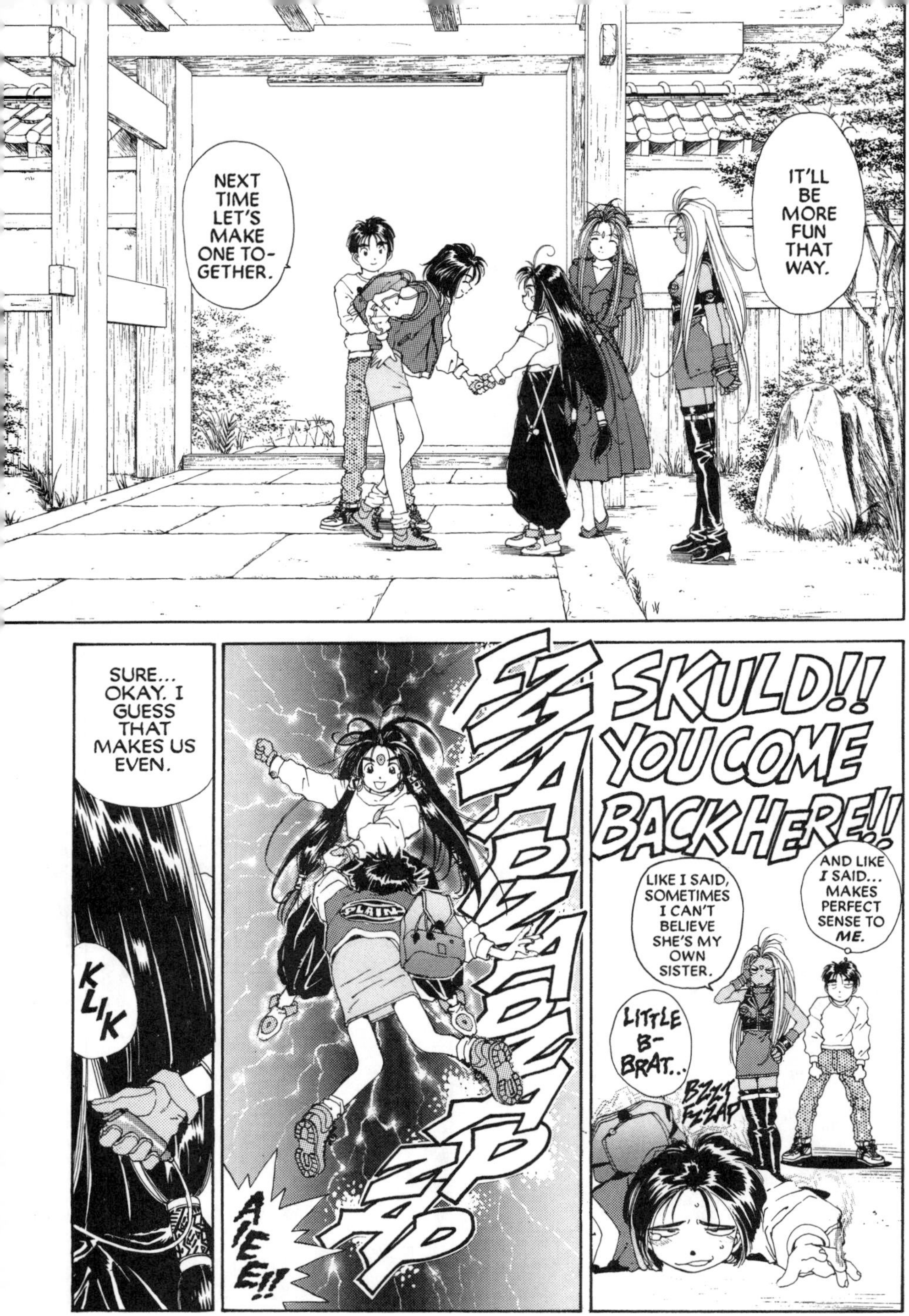
NEXT TIME LET'S MAKE ONE TO-GETHER.
IT'LL BE MORE FUN THAT WAY.
SURE... OKAY. I GUESS THAT MAKES US EVEN.
KLIK
ZAP
AIEEE!!
SKULD!! YOU COME BACK HERE!!
LITTLE B-BRAT...
BZZT FZZAP
LIKE I SAID, SOMETIMES I CAN'T BELIEVE SHE'S MY OWN SISTER.
AND LIKE *I* SAID... MAKES PERFECT SENSE TO *ME*.

The Trials of Morisato, part 1

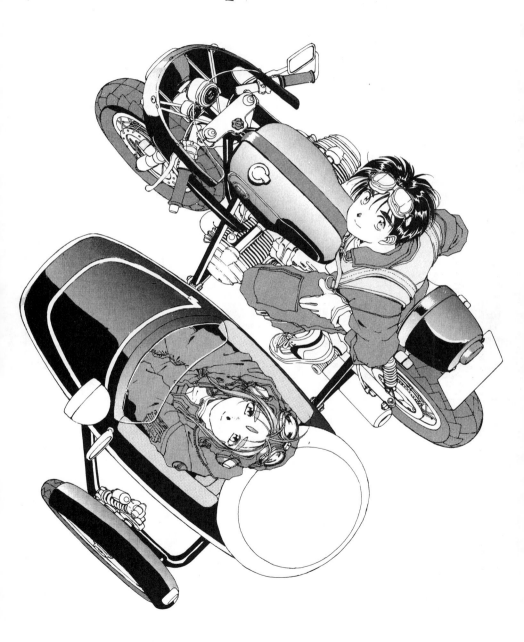

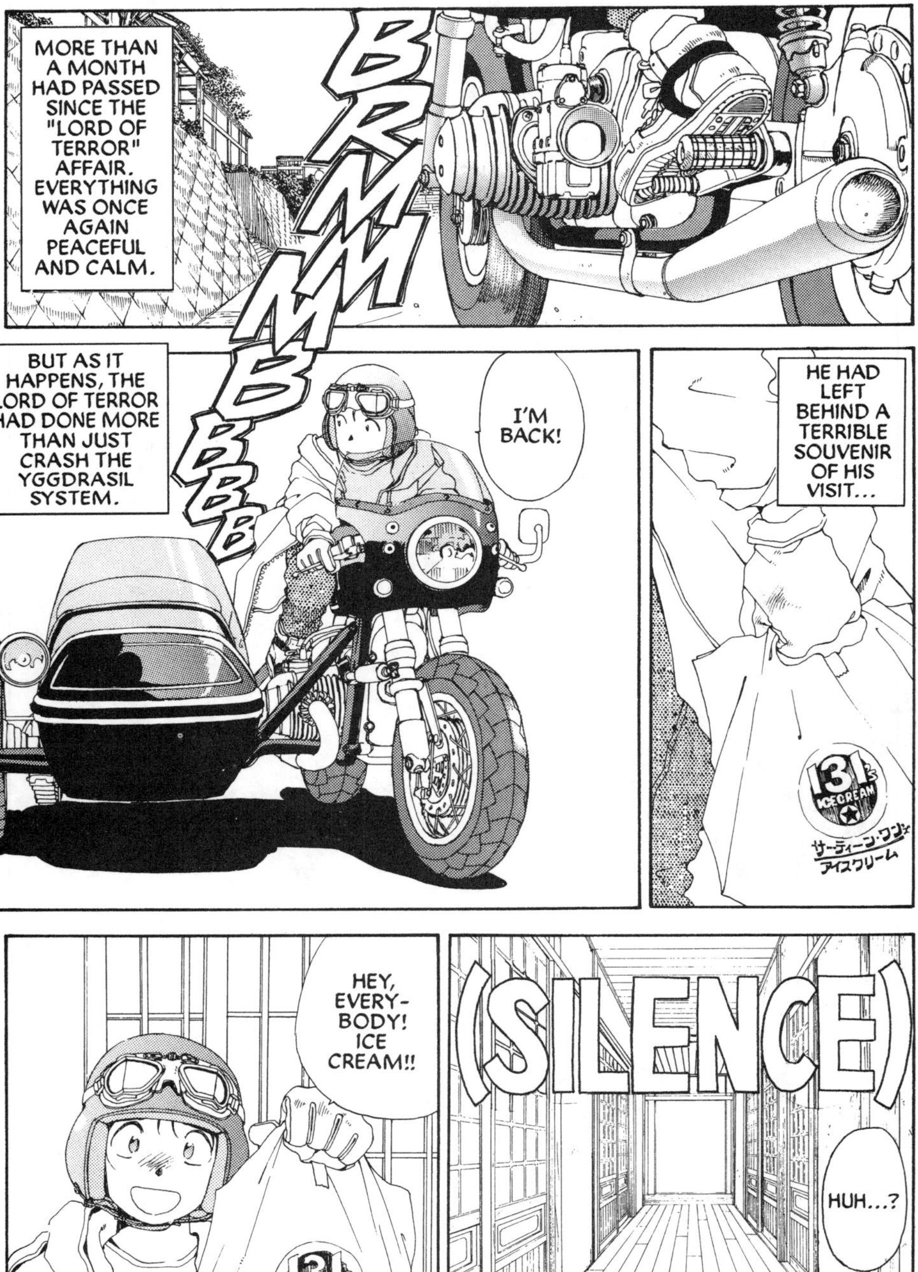
MORE THAN A MONTH HAD PASSED SINCE THE "LORD OF TERROR" AFFAIR. EVERYTHING WAS ONCE AGAIN PEACEFUL AND CALM.
BRMMMBBBB
BUT AS IT HAPPENS, THE LORD OF TERROR HAD DONE MORE THAN JUST CRASH THE YGGDRASIL SYSTEM.
I'M BACK!
HE HAD LEFT BEHIND A TERRIBLE SOUVENIR OF HIS VISIT...
31's ICECREAM
サーティーン・ワンズ
アイスクリーム
HEY, EVERY-BODY! ICE CREAM!!
31's ICECREAM
(SILENCE)
HUH...?

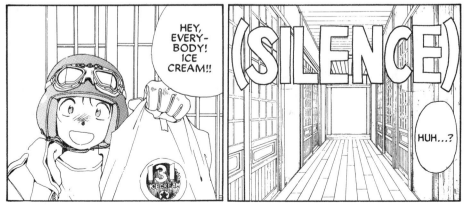

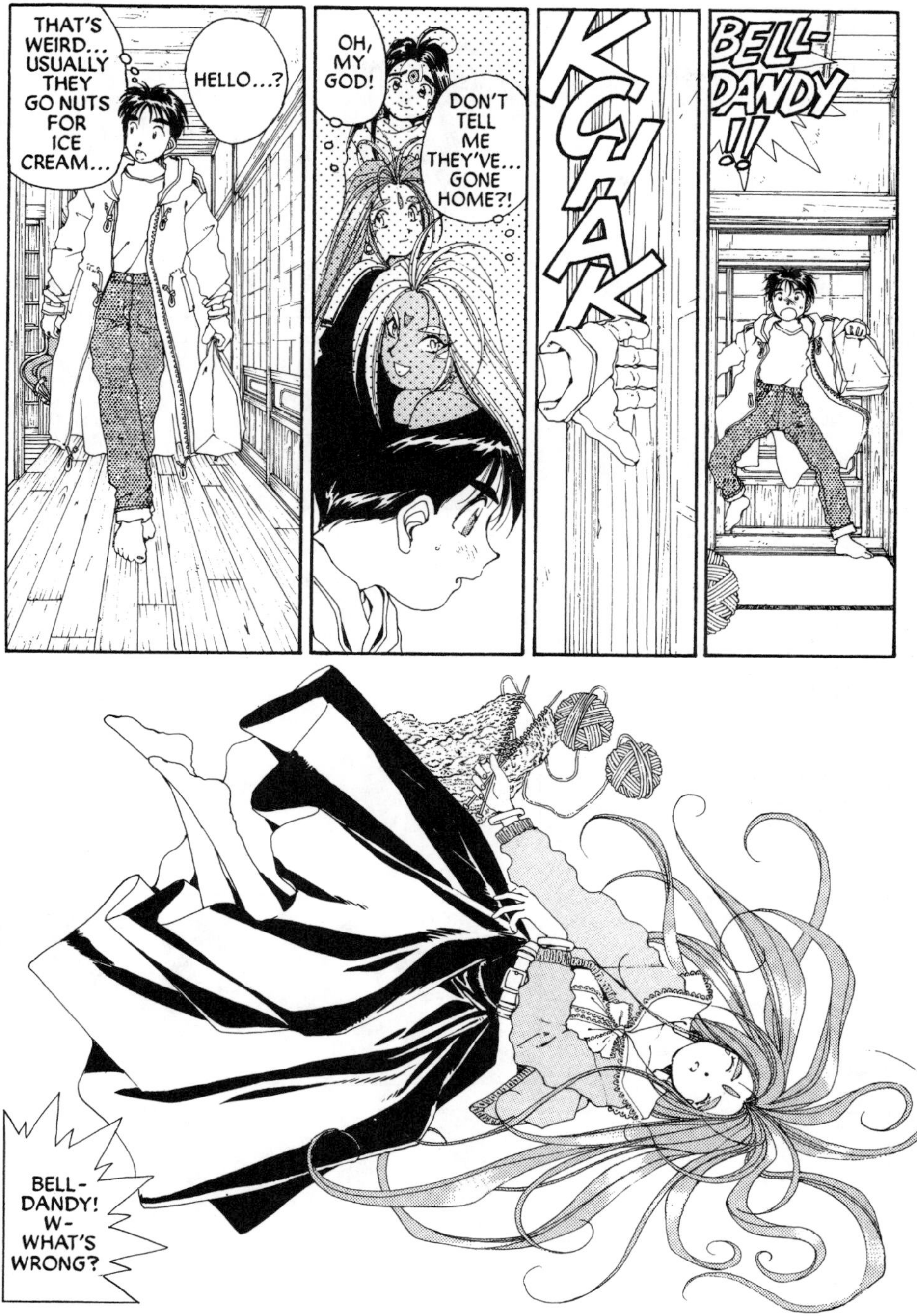

THAT'S WEIRD... USUALLY THEY GO NUTS FOR ICE CREAM...
HELLO...?
OH, MY GOD!
DON'T TELL ME THEY'VE... GONE HOME?!
KCHAK
BELL-DANDY!!
BELL-DANDY! W-WHAT'S WRONG?

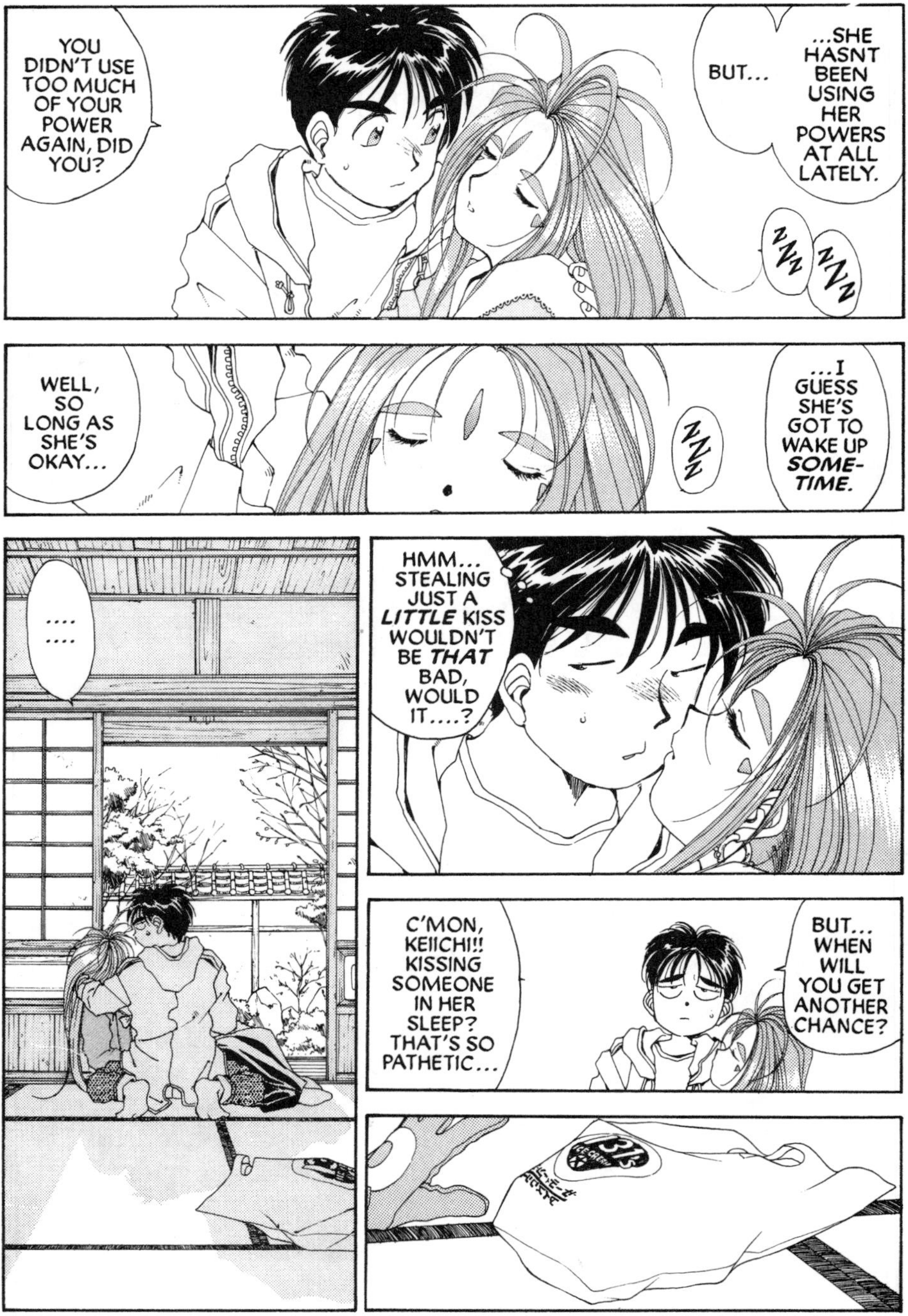
YOU DIDN'T USE TOO MUCH OF YOUR POWER AGAIN, DID YOU?
BUT...
...SHE HASNT BEEN USING HER POWERS AT ALL LATELY.
ZZZ
ZZZ
WELL, SO LONG AS SHE'S OKAY...
ZZZ
...I GUESS SHE'S GOT TO WAKE UP SOME-TIME.
....
....
HMM... STEALING JUST A LITTLE KISS WOULDN'T BE THAT BAD, WOULD IT....?
C'MON, KEIICHI!! KISSING SOMEONE IN HER SLEEP? THAT'S SO PATHETIC...
BUT... WHEN WILL YOU GET ANOTHER CHANCE?

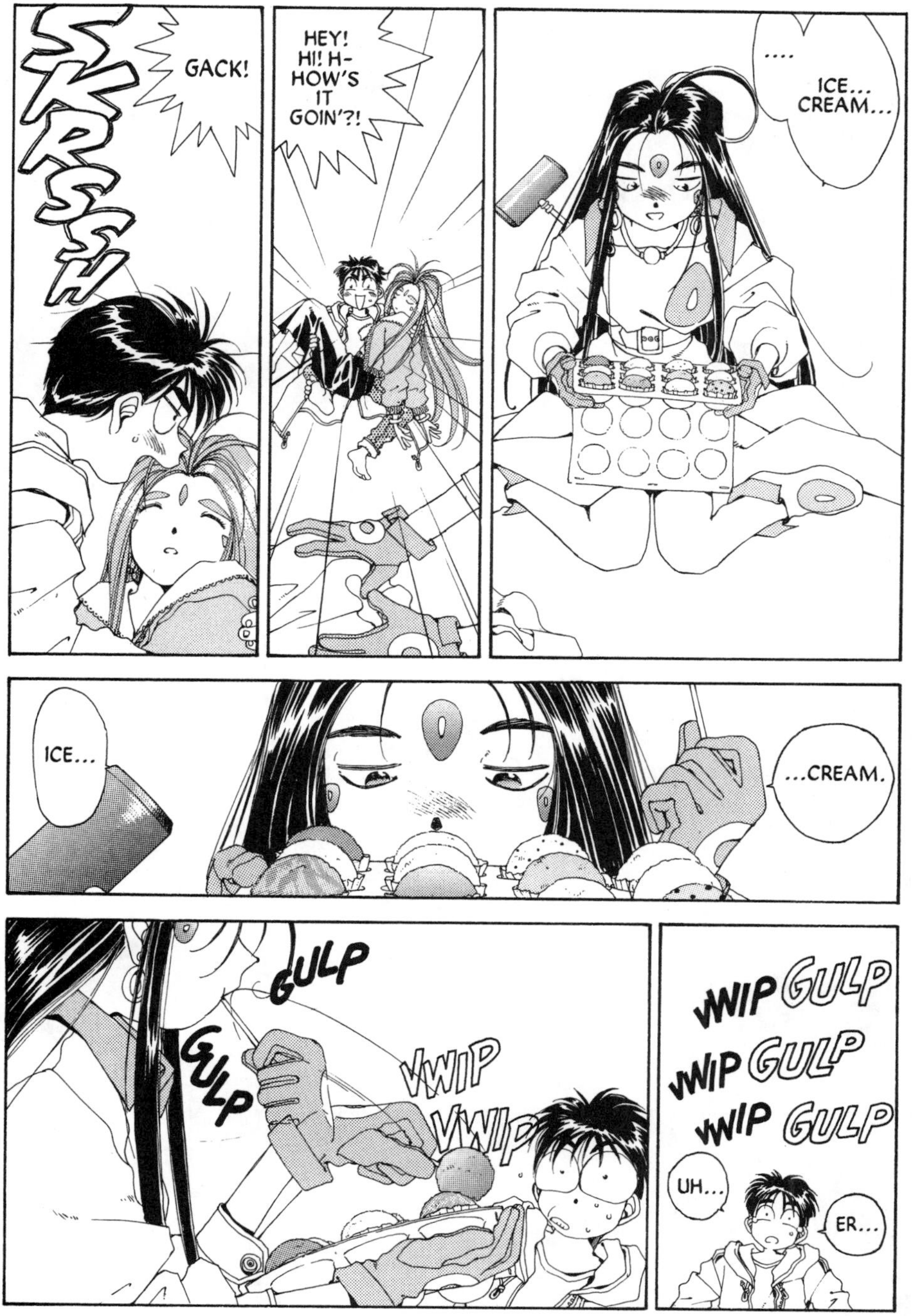
SKRSSH
GACK!
HEY! HI! H-HOW'S IT GOIN'?!
....
ICE... CREAM...
ICE...
...CREAM.
GULP
GULP
VWIP
VWIP
VWIP GULP
VWIP GULP
VWIP GULP
UH...
ER...

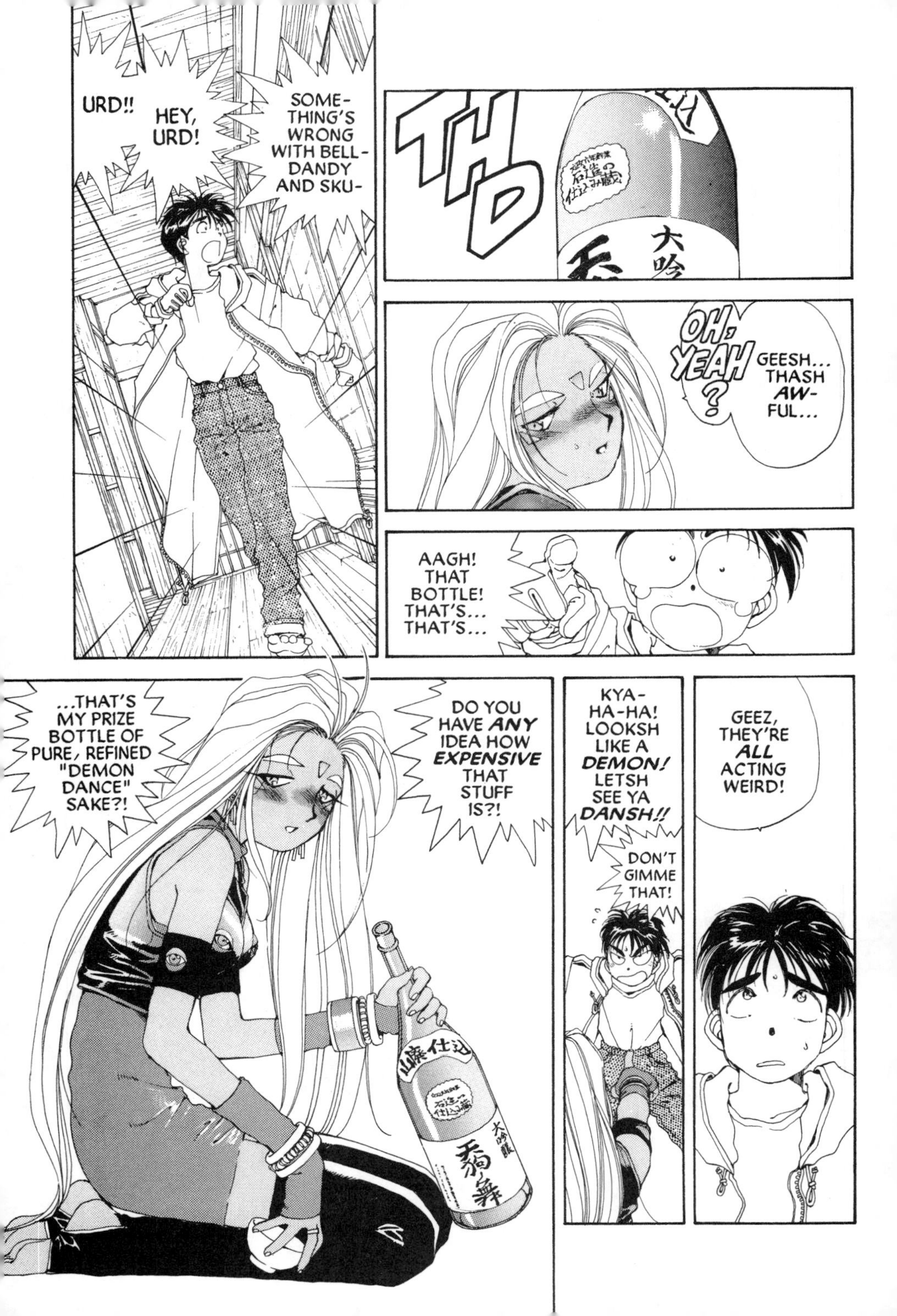
URD!!
HEY, URD!
SOME-THING'S WRONG WITH BELL-DANDY AND SKU-
THD
OH, YEAH?
GEESH... THASH AW-FUL...
AAGH! THAT BOTTLE! THAT'S... THAT'S...
...THAT'S MY PRIZE BOTTLE OF PURE, REFINED "DEMON DANCE" SAKE?!
DO YOU HAVE ANY IDEA HOW EXPENSIVE THAT STUFF IS?!
山廃仕込
大吟醸
天狗舞
KYA-HA-HA! LOOKSH LIKE A DEMON! LETSH SEE YA DANSH!!
DON'T GIMME THAT!
GEEZ, THEY'RE ALL ACTING WEIRD!

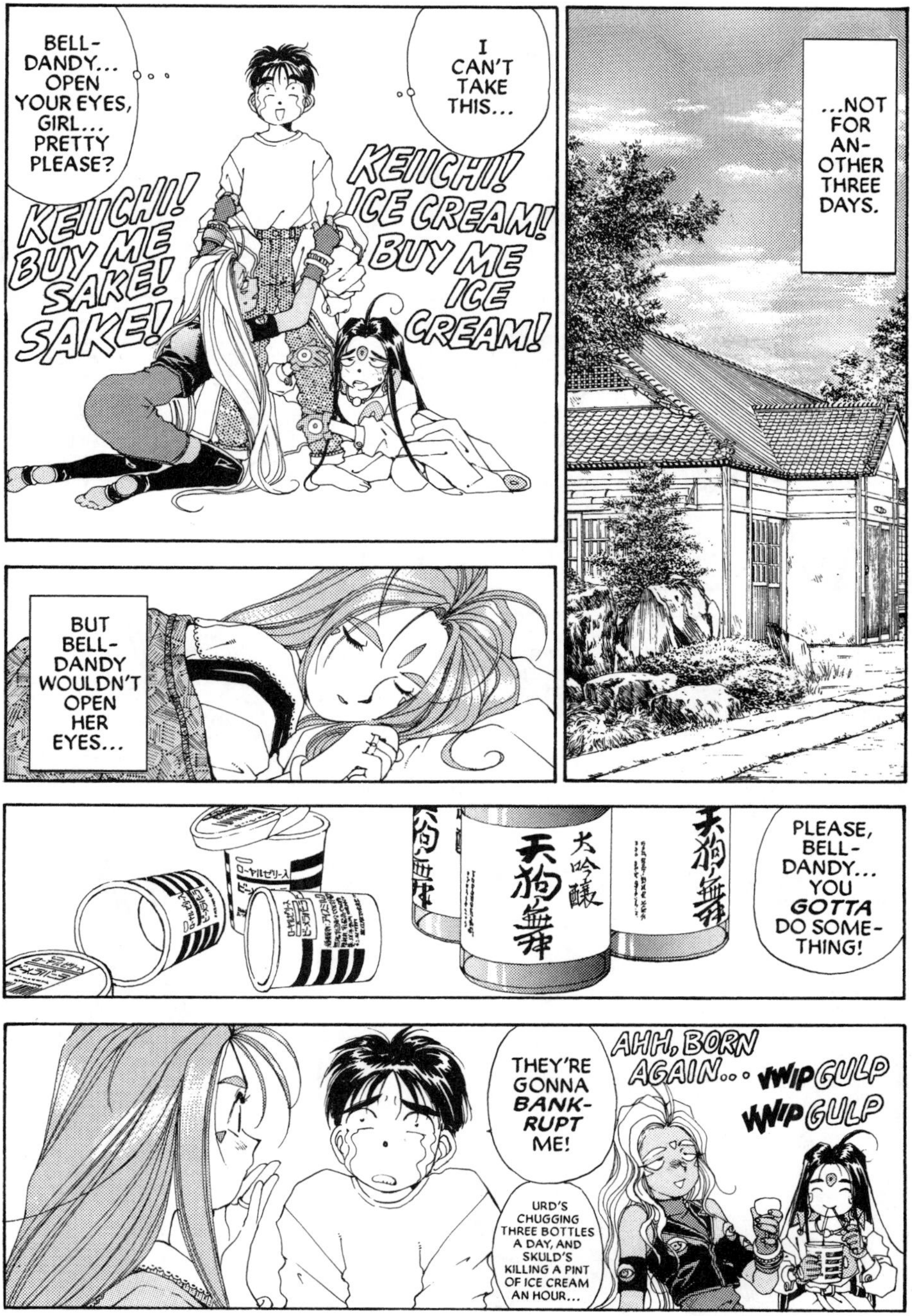
BELL-DANDY... OPEN YOUR EYES, GIRL... PRETTY PLEASE?
I CAN'T TAKE THIS...
KEIICHI! BUY ME SAKE! SAKE!
KEIICHI! ICE CREAM! BUY ME ICE CREAM!
BUT BELL-DANDY WOULDN'T OPEN HER EYES...
...NOT FOR AN-OTHER THREE DAYS.
天狗舞
大吟醸
天狗舞
天狗舞
PLEASE, BELL-DANDY... YOU *GOTTA* DO SOME-THING!
THEY'RE GONNA *BANK-RUPT* ME!
URD'S CHUGGING THREE BOTTLES A DAY, AND SKULD'S KILLING A PINT OF ICE CREAM AN HOUR...
AHH, BORN AGAIN...
VVVIP GULP
VVVIP GULP

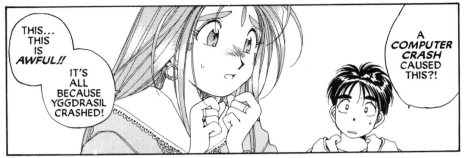

THIS... THIS IS AWFUL!!
IT'S ALL BECAUSE YGGDRASIL CRASHED!
A COMPUTER CRASH CAUSED THIS?!
YGGDRASIL IS OUR CONTROL SYSTEM. BUT AT THE SAME TIME...
...IT'S OUR LIFE-SUPPORT SYSTEM, TOO.
FOR US TO STAY HERE ON EARTH WE HAVE TO TAP ENERGY...
FROM THE EARTH...
THE TREES...
WIND AND CLOUDS...
EVEN THE SEA.
WE BORROW ENERGY FROM ALL OF NATURE.
THESE NATURAL ENERGIES ARE WHAT POWER THE LOCAL EARTH SPIRITS.
BUT WE CAN'T PROCESS THEM UNTIL THEY'VE BEEN CONVERTED BY YGGDRASIL.

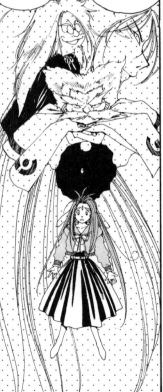

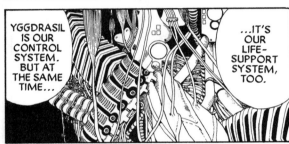

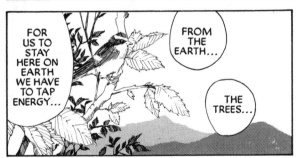

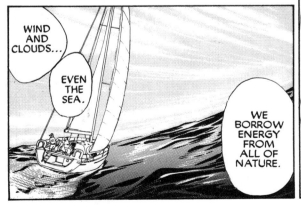

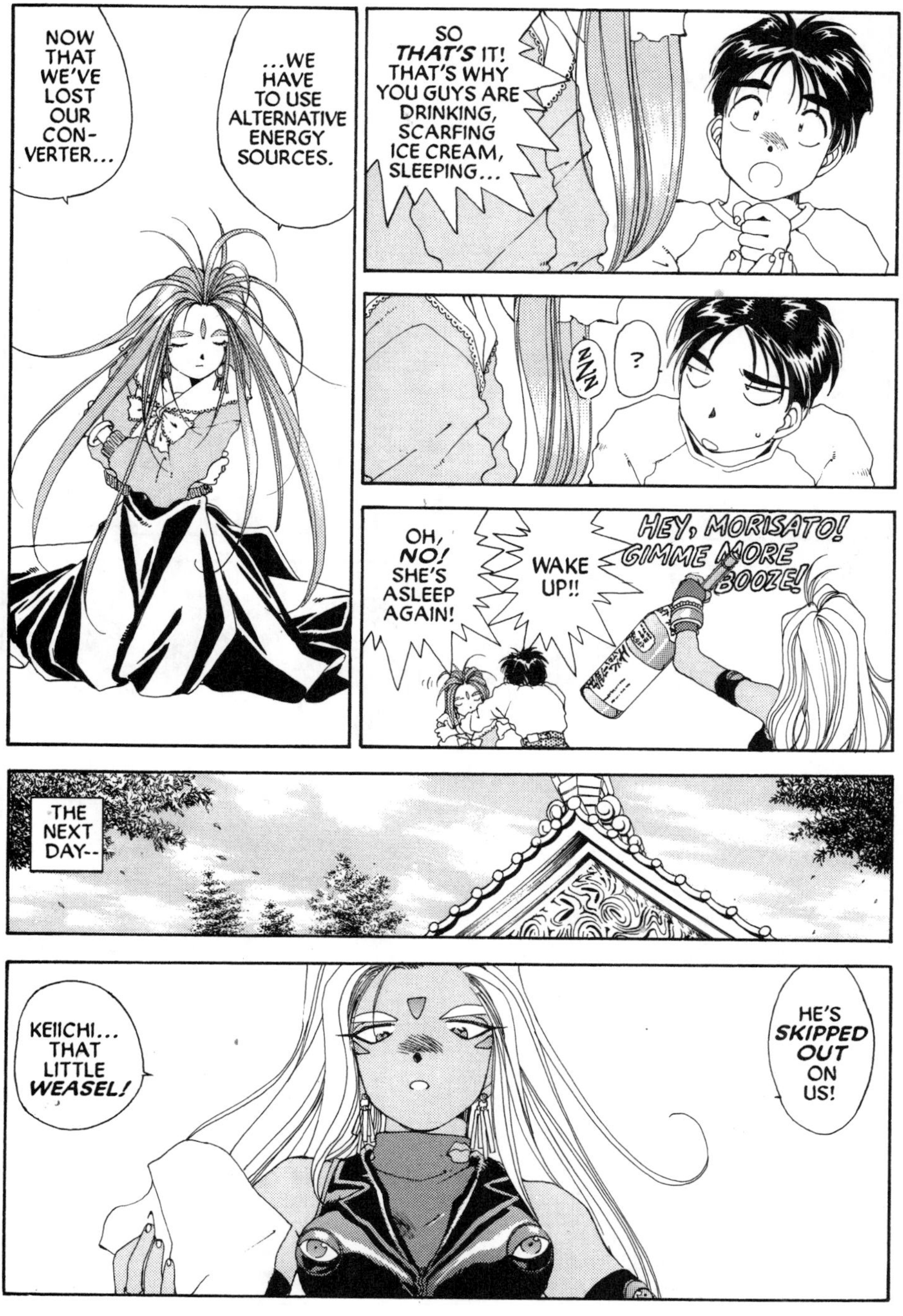
NOW THAT WE'VE LOST OUR CON-VERTER...
...WE HAVE TO USE ALTERNATIVE ENERGY SOURCES.
SO THAT'S IT! THAT'S WHY YOU GUYS ARE DRINKING, SCARFING ICE CREAM, SLEEPING...
ZZZ
?
OH, NO! SHE'S ASLEEP AGAIN!
WAKE UP!!
HEY, MORISATO! GIMME MORE BOOZE!
THE NEXT DAY--
KEIICHI... THAT LITTLE WEASEL!
HE'S SKIPPED OUT ON US!

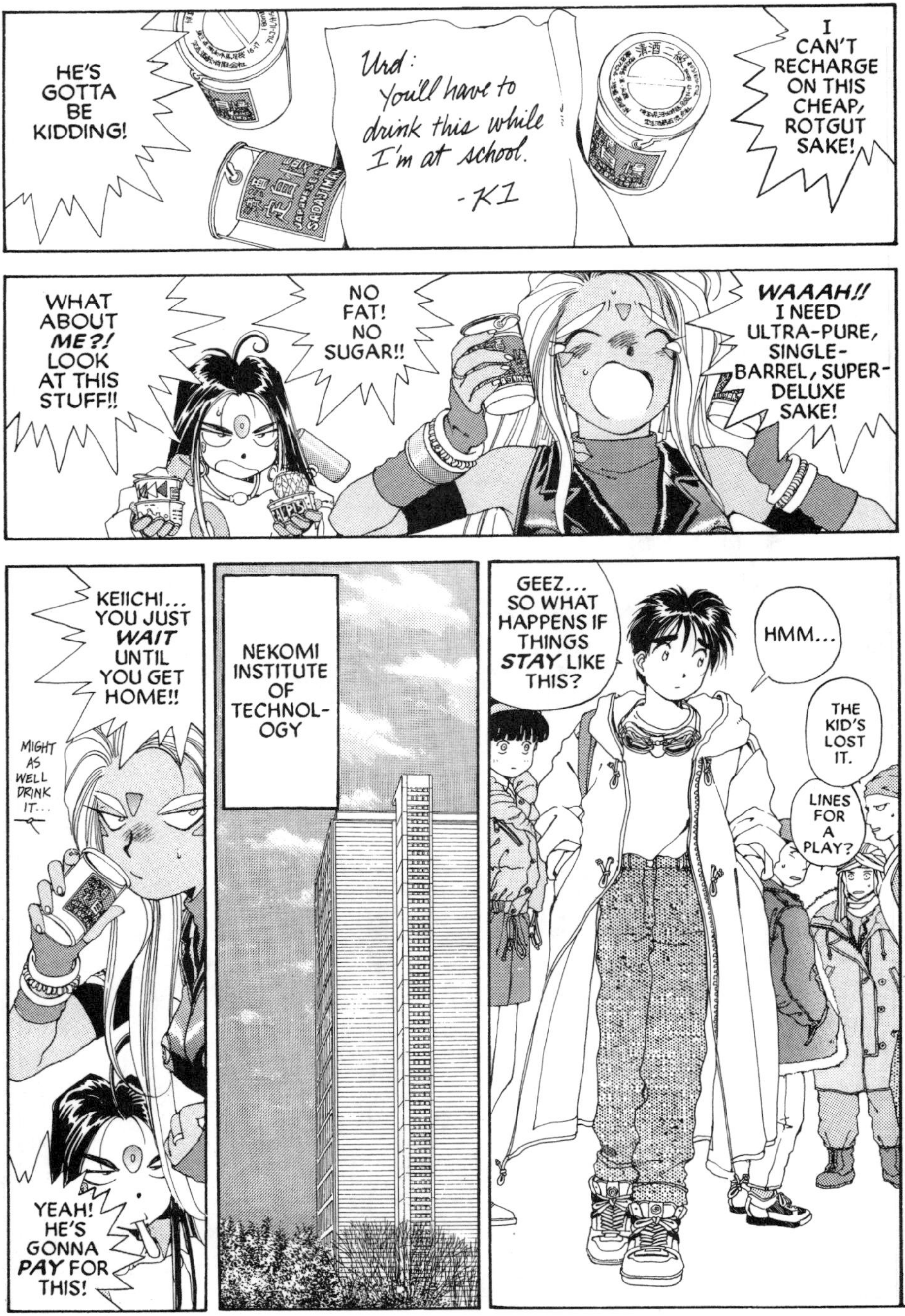
HE'S GOTTA BE KIDDING!
Urd: You'll have to drink this while I'm at school. -K1
I CAN'T RECHARGE ON THIS CHEAP, ROTGUT SAKE!
WHAT ABOUT *ME?!* LOOK AT THIS STUFF!!
NO FAT! NO SUGAR!!
WAAAH!! I NEED ULTRA-PURE, SINGLE-BARREL, SUPER-DELUXE SAKE!
KEIICHI... YOU JUST *WAIT* UNTIL YOU GET HOME!!
MIGHT AS WELL DRINK IT...
YEAH! HE'S GONNA *PAY* FOR THIS!
NEKOMI INSTITUTE OF TECHNOLOGY
GEEZ... SO WHAT HAPPENS IF THINGS *STAY* LIKE THIS?
HMM...
THE KID'S LOST IT.
LINES FOR A PLAY?

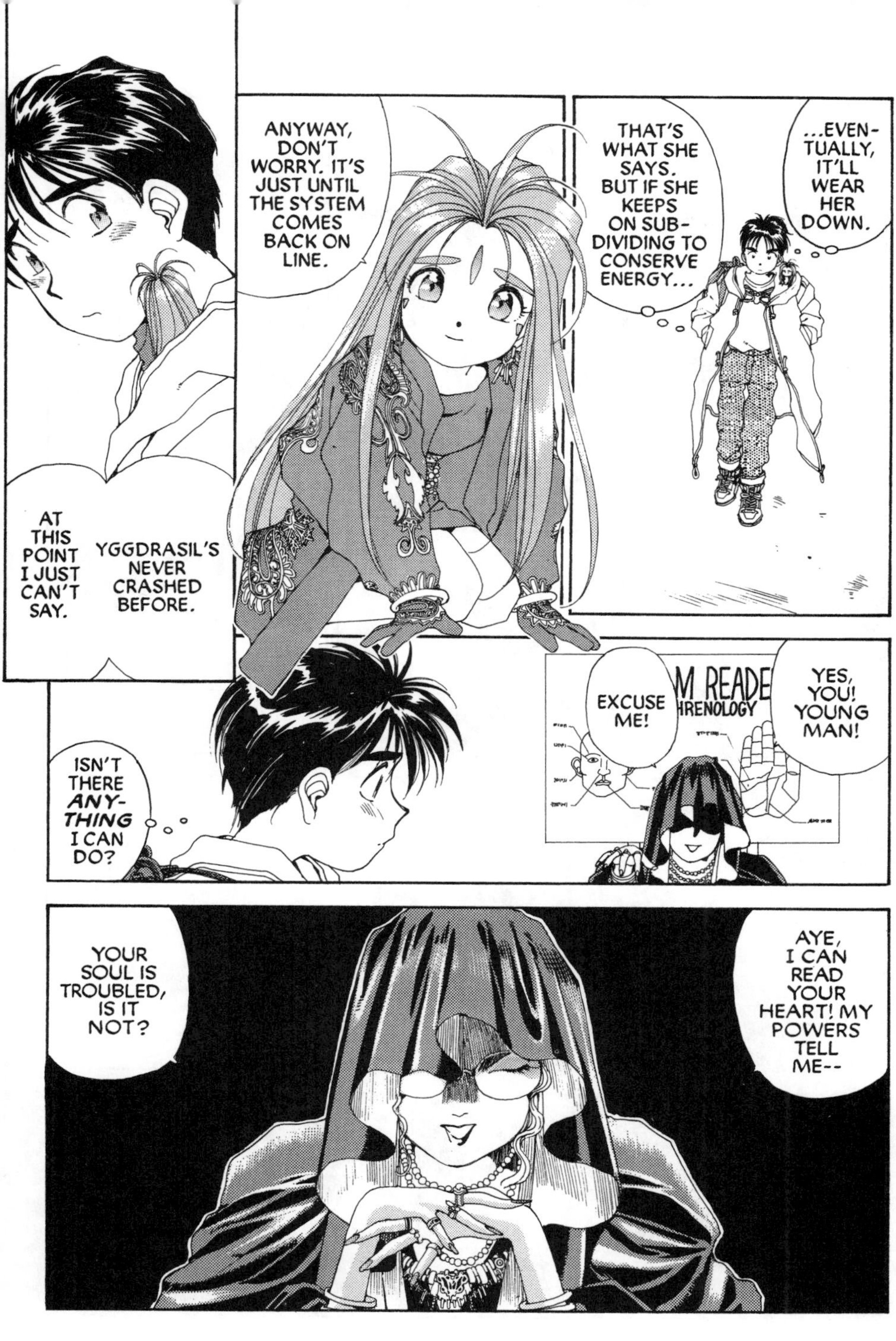
AT THIS POINT I JUST CAN'T SAY.
YGGDRASIL'S NEVER CRASHED BEFORE.
ANYWAY, DON'T WORRY. IT'S JUST UNTIL THE SYSTEM COMES BACK ON LINE.
THAT'S WHAT SHE SAYS. BUT IF SHE KEEPS ON SUB-DIVIDING TO CONSERVE ENERGY...
...EVEN-TUALLY, IT'LL WEAR HER DOWN.
ISN'T THERE *ANYTHING* I CAN DO?
EXCUSE ME!
YES, YOU! YOUNG MAN!
YOUR SOUL IS TROUBLED, IS IT NOT?
AYE, I CAN READ YOUR HEART! MY POWERS TELL ME--

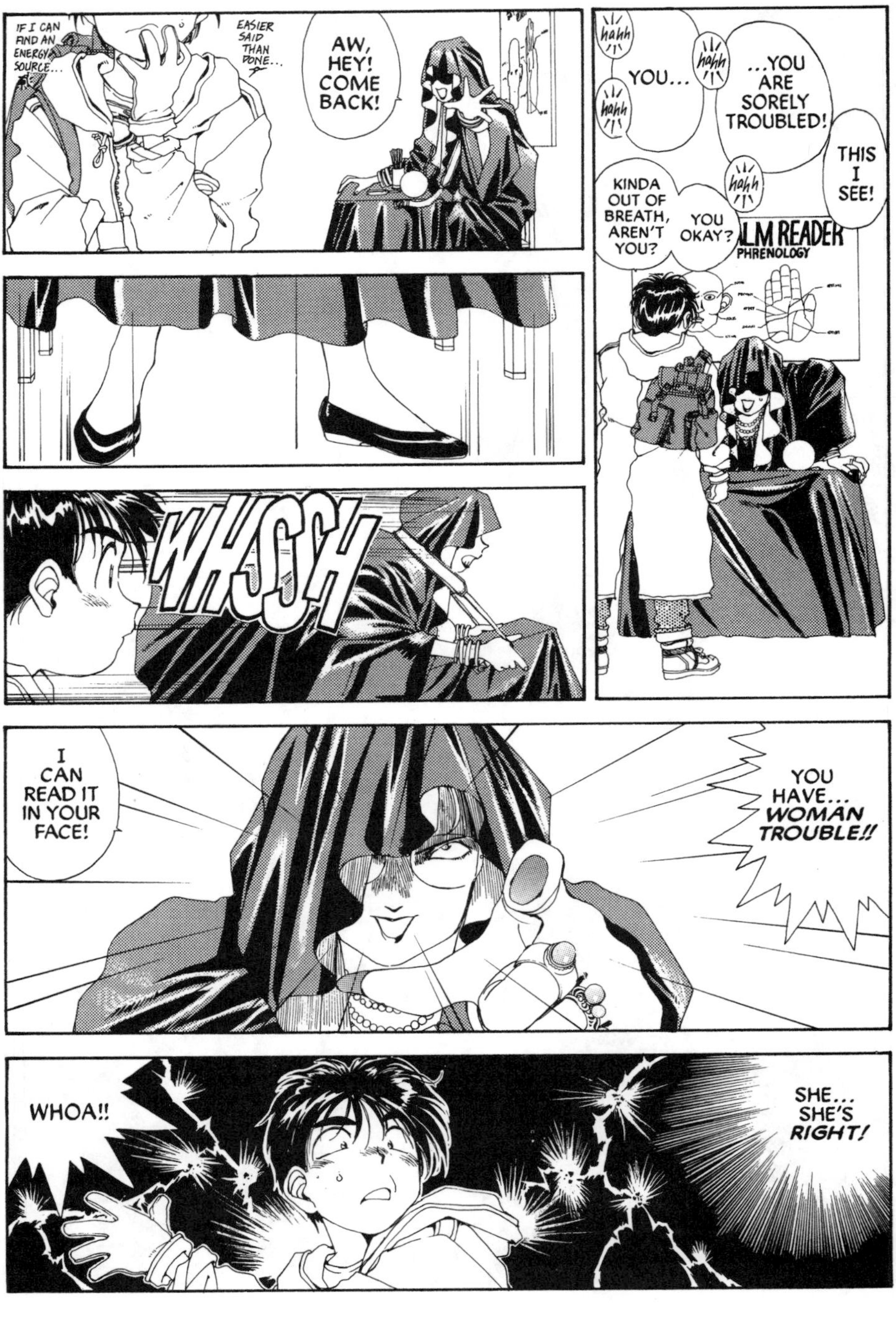
IF I CAN FIND AN ENERGY SOURCE...
EASIER SAID THAN DONE...
AW, HEY! COME BACK!
WHSCH
hahh
YOU...
hahh
hahh
...YOU ARE SORELY TROUBLED!
THIS I SEE!
hahh
KINDA OUT OF BREATH, AREN'T YOU?
YOU OKAY?
ALM READER
PHRENOLOGY
I CAN READ IT IN YOUR FACE!
YOU HAVE... *WOMAN TROUBLE!!*
WHOA!!
SHE... SHE'S *RIGHT!*

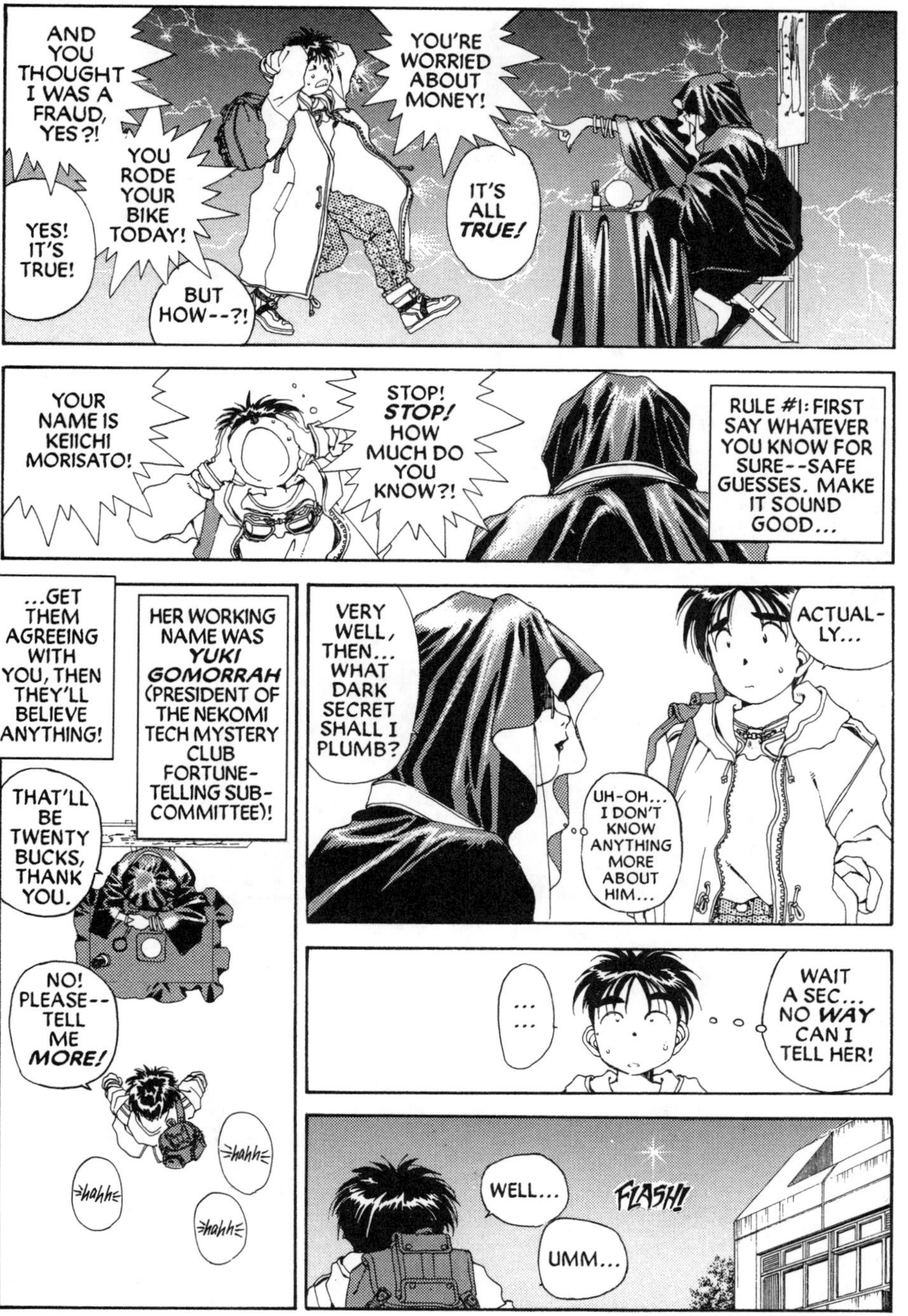
AND YOU THOUGHT I WAS A FRAUD, YES?!
YES! IT'S TRUE!
YOU RODE YOUR BIKE TODAY!
BUT HOW--?!
YOU'RE WORRIED ABOUT MONEY!
IT'S ALL *TRUE!*
YOUR NAME IS KEIICHI MORISATO!
STOP! *STOP!* HOW MUCH DO YOU KNOW?!
RULE #1: FIRST SAY WHATEVER YOU KNOW FOR SURE--SAFE GUESSES. MAKE IT SOUND GOOD...
...GET THEM AGREEING WITH YOU, THEN THEY'LL BELIEVE ANYTHING!
HER WORKING NAME WAS *YUKI GOMORRAH* (PRESIDENT OF THE NEKOMI TECH MYSTERY CLUB FORTUNE-TELLING SUB-COMMITTEE)!
THAT'LL BE TWENTY BUCKS, THANK YOU.
NO! PLEASE--TELL ME *MORE!*
hahh
hahh
hahh
VERY WELL, THEN... WHAT DARK SECRET SHALL I PLUMB?
ACTUAL-LY...
UH-OH... I DON'T KNOW ANYTHING MORE ABOUT HIM...
... ...
WAIT A SEC... NO *WAY* CAN I TELL HER!
WELL...
FLASH!
UMM...

FZZZAP

FZZZT

PALM READER
PHRENOLOGY

URK!

AHHH...?!

ER... ARE YOU OKAY, MA'AM?

THOU...

THOU SEEKEST A SOURCE OF POWERS.

VERILY, IT RIDETH HIGH IN THE HEAVENS.

PSST! WHAT HAPPENED TO *HER*, ALL OF A SUDDEN?

SHSHH! JUST LISTEN!

SHADOW OF SUN, DRINKING DEEP OF ALL ITS FORCES...

FRAGMENTS... SCATTERED ACROSS THE LAND...

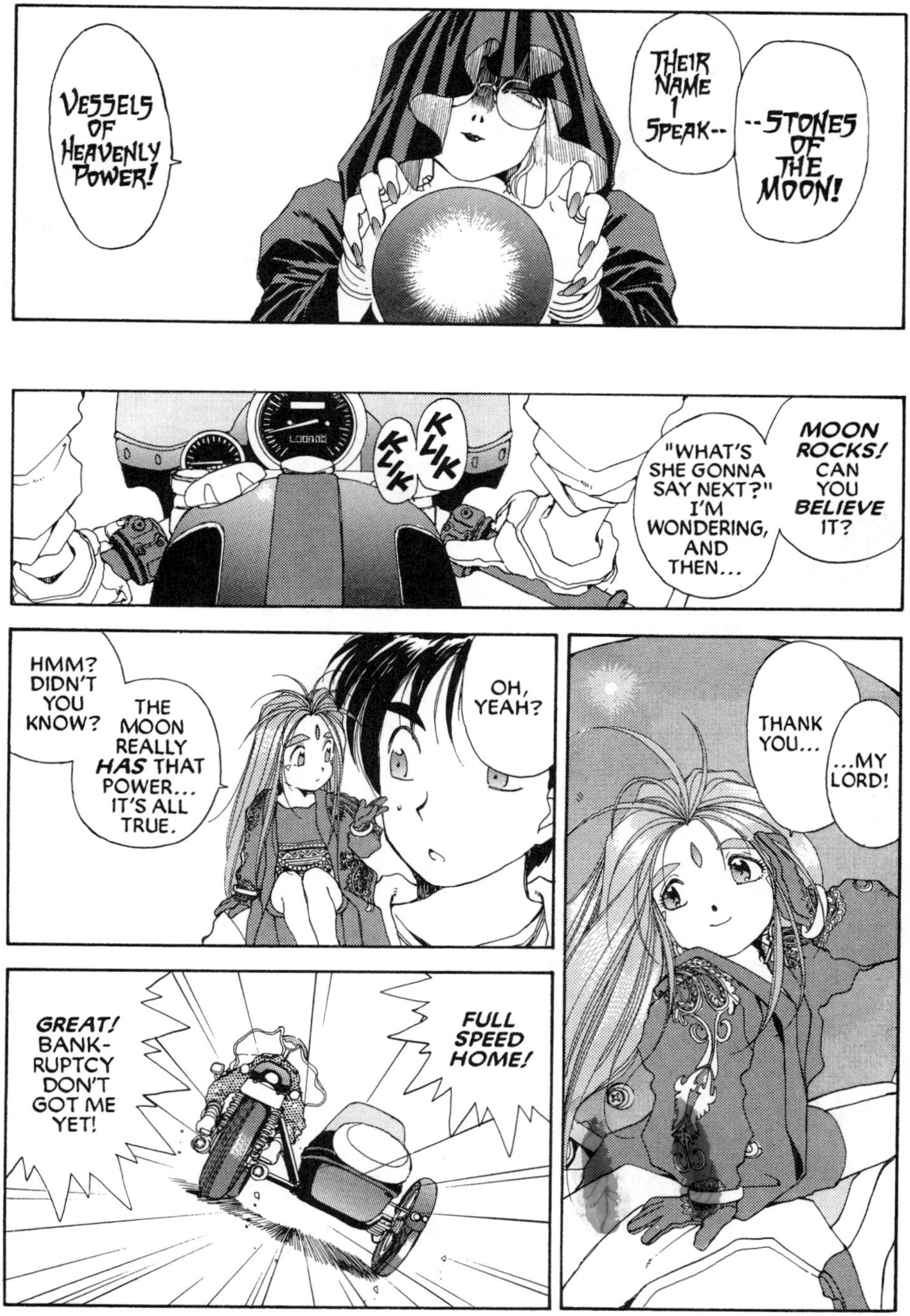
VESSELS OF HEAVENLY POWER!
THEIR NAME I SPEAK--
--STONES OF THE MOON!
KLIK
KLIK
"WHAT'S SHE GONNA SAY NEXT?" I'M WONDERING, AND THEN...
MOON ROCKS! CAN YOU BELIEVE IT?
HMM? DIDN'T YOU KNOW?
THE MOON REALLY HAS THAT POWER... IT'S ALL TRUE.
OH, YEAH?
GREAT! BANK-RUPTCY DON'T GOT ME YET!
FULL SPEED HOME!
THANK YOU...
...MY LORD!

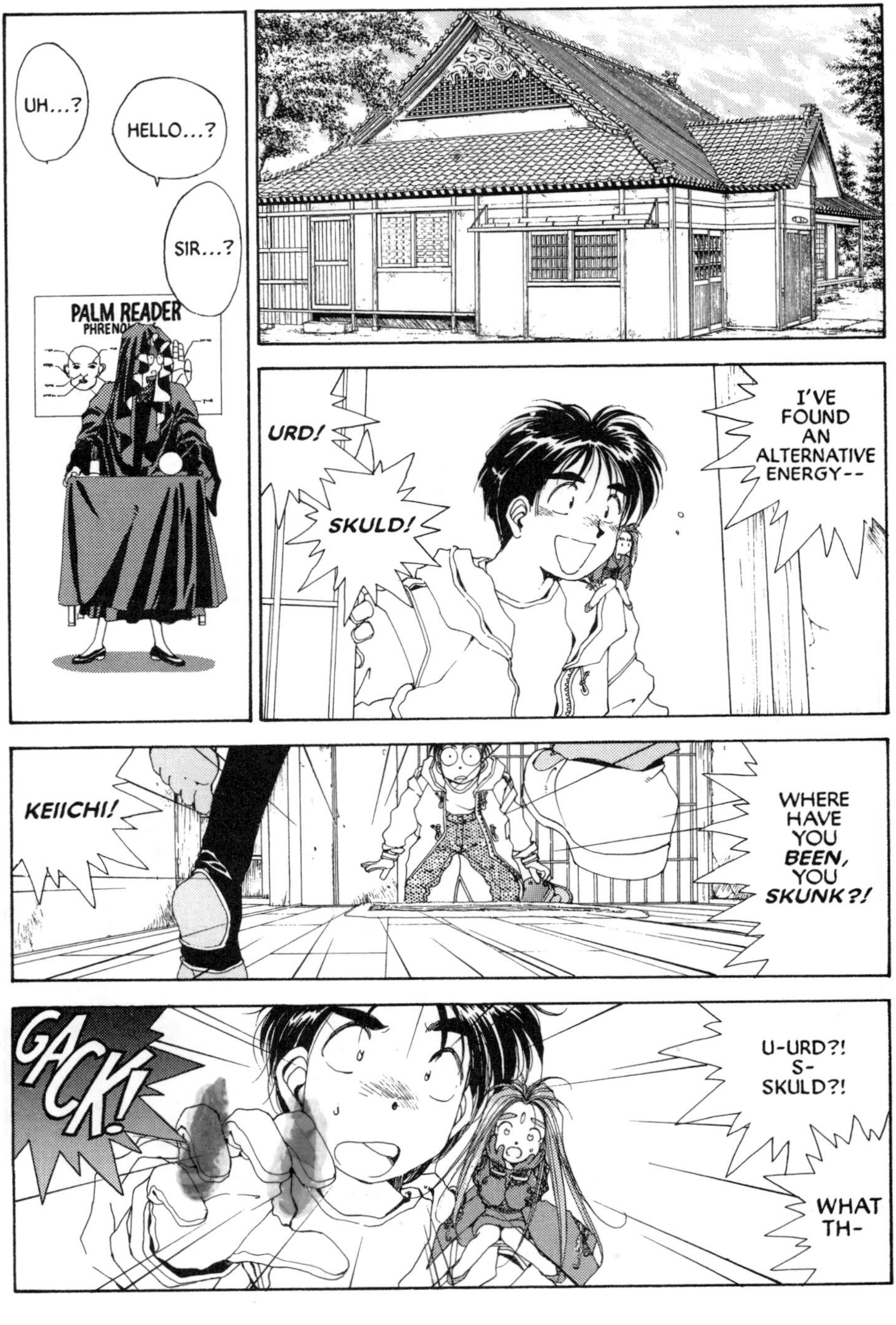

UH...?
HELLO...?
SIR...?
PALM READER
URD!
SKULD!
I'VE FOUND AN ALTERNATIVE ENERGY--
KEIICHI!
WHERE HAVE YOU BEEN, YOU SKUNK?!
GACK!
U-URD?! S-SKULD?!
WHAT TH-

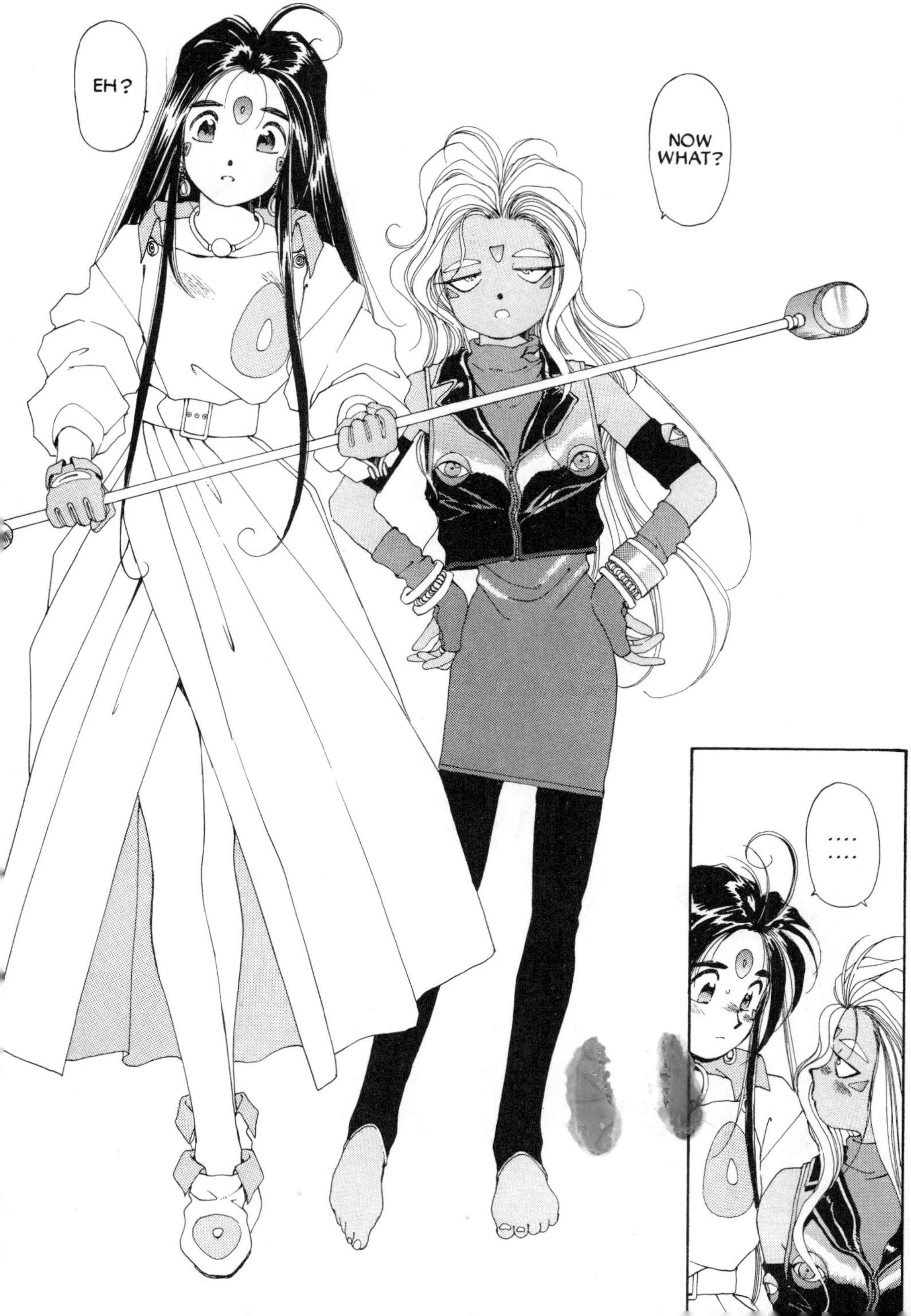
EH?
NOW WHAT?
....
....

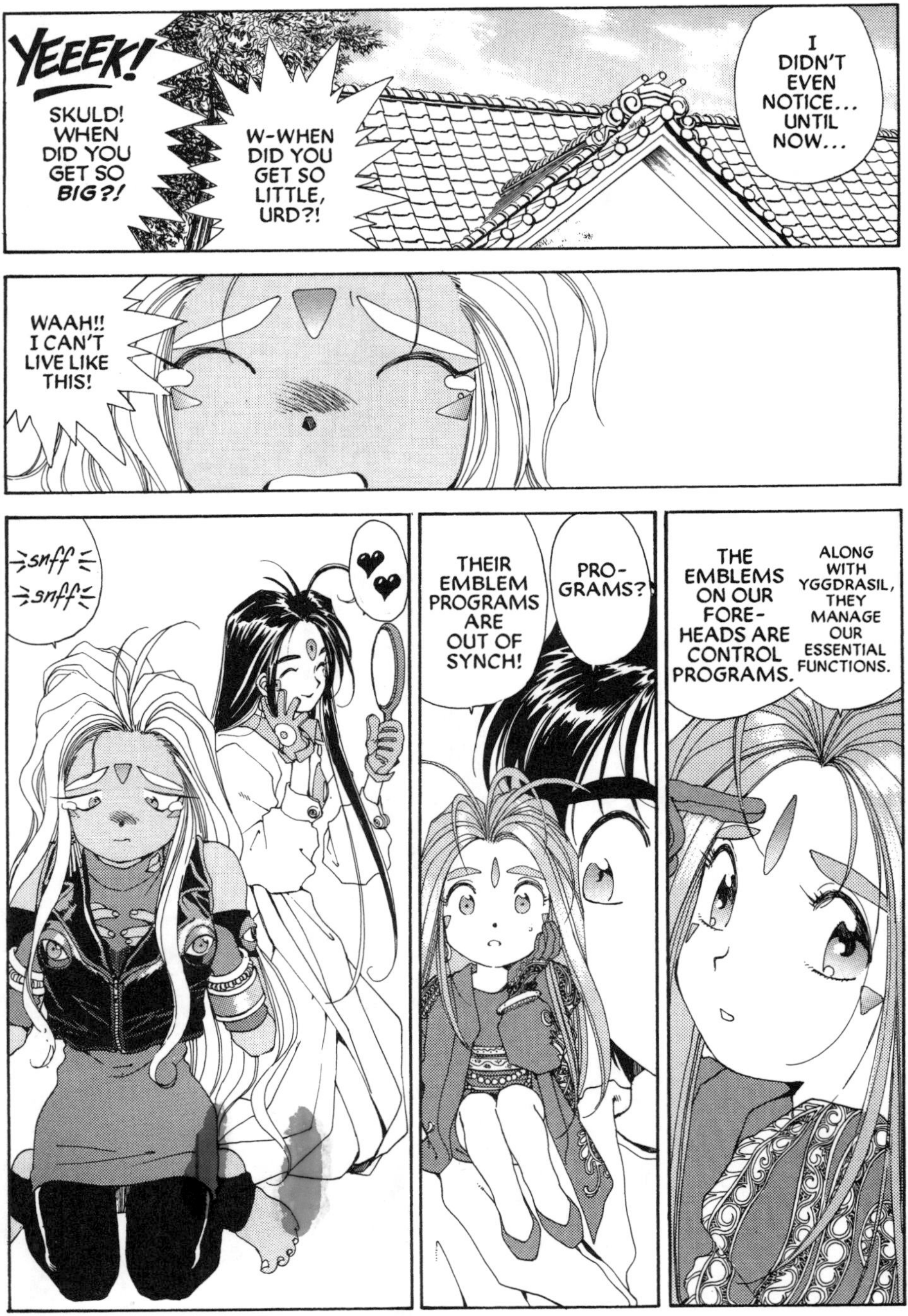
YEEEK!
SKULD! WHEN DID YOU GET SO *BIG?!*
W-WHEN DID YOU GET SO LITTLE, URD?!
I DIDN'T EVEN NOTICE... UNTIL NOW...
WAAH!! I CAN'T LIVE LIKE THIS!
snff snff
THEIR EMBLEM PROGRAMS ARE OUT OF SYNCH!
PRO-GRAMS?
THE EMBLEMS ON OUR FORE-HEADS ARE CONTROL PROGRAMS.
ALONG WITH YGGDRASIL, THEY MANAGE OUR ESSENTIAL FUNCTIONS.

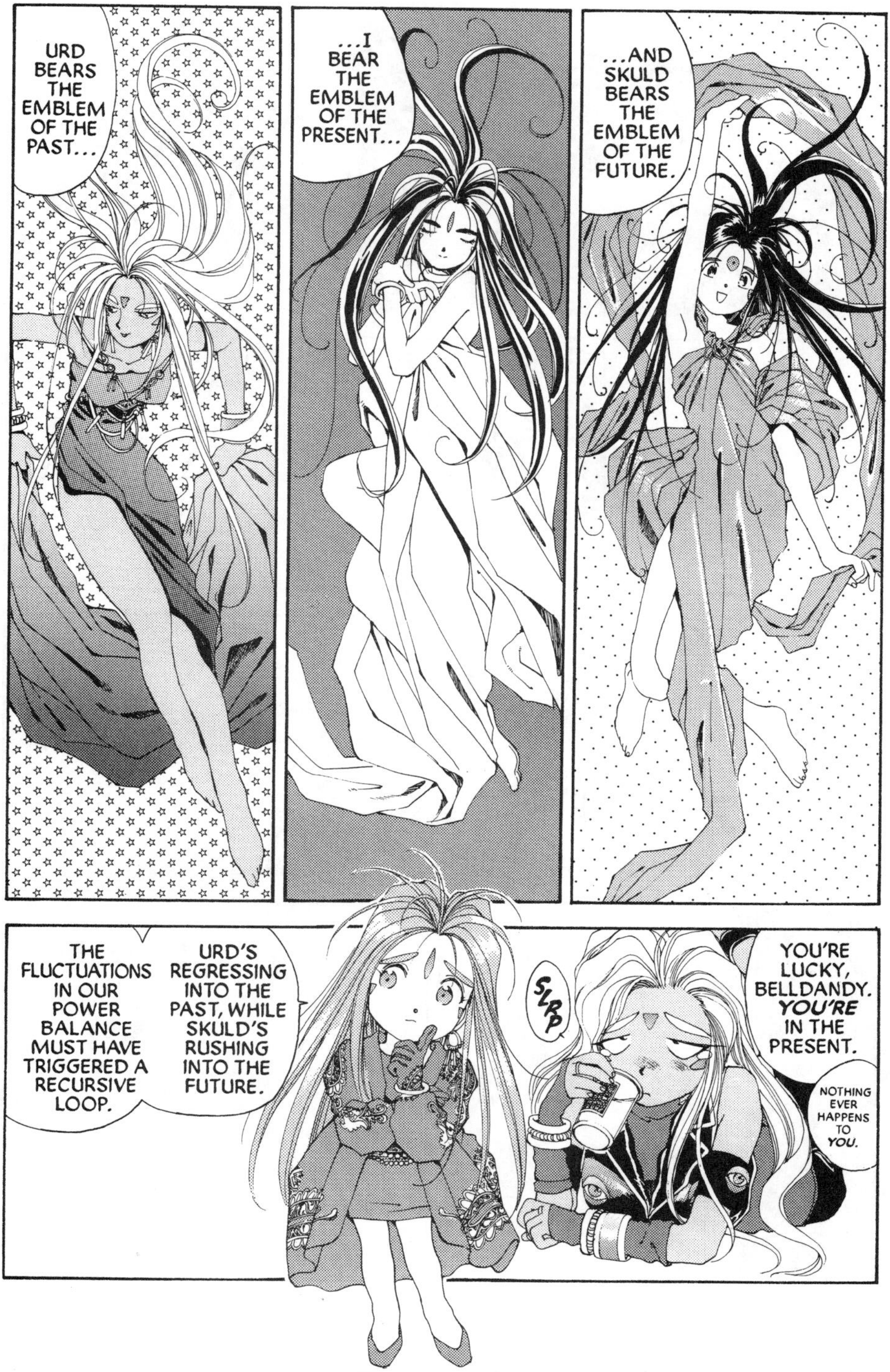
URD BEARS THE EMBLEM OF THE PAST...
...I BEAR THE EMBLEM OF THE PRESENT...
...AND SKULD BEARS THE EMBLEM OF THE FUTURE.
THE FLUCTUATIONS IN OUR POWER BALANCE MUST HAVE TRIGGERED A RECURSIVE LOOP.
URD'S REGRESSING INTO THE PAST, WHILE SKULD'S RUSHING INTO THE FUTURE.
SLRP
YOU'RE LUCKY, BELLDANDY. *YOU'RE* IN THE PRESENT.
NOTHING EVER HAPPENS TO *YOU*.

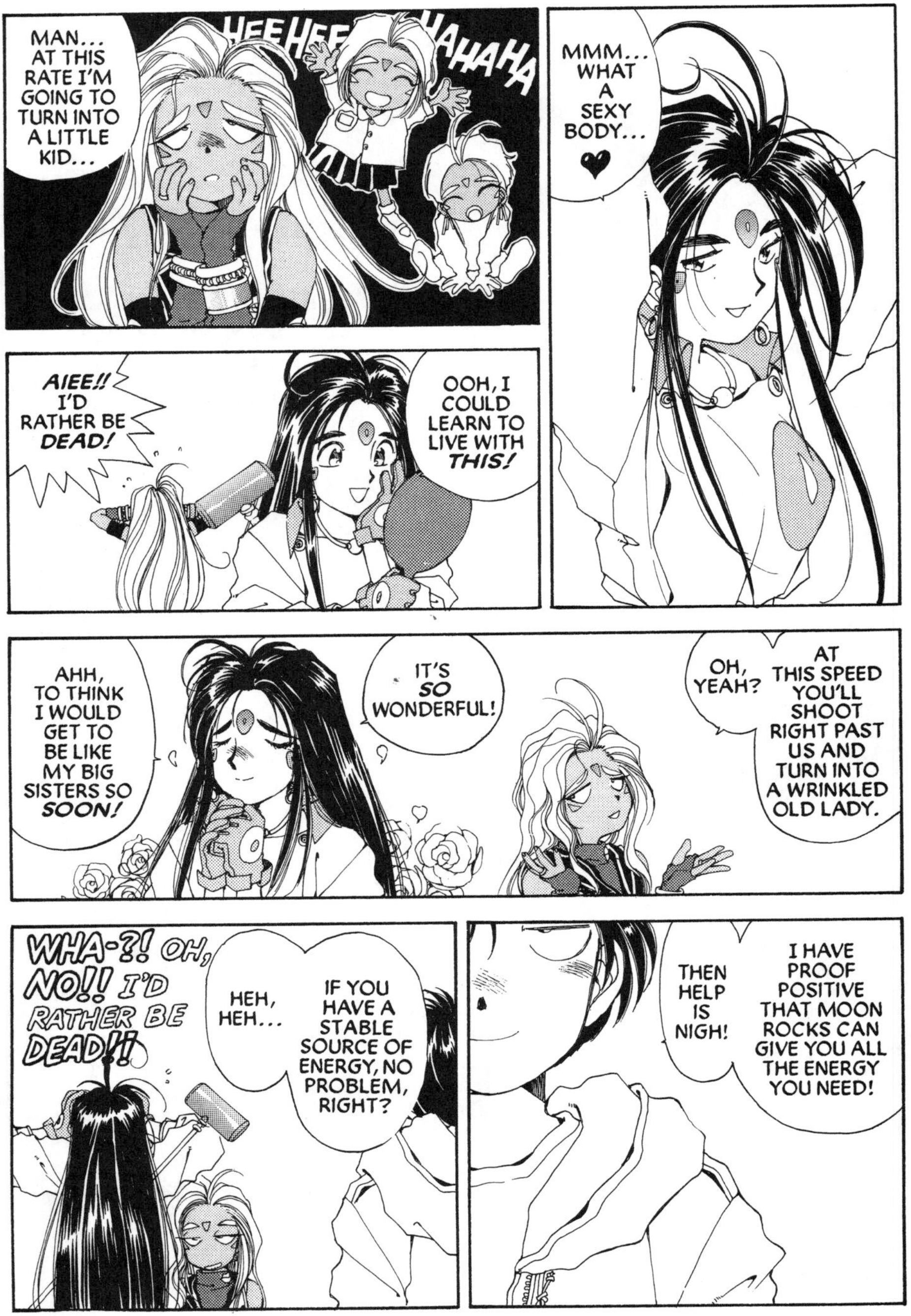
MAN... AT THIS RATE I'M GOING TO TURN INTO A LITTLE KID...
HEEHEE
HAHAHA
AIEE!! I'D RATHER BE DEAD!
OOH, I COULD LEARN TO LIVE WITH THIS!
MMM... WHAT A SEXY BODY... ♥
AHH, TO THINK I WOULD GET TO BE LIKE MY BIG SISTERS SO SOON!
IT'S SO WONDERFUL!
OH, YEAH?
AT THIS SPEED YOU'LL SHOOT RIGHT PAST US AND TURN INTO A WRINKLED OLD LADY.
WHA-?! OH, NO!! I'D RATHER BE DEAD!!
HEH, HEH...
IF YOU HAVE A STABLE SOURCE OF ENERGY, NO PROBLEM, RIGHT?
THEN HELP IS NIGH!
I HAVE PROOF POSITIVE THAT MOON ROCKS CAN GIVE YOU ALL THE ENERGY YOU NEED!

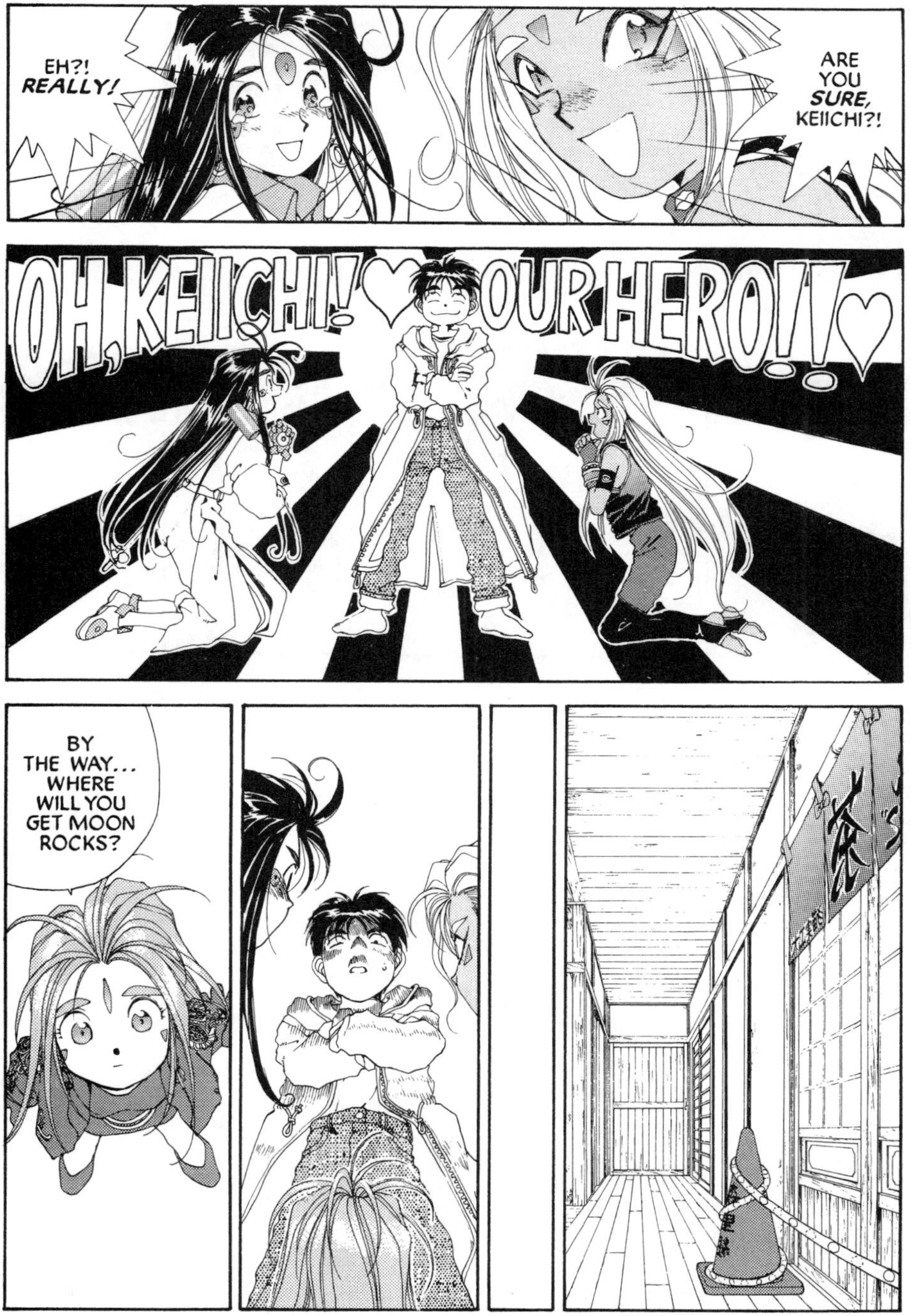
EH?! REALLY!
ARE YOU SURE, KEIICHI?!
OH, KEIICHI! ♥ OUR HERO!! ♥
BY THE WAY... WHERE WILL YOU GET MOON ROCKS?

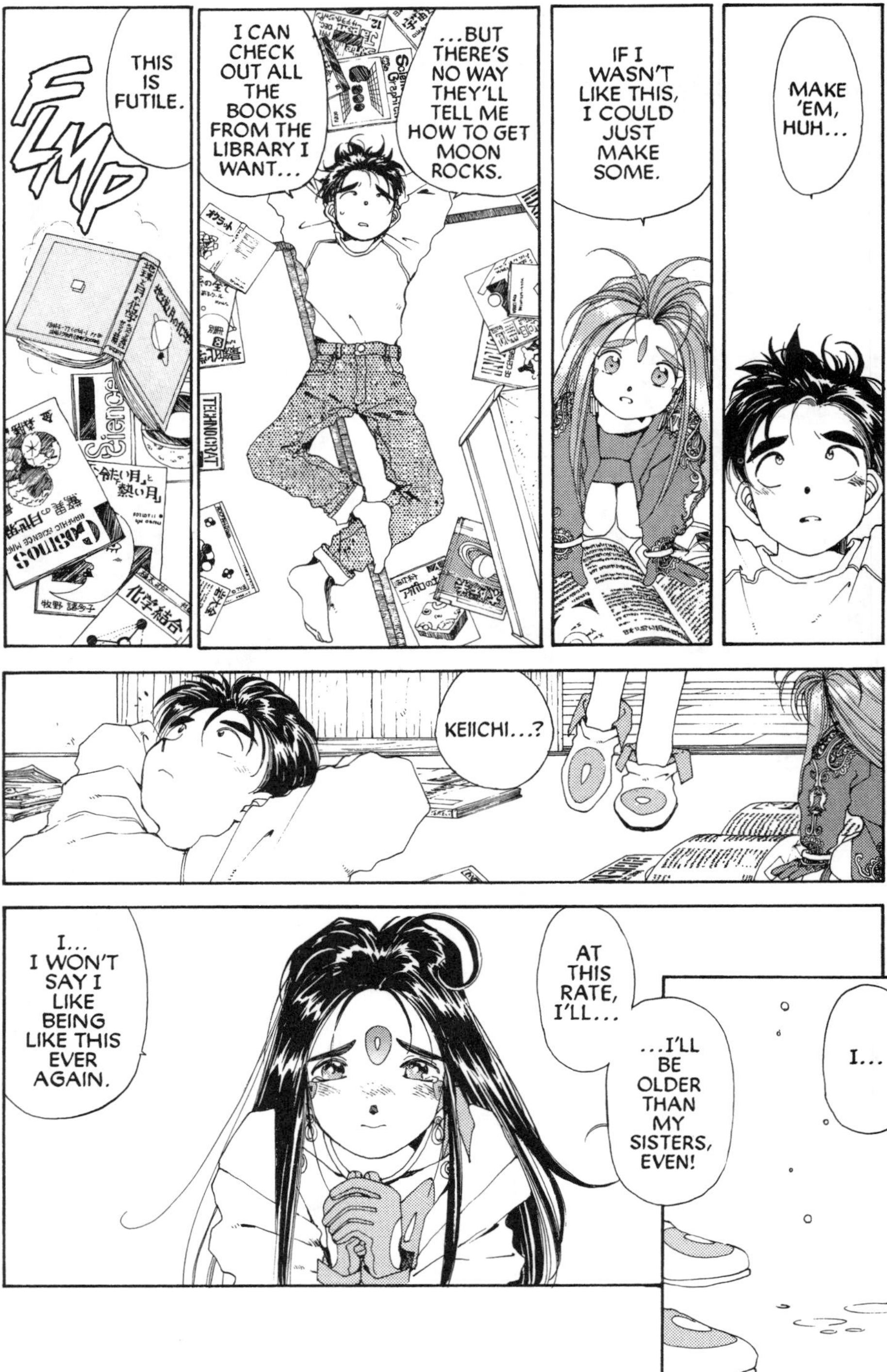
FLMP
THIS IS FUTILE.
I CAN CHECK OUT ALL THE BOOKS FROM THE LIBRARY I WANT...
...BUT THERE'S NO WAY THEY'LL TELL ME HOW TO GET MOON ROCKS.
IF I WASN'T LIKE THIS, I COULD JUST MAKE SOME.
MAKE 'EM, HUH...
KEIICHI...?
I... I WON'T SAY I LIKE BEING LIKE THIS EVER AGAIN.
AT THIS RATE, I'LL...
...I'LL BE OLDER THAN MY SISTERS, EVEN!
I...

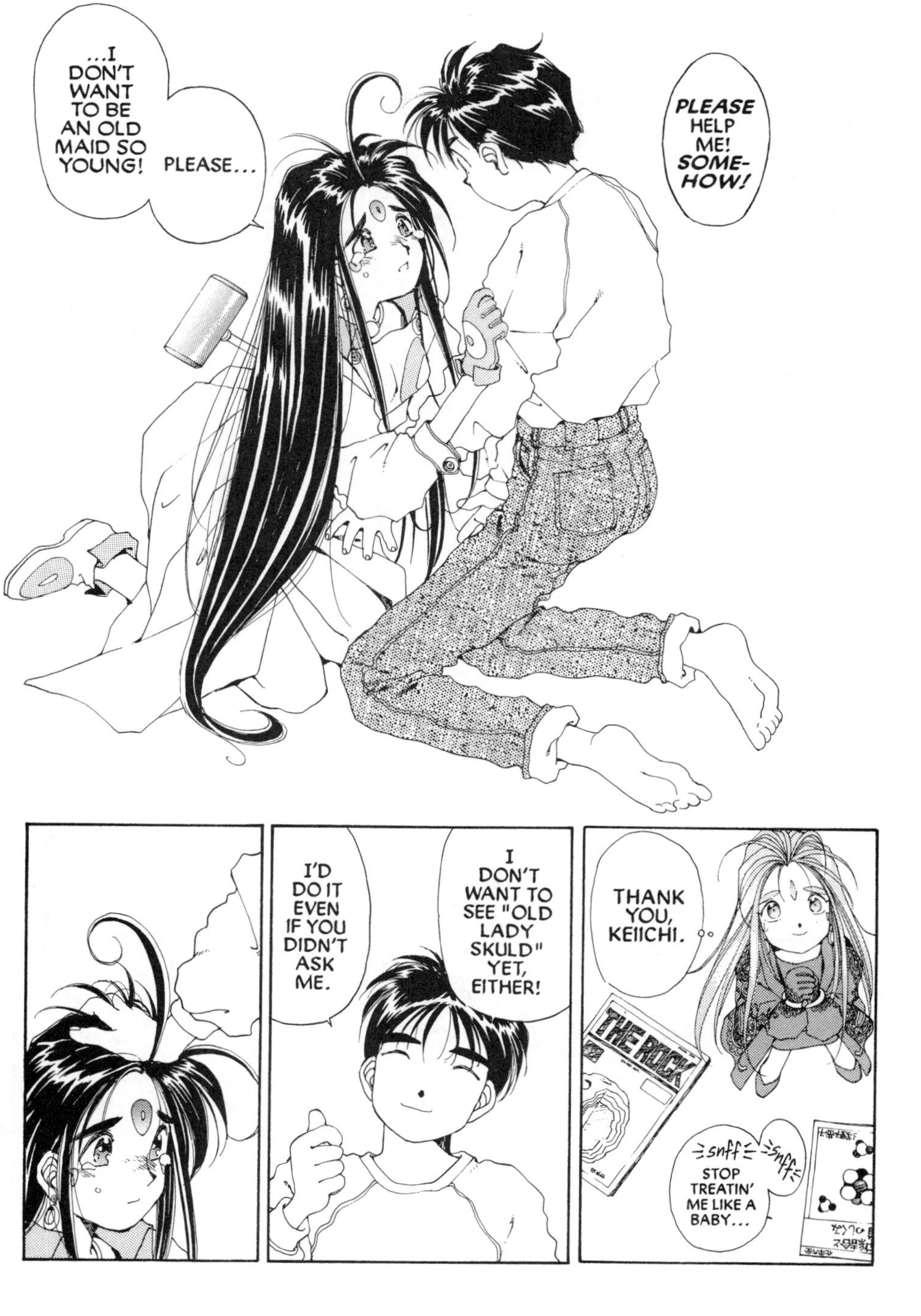
...I DON'T WANT TO BE AN OLD MAID SO YOUNG!
PLEASE...
PLEASE HELP ME! SOMEHOW!
I'D DO IT EVEN IF YOU DIDN'T ASK ME.
I DON'T WANT TO SEE "OLD LADY SKULD" YET, EITHER!
THANK YOU, KEIICHI.
THE ROCK
snff snff
STOP TREATIN' ME LIKE A BABY...

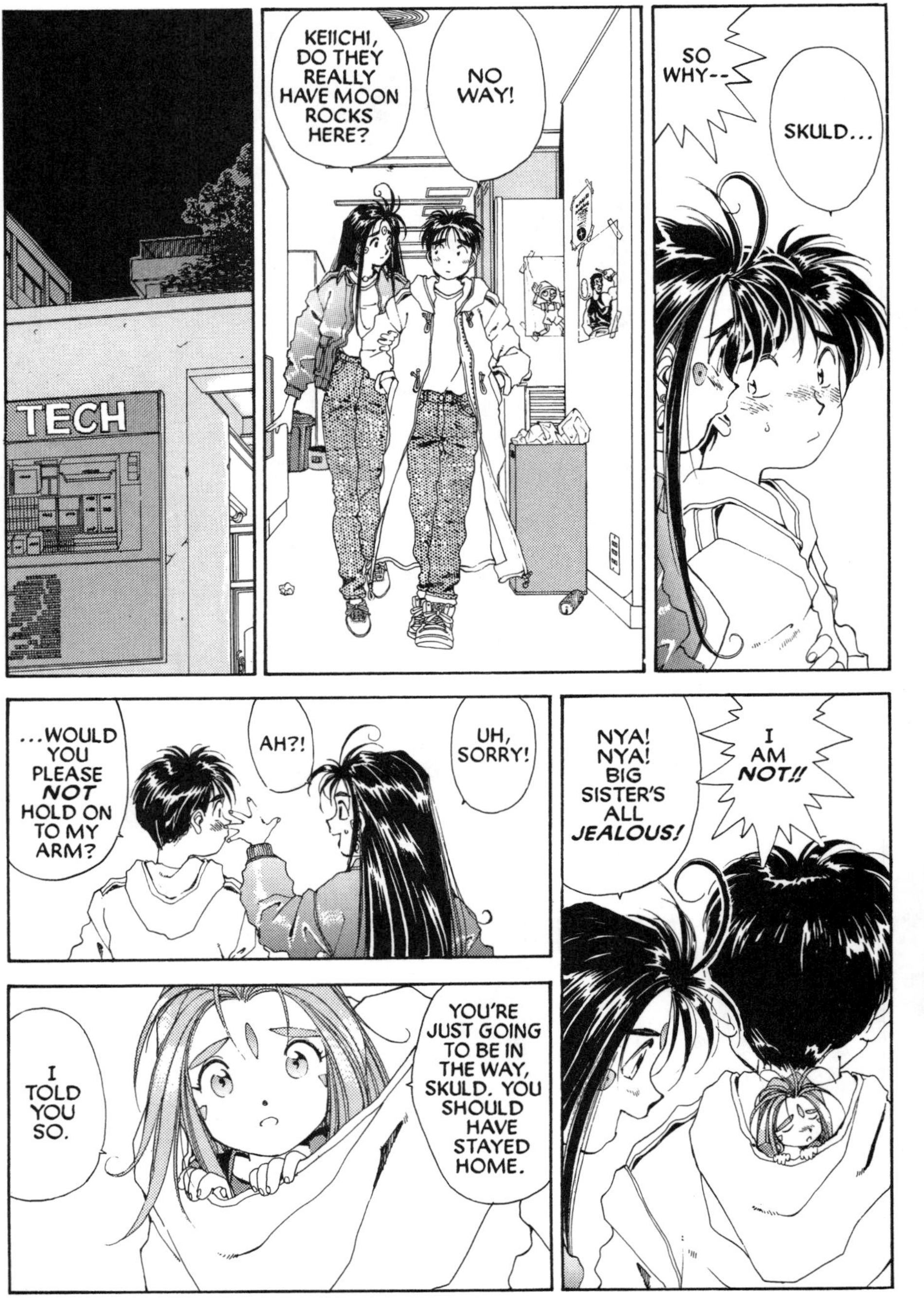
TECH
KEIICHI, DO THEY REALLY HAVE MOON ROCKS HERE?
NO WAY!
SO WHY--
SKULD...
...WOULD YOU PLEASE NOT HOLD ON TO MY ARM?
AH?!
UH, SORRY!
I TOLD YOU SO.
YOU'RE JUST GOING TO BE IN THE WAY, SKULD. YOU SHOULD HAVE STAYED HOME.
NYA! NYA! BIG SISTER'S ALL JEALOUS!
I AM NOT!!

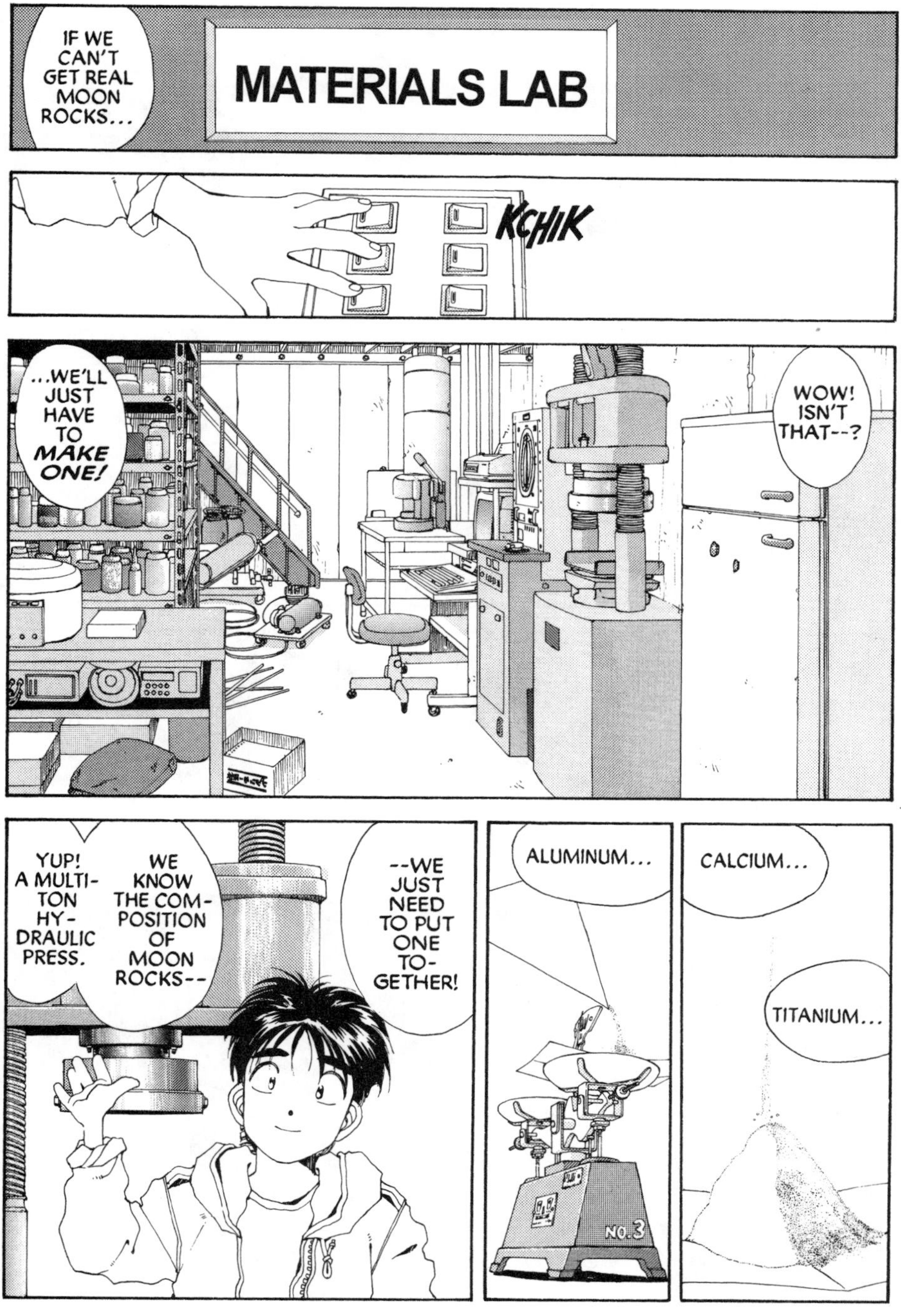
IF WE CAN'T GET REAL MOON ROCKS...
MATERIALS LAB
KCHIK
...WE'LL JUST HAVE TO *MAKE ONE!*
WOW! ISN'T THAT--?
YUP! A MULTITON HYDRAULIC PRESS.
WE KNOW THE COMPOSITION OF MOON ROCKS--
--WE JUST NEED TO PUT ONE TOGETHER!
ALUMINUM...
NO.3
CALCIUM...
TITANIUM...

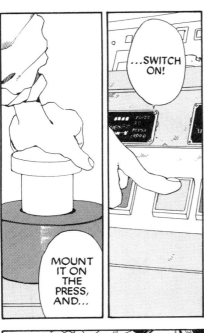

MOUNT IT ON THE PRESS, AND...
...SWITCH ON!
GRMMMM
THERE-- IT SHOULD BE READY BY SUNRISE.
YOU DID IT!
GRMMMMMM
MMMMMM
MMMMMM

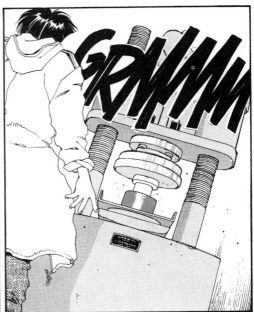

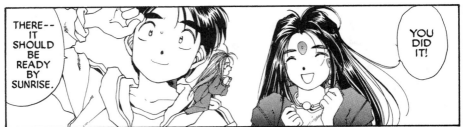

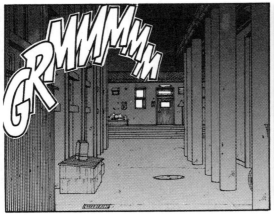

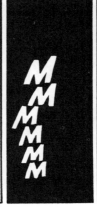

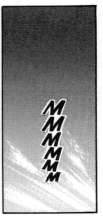

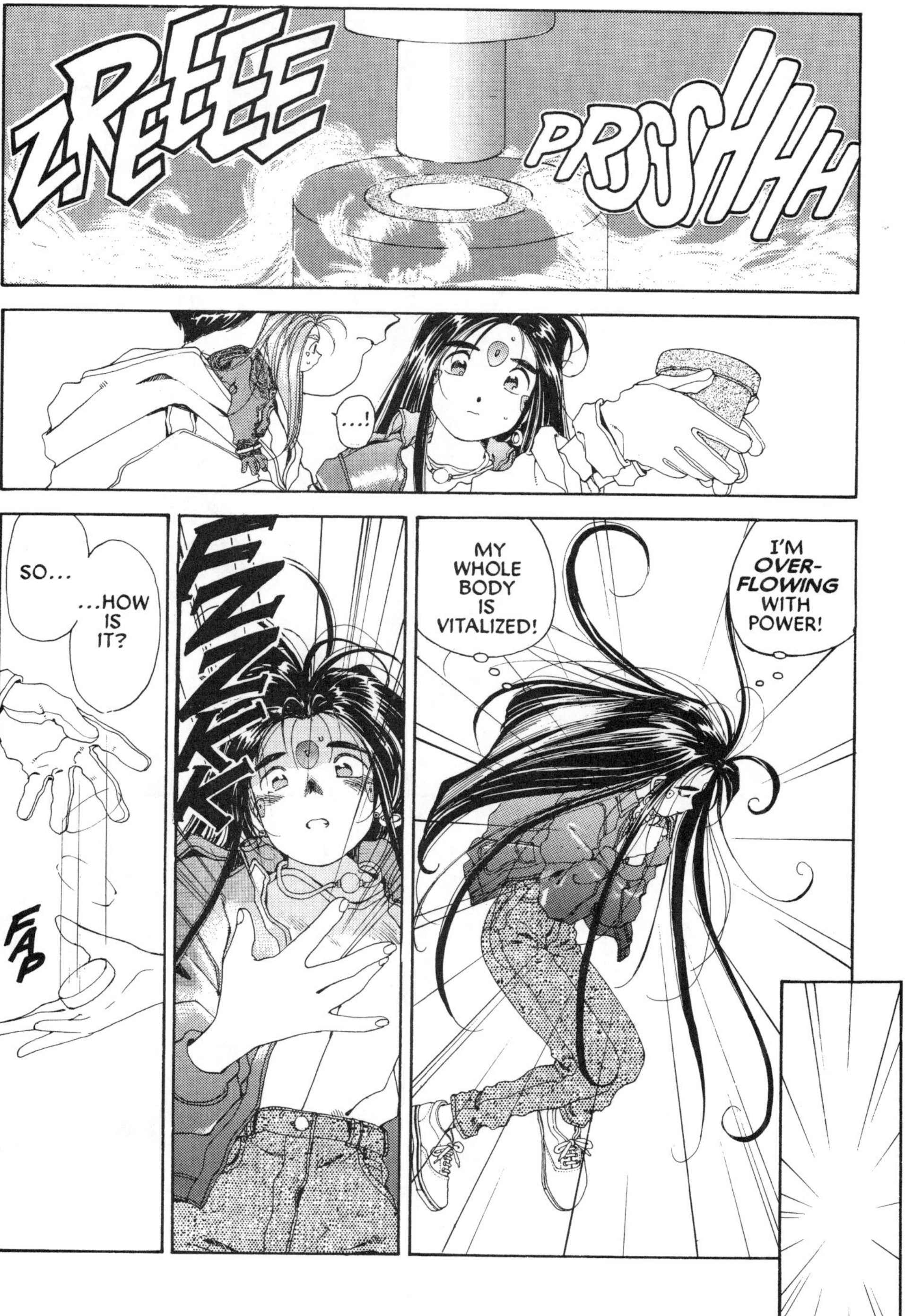
ZREEEE
PRSSHHH
....!
SO...
...HOW IS IT?
FAP
MY WHOLE BODY IS VITALIZED!
I'M *OVERFLOWING* WITH POWER!

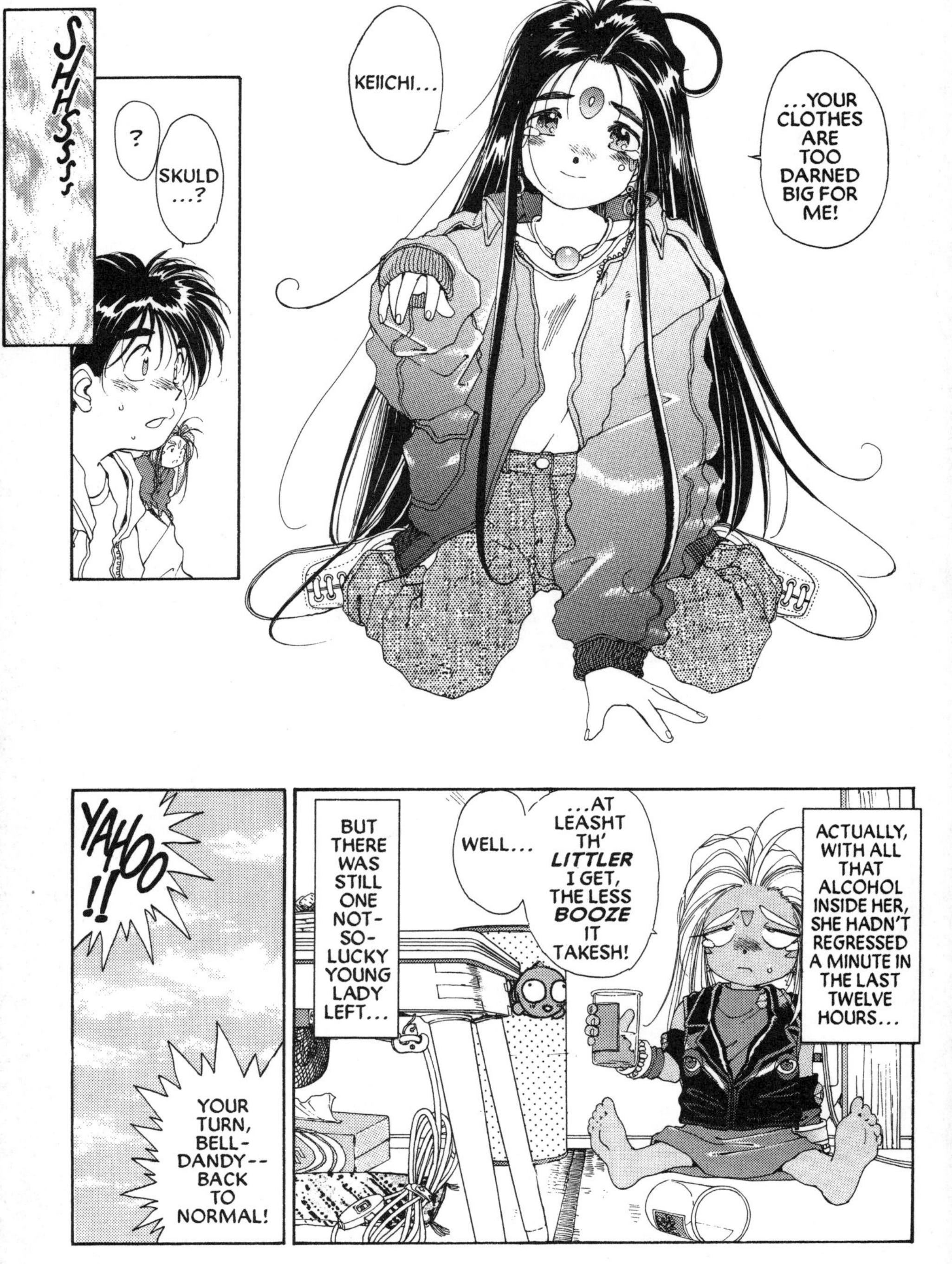
SHHSSSS
?
SKULD ...?
KEIICHI...
...YOUR CLOTHES ARE TOO DARNED BIG FOR ME!
YAHOO!!
YOUR TURN, BELL-DANDY-- BACK TO NORMAL!
BUT THERE WAS STILL ONE NOT-SO-LUCKY YOUNG LADY LEFT...
WELL...
...AT LEASHT TH' LITTLER I GET, THE LESS BOOZE IT TAKESH!
ACTUALLY, WITH ALL THAT ALCOHOL INSIDE HER, SHE HADN'T REGRESSED A MINUTE IN THE LAST TWELVE HOURS...

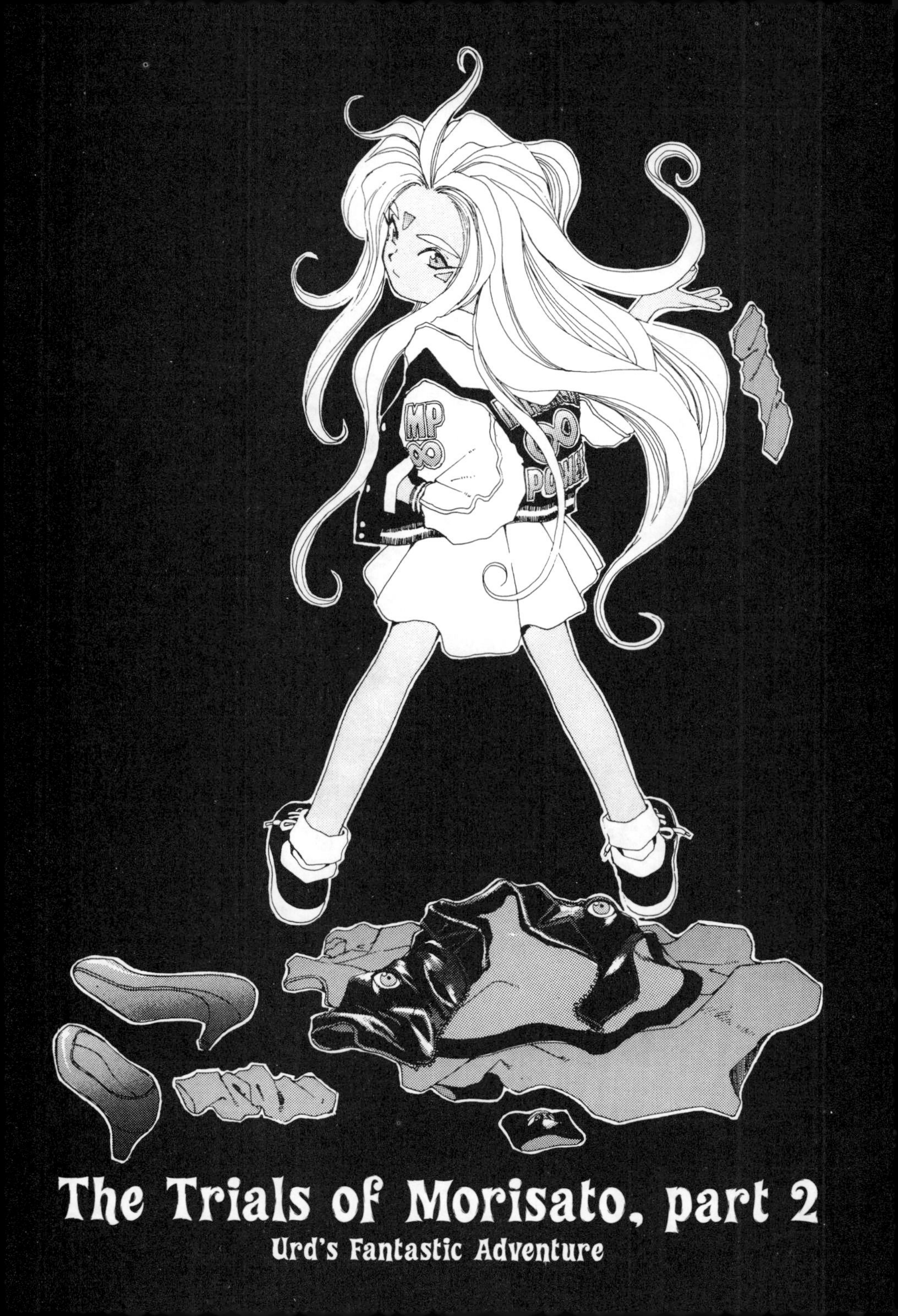

The Trials of Morisato, part 2

Urd's Fantastic Adventure

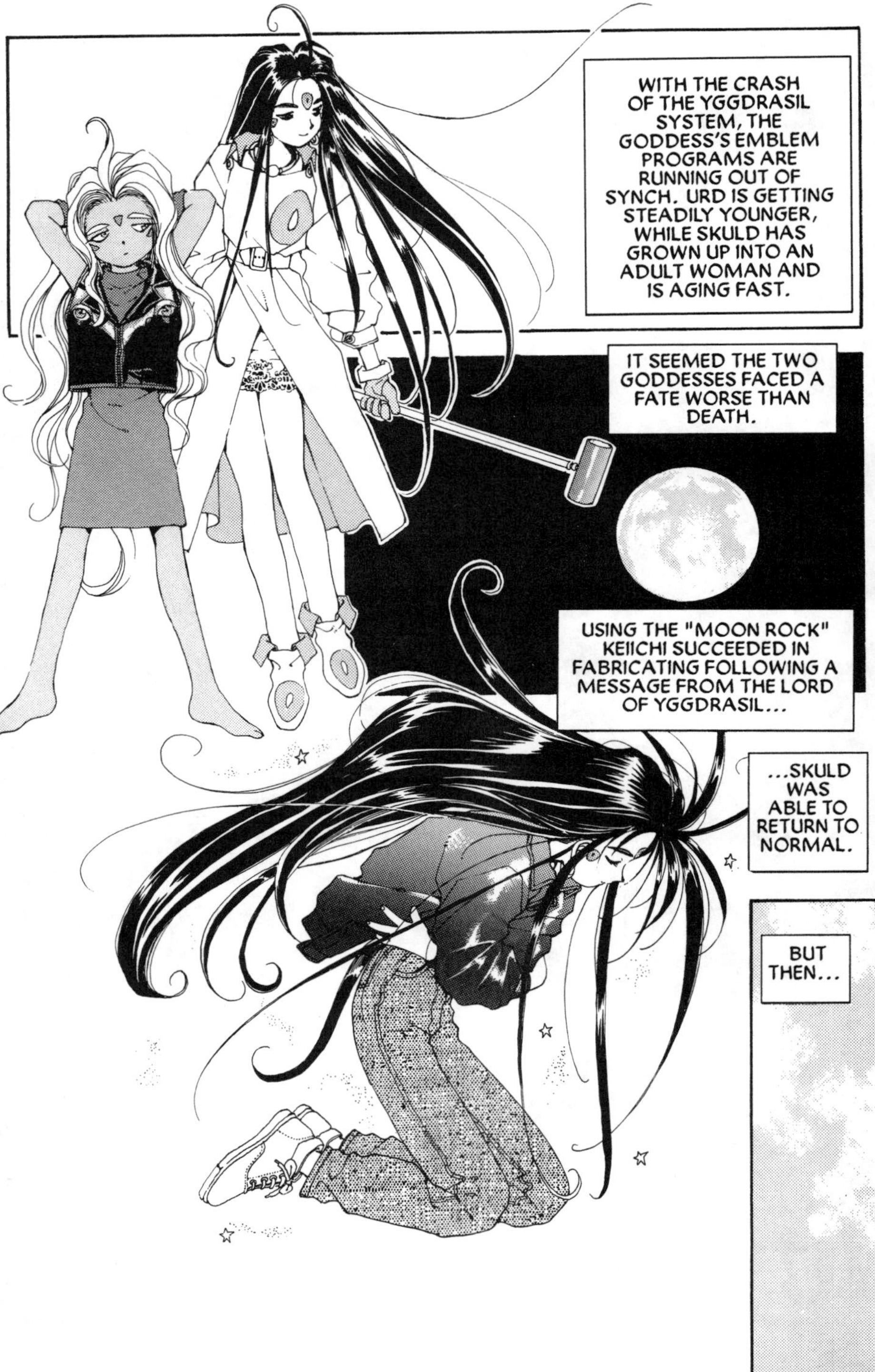
WITH THE CRASH OF THE YGGDRASIL SYSTEM, THE GODDESS'S EMBLEM PROGRAMS ARE RUNNING OUT OF SYNCH. URD IS GETTING STEADILY YOUNGER, WHILE SKULD HAS GROWN UP INTO AN ADULT WOMAN AND IS AGING FAST.
IT SEEMED THE TWO GODDESSES FACED A FATE WORSE THAN DEATH.
USING THE "MOON ROCK" KEIICHI SUCCEEDED IN FABRICATING FOLLOWING A MESSAGE FROM THE LORD OF YGGDRASIL...
...SKULD WAS ABLE TO RETURN TO NORMAL.
BUT THEN...

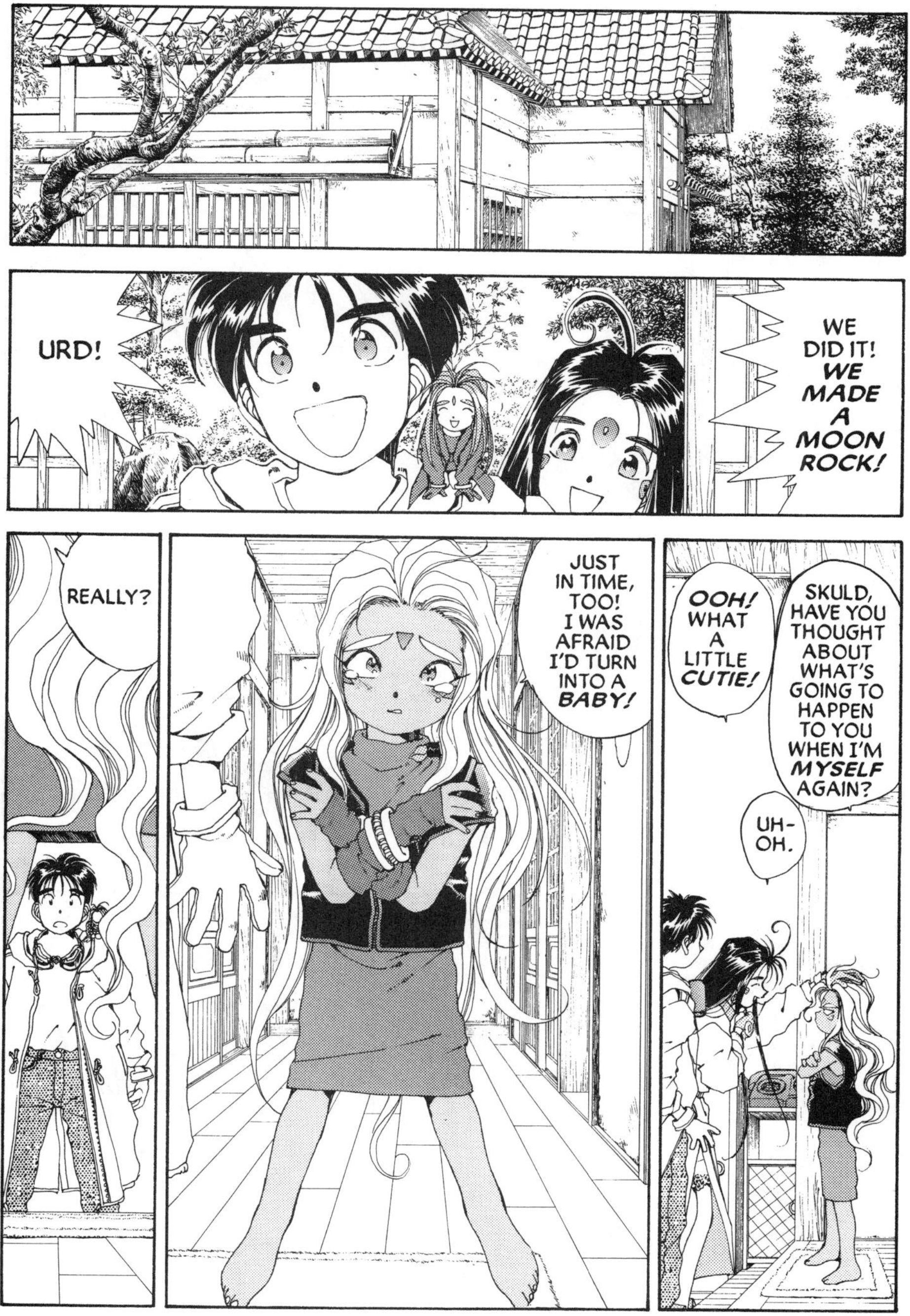
URD!
WE DID IT! WE MADE A MOON ROCK!
REALLY?
JUST IN TIME, TOO! I WAS AFRAID I'D TURN INTO A BABY!
OOH! WHAT A LITTLE CUTIE!
SKULD, HAVE YOU THOUGHT ABOUT WHAT'S GOING TO HAPPEN TO YOU WHEN I'M MYSELF AGAIN?
UH-OH.

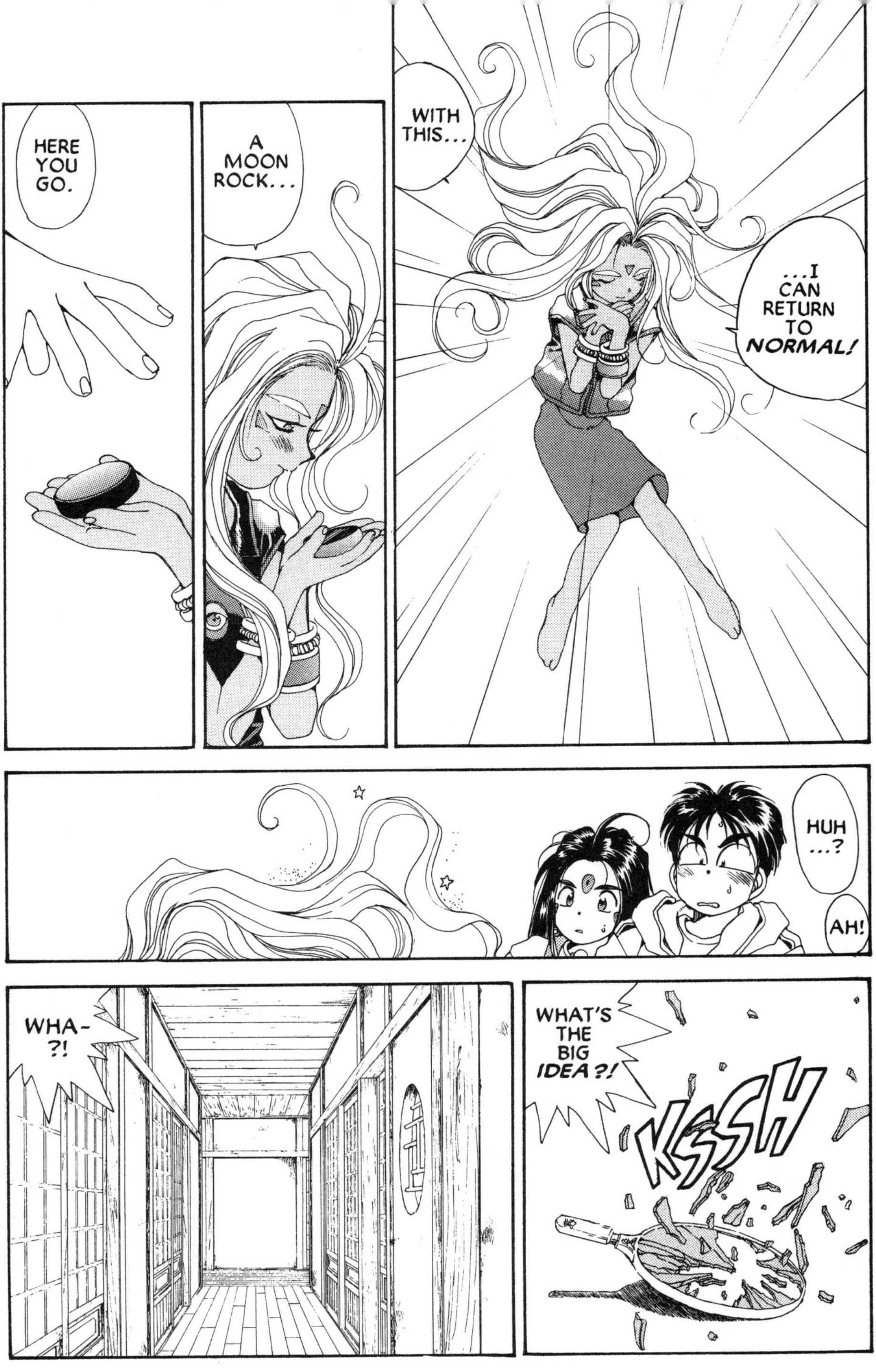
HERE YOU GO.
A MOON ROCK...
WITH THIS...
...I CAN RETURN TO *NORMAL!*
HUH ...?
AH!
WHA- ?!
WHAT'S THE BIG *IDEA?!*
KSSH

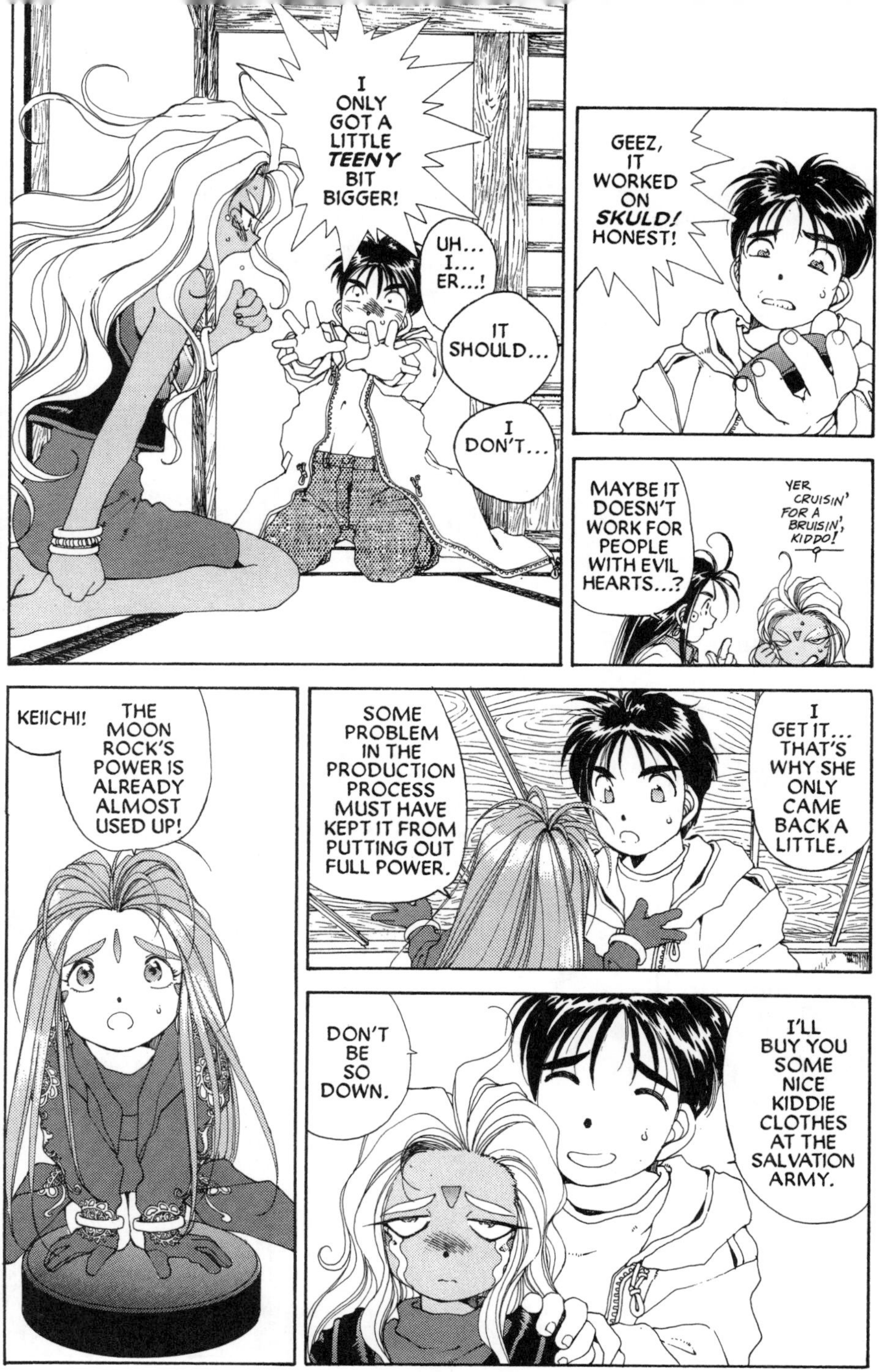
I ONLY GOT A LITTLE TEENY BIT BIGGER!
UH... I... ER...!
IT SHOULD...
I DON'T...
GEEZ, IT WORKED ON SKULD! HONEST!
MAYBE IT DOESN'T WORK FOR PEOPLE WITH EVIL HEARTS...?
YER CRUISIN' FOR A BRUISIN', KIDDO!
KEIICHI!
THE MOON ROCK'S POWER IS ALREADY ALMOST USED UP!
SOME PROBLEM IN THE PRODUCTION PROCESS MUST HAVE KEPT IT FROM PUTTING OUT FULL POWER.
I GET IT... THAT'S WHY SHE ONLY CAME BACK A LITTLE.
DON'T BE SO DOWN.
I'LL BUY YOU SOME NICE KIDDIE CLOTHES AT THE SALVATION ARMY.

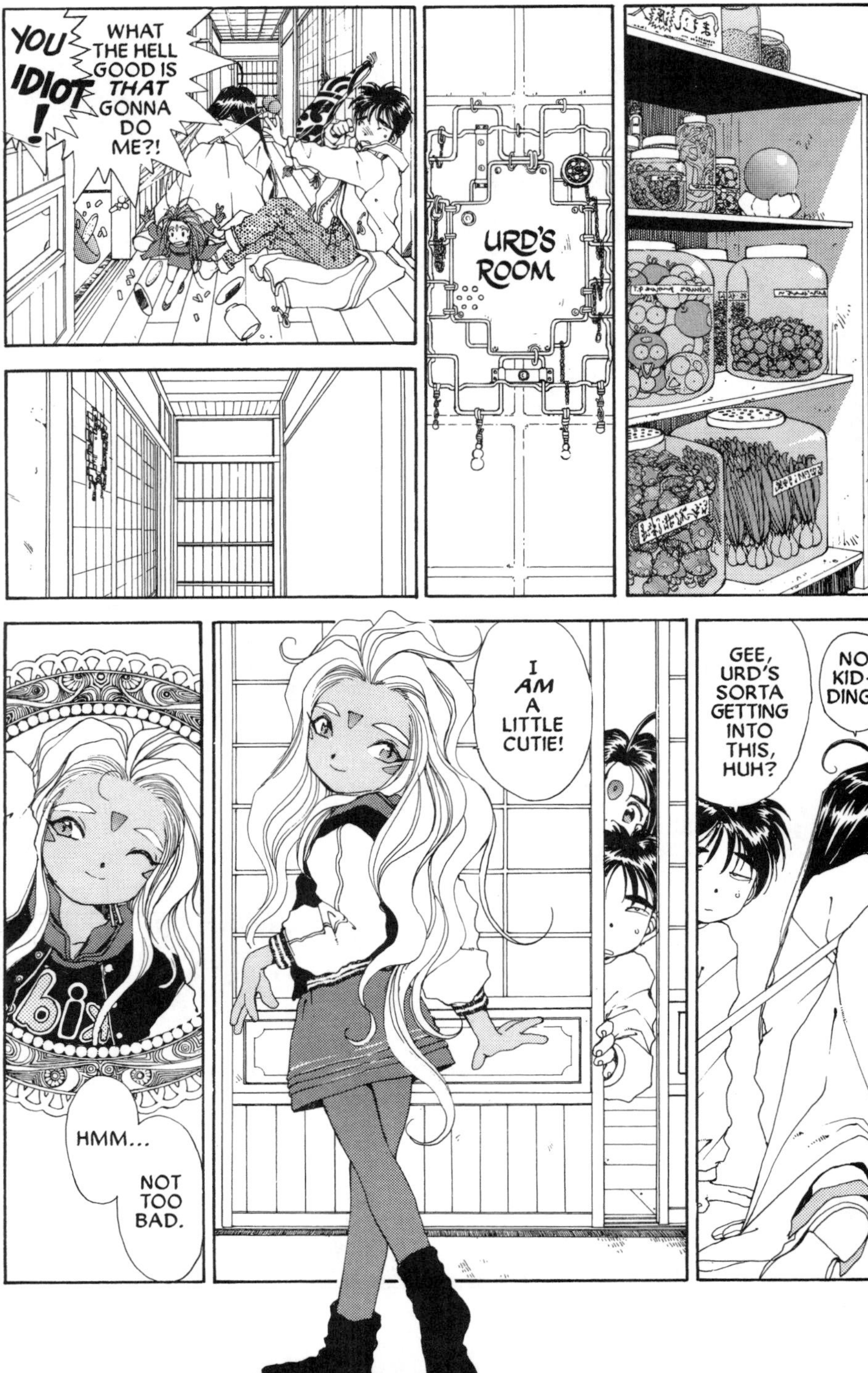
YOU IDIOT!
WHAT THE HELL GOOD IS *THAT* GONNA DO ME?!
URD'S ROOM
HMM...
NOT TOO BAD.
I *AM* A LITTLE CUTIE!
GEE, URD'S SORTA GETTING INTO THIS, HUH?
NO KID-DING.

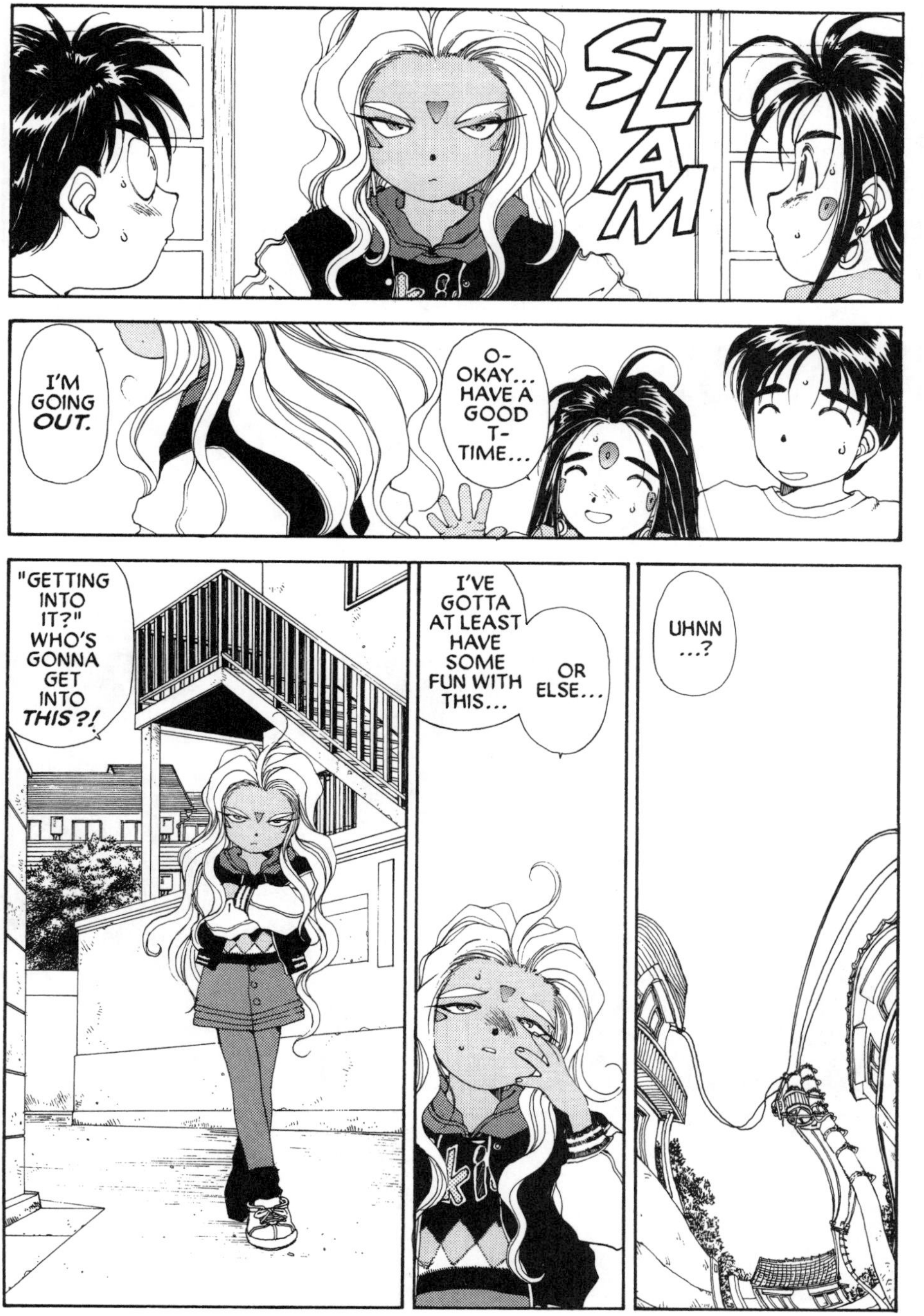
SLAM
I'M GOING OUT.
O-OKAY... HAVE A GOOD T-TIME...
"GETTING INTO IT?" WHO'S GONNA GET INTO THIS?!
I'VE GOTTA AT LEAST HAVE SOME FUN WITH THIS...
OR ELSE...
UHNN ...?

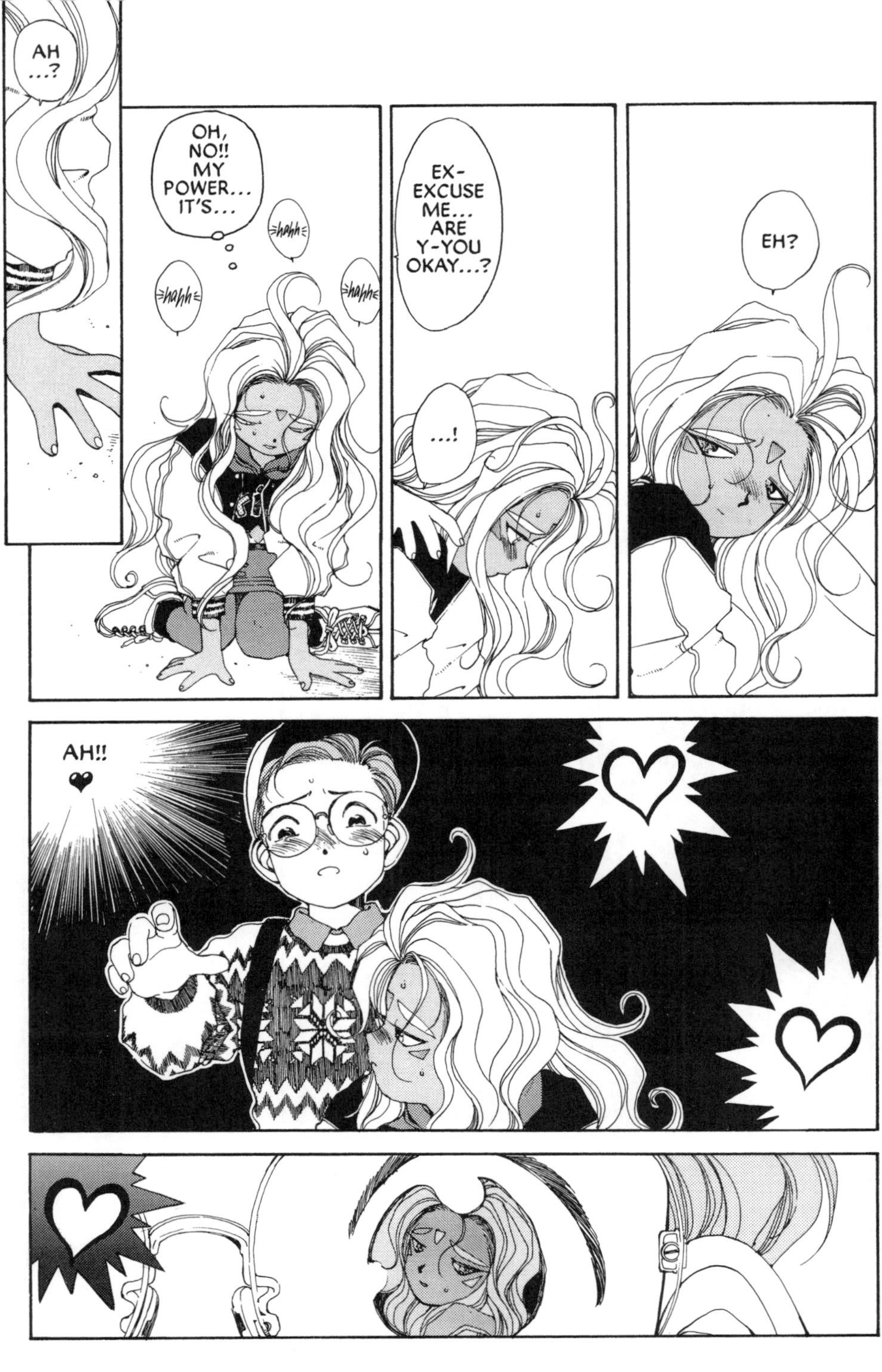
AH ...?
OH, NO!! MY POWER... IT'S...
hahh
hahh
hahh
EX-EXCUSE ME... ARE Y-YOU OKAY...?
...!
EH?
AH!!

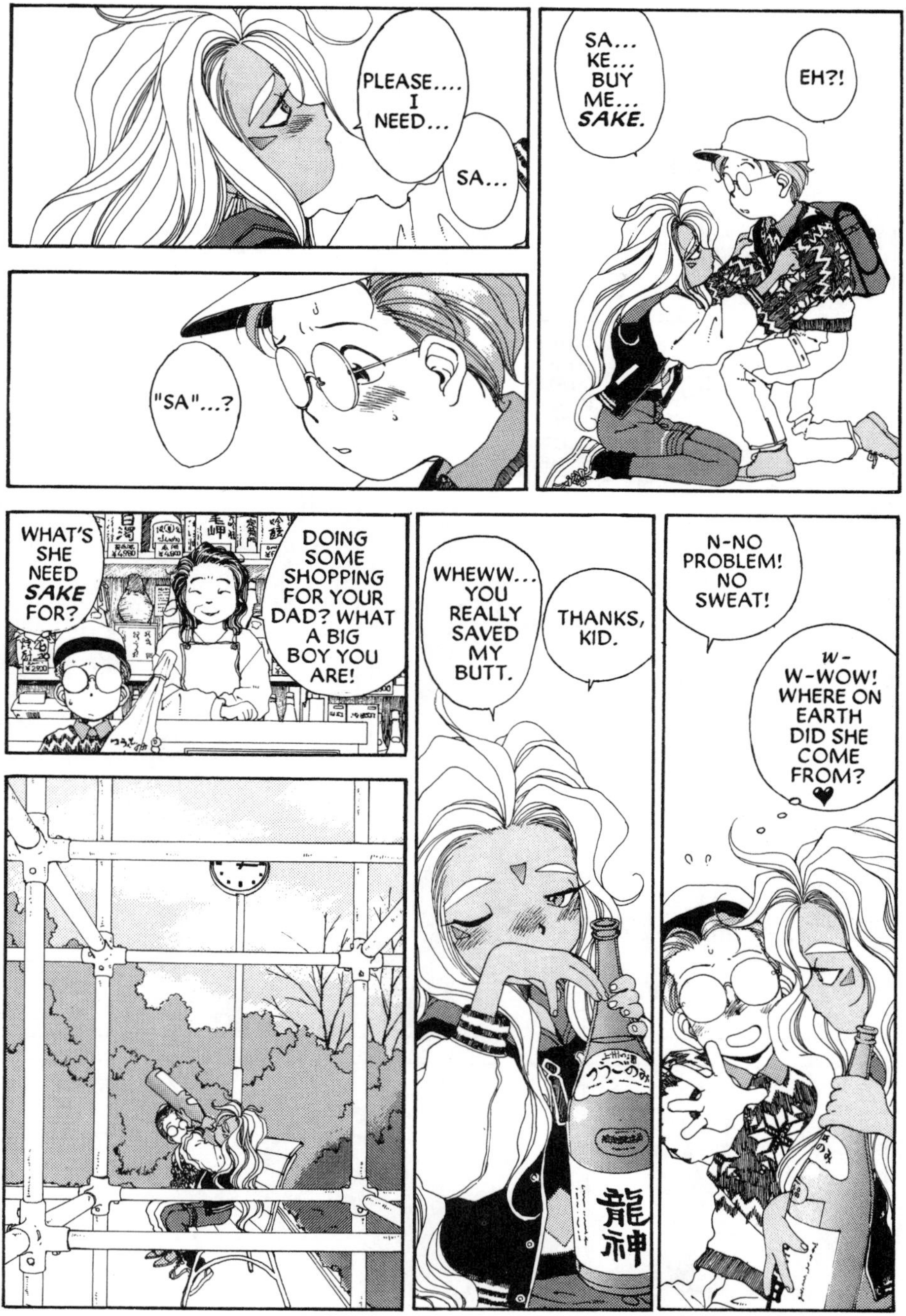
PLEASE.... I NEED...
SA...
"SA"...?
SA... KE... BUY ME... ***SAKE.***
EH?!
WHAT'S SHE NEED ***SAKE*** FOR?
DOING SOME SHOPPING FOR YOUR DAD? WHAT A BIG BOY YOU ARE!
WHEWW... YOU REALLY SAVED MY BUTT.
THANKS, KID.
N-NO PROBLEM! NO SWEAT!
W-W-WOW! WHERE ON EARTH DID SHE COME FROM?
龍神

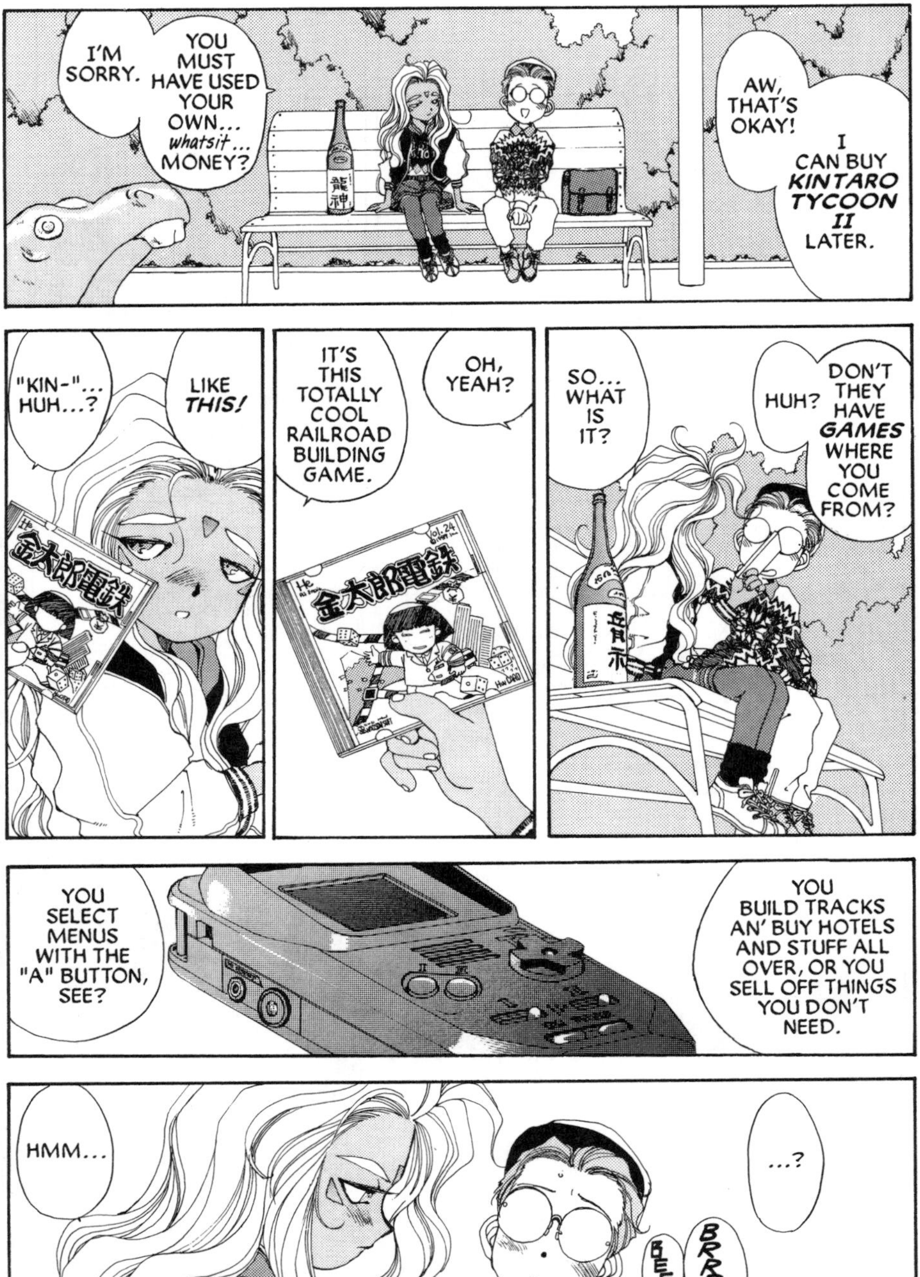
I'M SORRY.
YOU MUST HAVE USED YOUR OWN... *whatsit*... MONEY?
龍神
AW, THAT'S OKAY!
I CAN BUY ***KINTARO TYCOON II*** LATER.
"KIN-"... HUH...?
LIKE ***THIS!***
金太郎電鉄
IT'S THIS TOTALLY COOL RAILROAD BUILDING GAME.
OH, YEAH?
金太郎電鉄
SO... WHAT IS IT?
HUH?
DON'T THEY HAVE ***GAMES*** WHERE YOU COME FROM?
YOU SELECT MENUS WITH THE "A" BUTTON, SEE?
YOU BUILD TRACKS AN' BUY HOTELS AND STUFF ALL OVER, OR YOU SELL OFF THINGS YOU DON'T NEED.
HMM...
...?
BEEP
BRRRING!

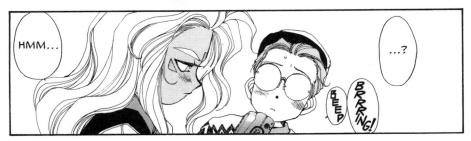

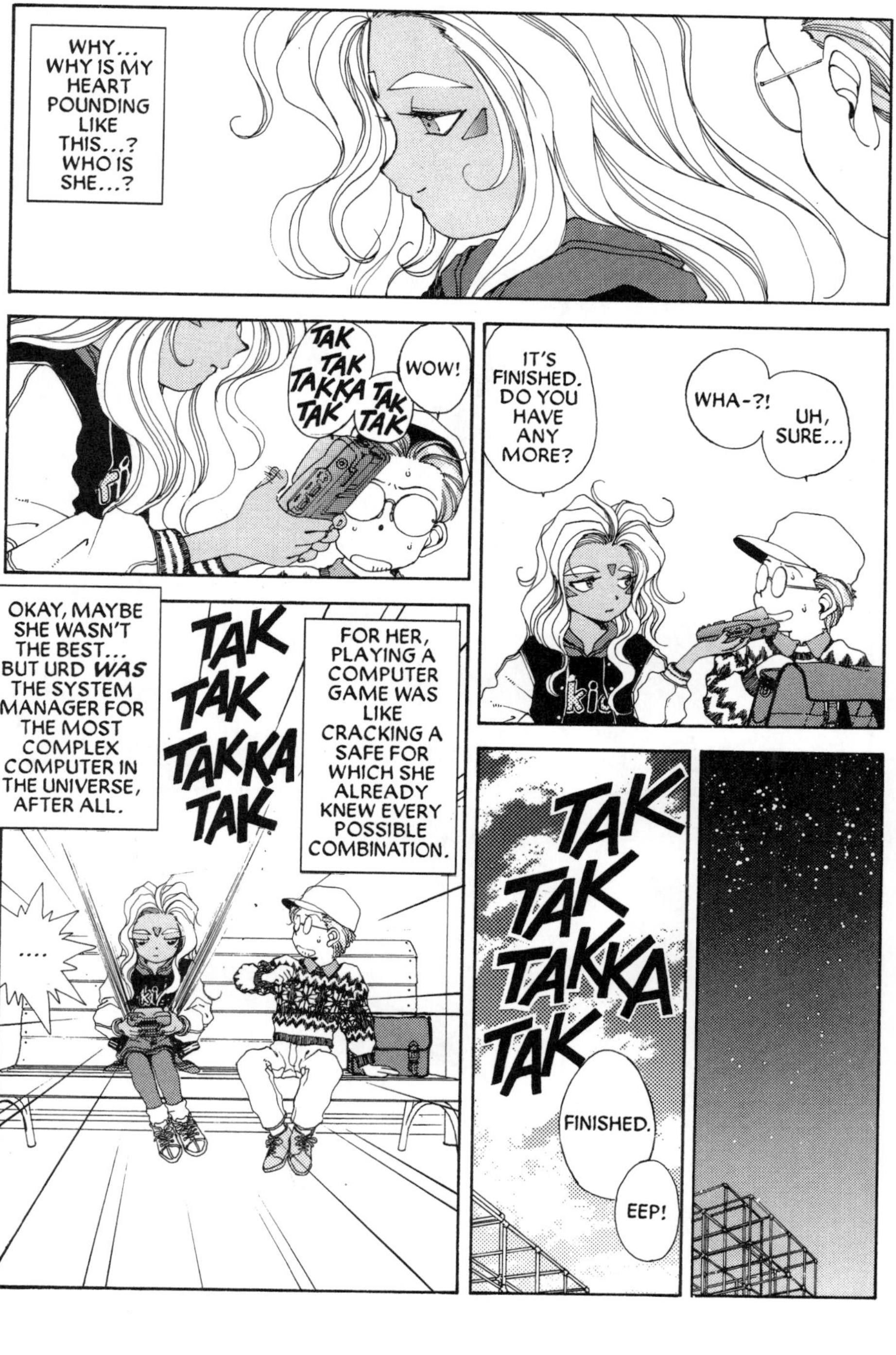
WHY... WHY IS MY HEART POUNDING LIKE THIS...? WHO IS SHE...?
TAK TAK TAKKA TAK
TAK TAK
WOW!
IT'S FINISHED. DO YOU HAVE ANY MORE?
WHA-?!
UH, SURE...
OKAY, MAYBE SHE WASN'T THE BEST... BUT URD WAS THE SYSTEM MANAGER FOR THE MOST COMPLEX COMPUTER IN THE UNIVERSE, AFTER ALL.
TAK TAK TAKKA TAK
FOR HER, PLAYING A COMPUTER GAME WAS LIKE CRACKING A SAFE FOR WHICH SHE ALREADY KNEW EVERY POSSIBLE COMBINATION.
....
TAK TAK TAKKA TAK
FINISHED.
EEP!

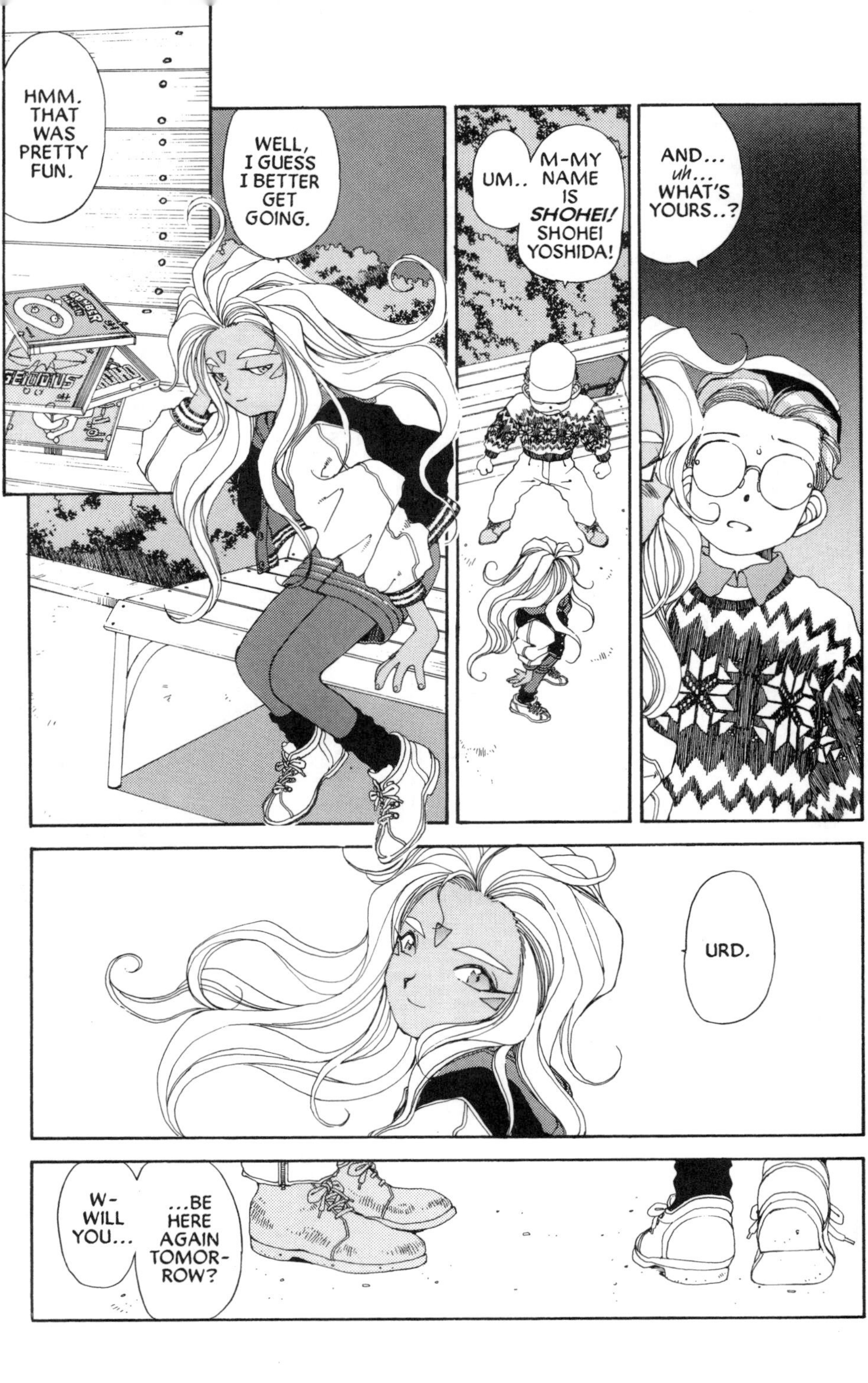
HMM. THAT WAS PRETTY FUN.
WELL, I GUESS I BETTER GET GOING.
UM..
M-MY NAME IS *SHOHEI!* SHOHEI YOSHIDA!
AND... *uh*... WHAT'S YOURS..?
URD.
W-WILL YOU...
...BE HERE AGAIN TOMOR-ROW?

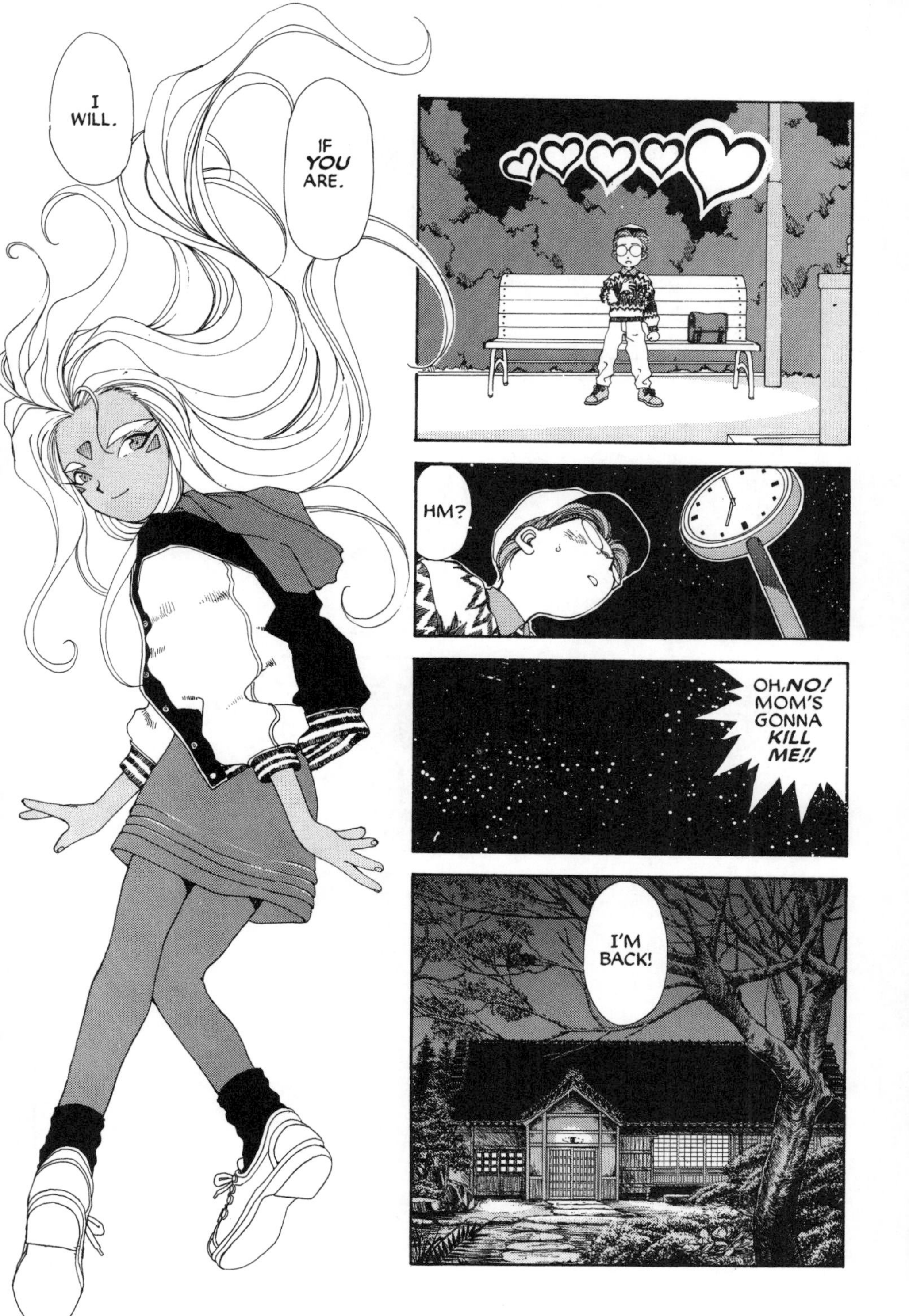
I WILL.
IF YOU ARE.
HM?
OH, NO! MOM'S GONNA KILL ME!!
I'M BACK!

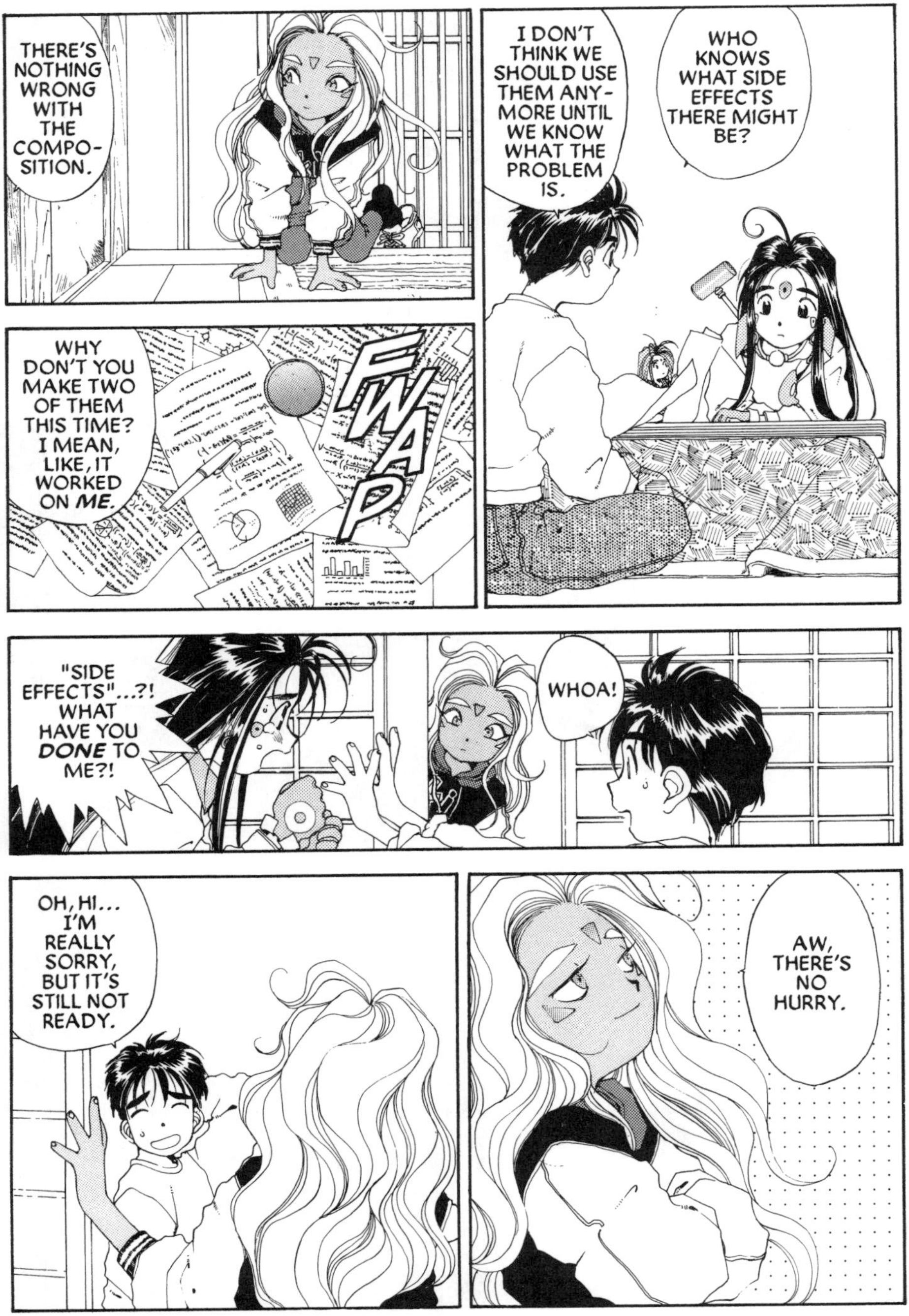
THERE'S NOTHING WRONG WITH THE COMPOSITION.
WHY DON'T YOU MAKE TWO OF THEM THIS TIME? I MEAN, LIKE, IT WORKED ON *ME*.
FWAP
I DON'T THINK WE SHOULD USE THEM ANY-MORE UNTIL WE KNOW WHAT THE PROBLEM IS.
WHO KNOWS WHAT SIDE EFFECTS THERE MIGHT BE?
"SIDE EFFECTS"...?! WHAT HAVE YOU *DONE* TO ME?!
WHOA!
OH, HI... I'M REALLY SORRY, BUT IT'S STILL NOT READY.
AW, THERE'S NO HURRY.

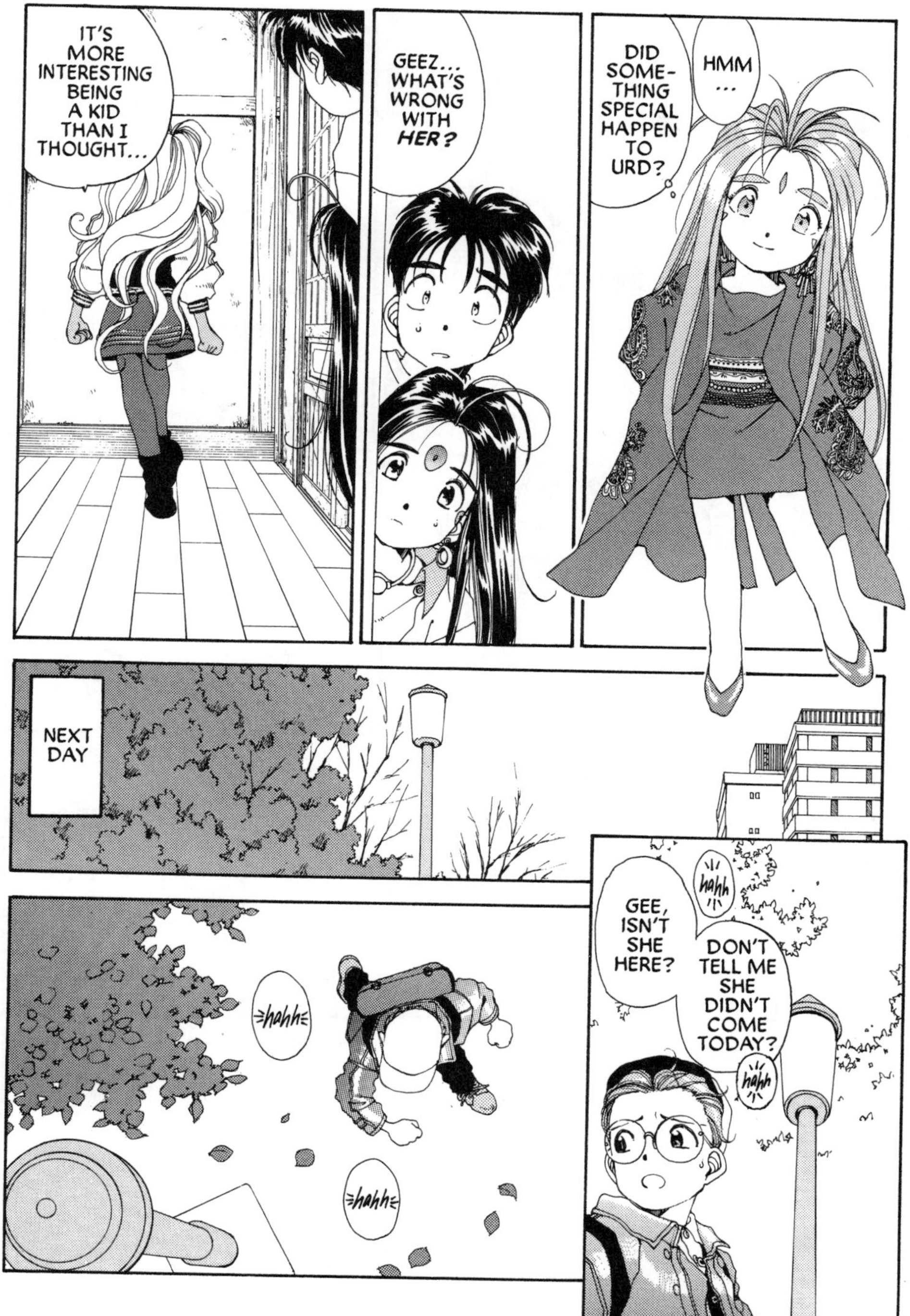
IT'S MORE INTERESTING BEING A KID THAN I THOUGHT...
GEEZ... WHAT'S WRONG WITH *HER*?
DID SOME-THING SPECIAL HAPPEN TO URD?
HMM...
NEXT DAY
hahh
hahh
hahh
GEE, ISN'T SHE HERE?
DON'T TELL ME SHE DIDN'T COME TODAY?
hahh

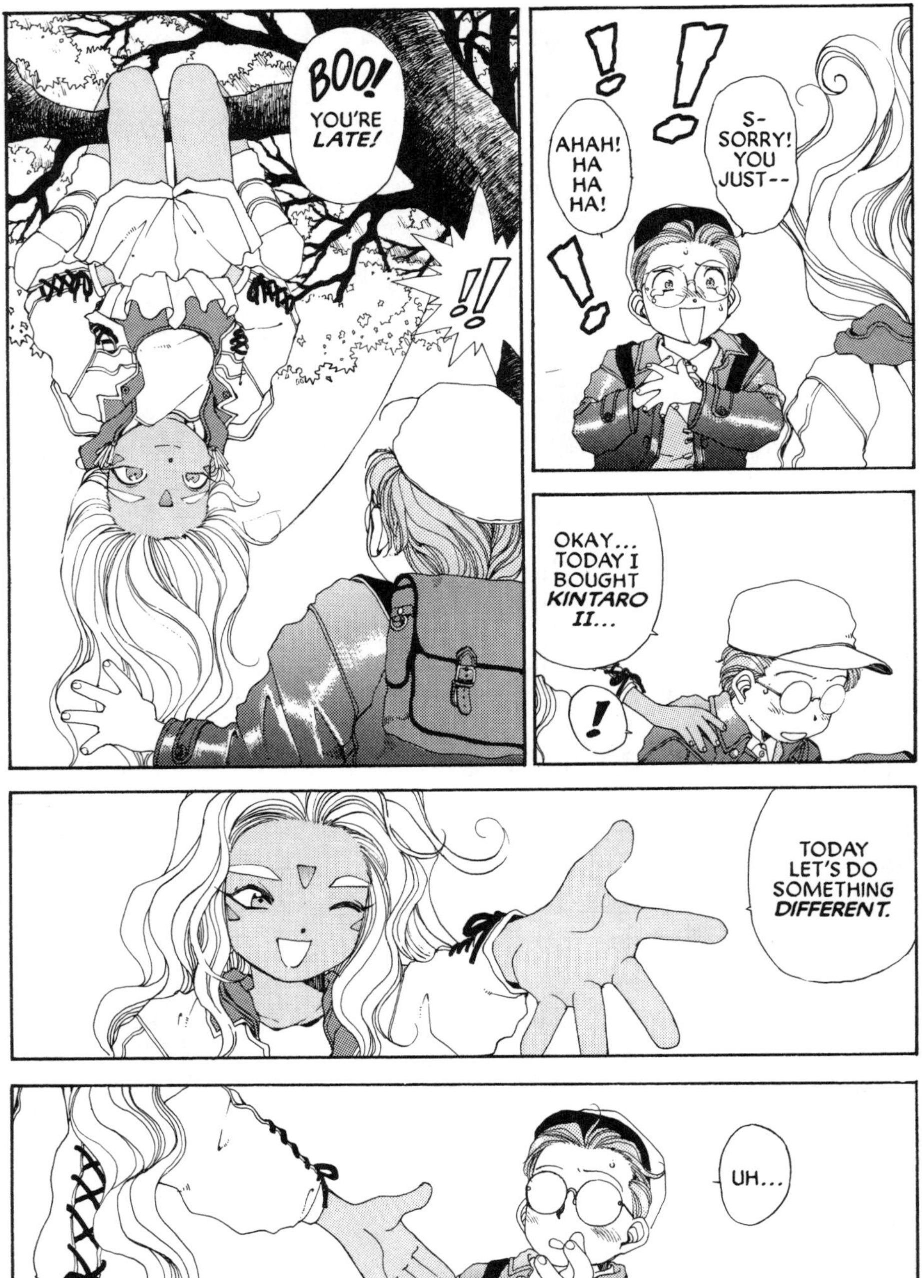
BOO! YOU'RE *LATE!*
!!
AHAH! HA HA HA!
!
!
!
S-SORRY! YOU JUST--
OKAY... TODAY I BOUGHT *KINTARO II*...
!
TODAY LET'S DO SOMETHING *DIFFERENT.*
UH...

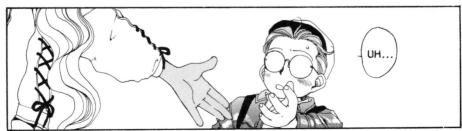

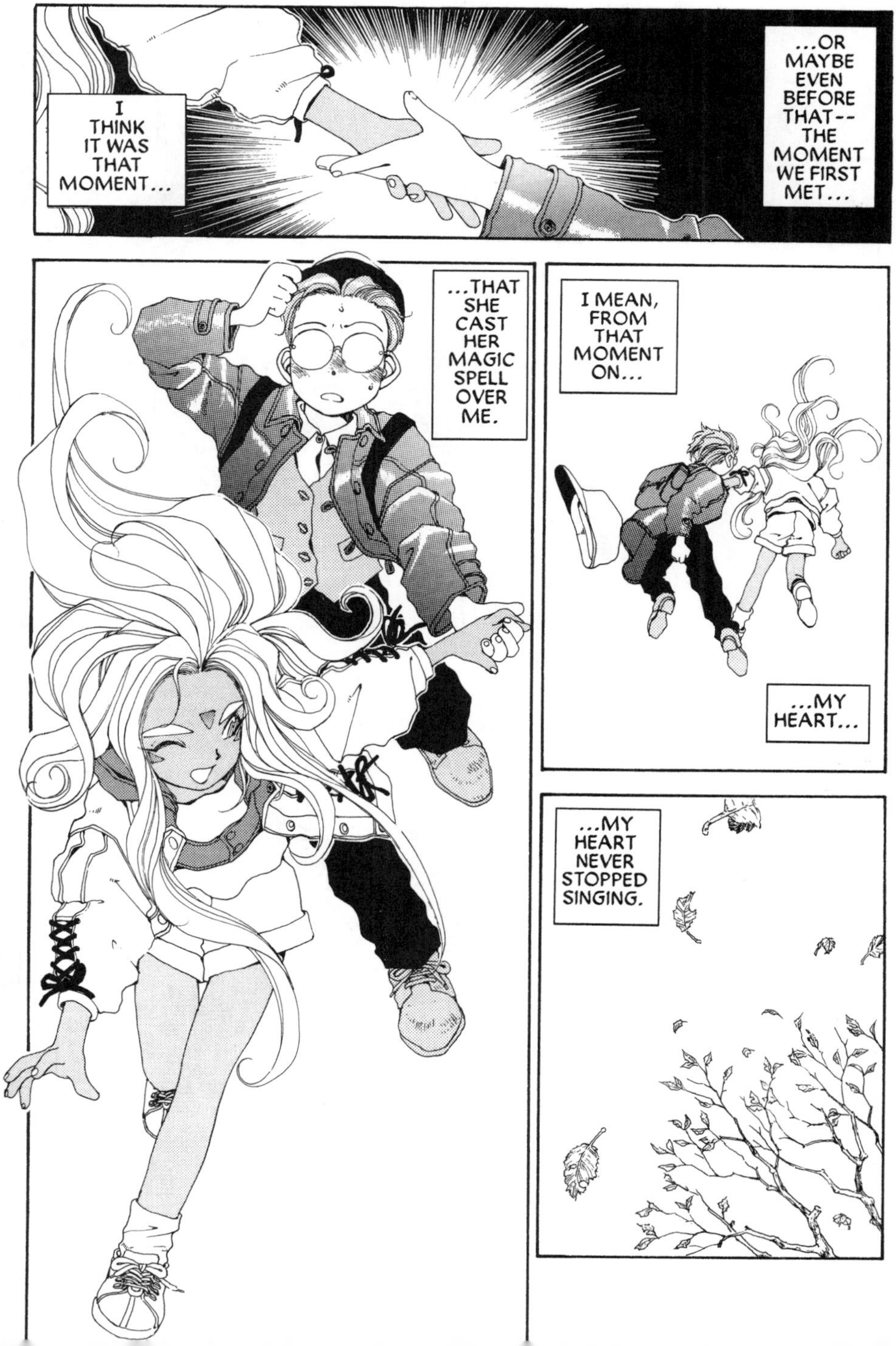
I THINK IT WAS THAT MOMENT...
...OR MAYBE EVEN BEFORE THAT-- THE MOMENT WE FIRST MET...
...THAT SHE CAST HER MAGIC SPELL OVER ME.
I MEAN, FROM THAT MOMENT ON...
...MY HEART...
...MY HEART NEVER STOPPED SINGING.

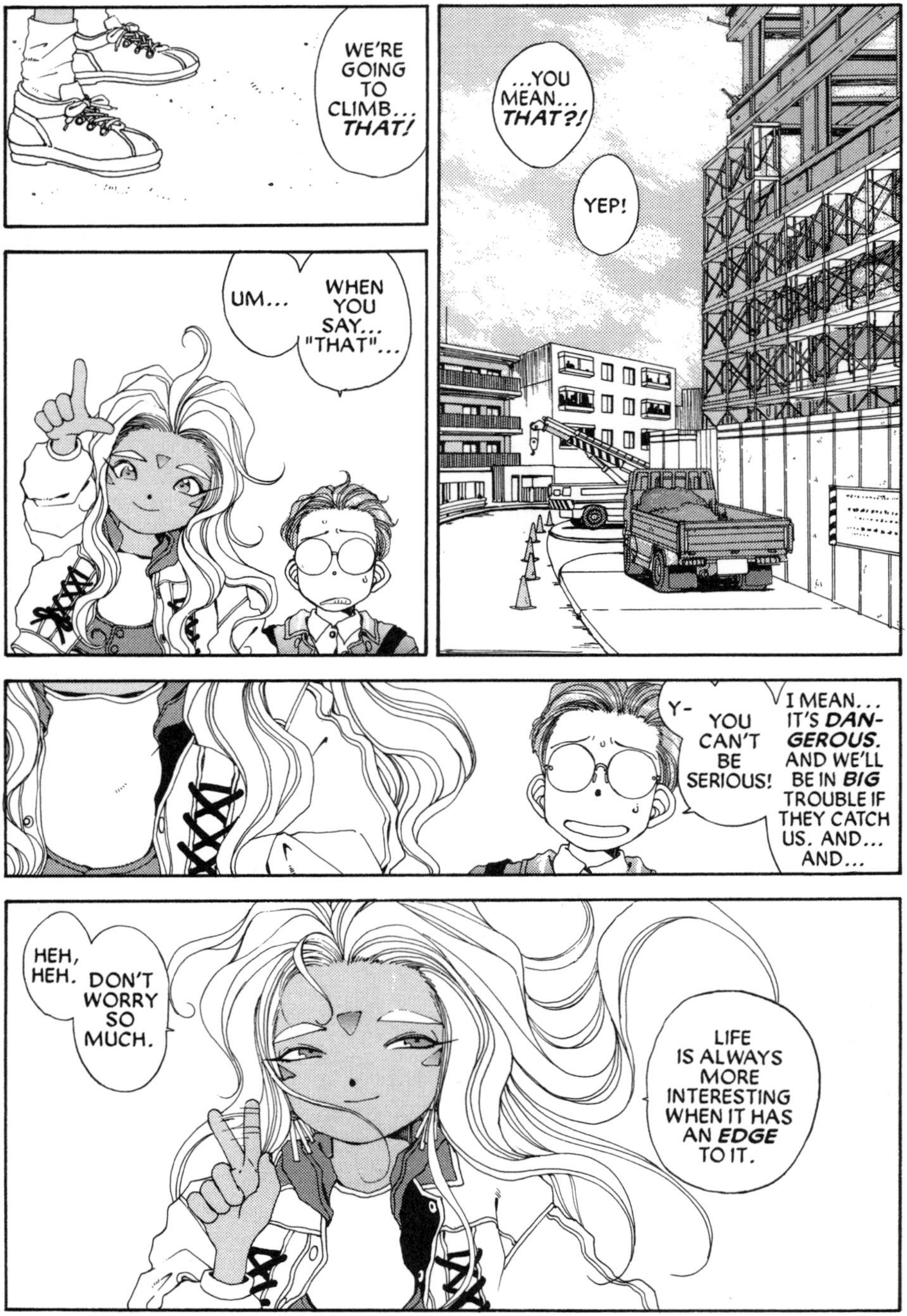
WE'RE GOING TO CLIMB... THAT!
UM...
WHEN YOU SAY... "THAT"...
...YOU MEAN... THAT?!
YEP!
Y-
YOU CAN'T BE SERIOUS!
I MEAN... IT'S DANGEROUS. AND WE'LL BE IN BIG TROUBLE IF THEY CATCH US. AND... AND...
HEH, HEH.
DON'T WORRY SO MUCH.
LIFE IS ALWAYS MORE INTERESTING WHEN IT HAS AN EDGE TO IT.

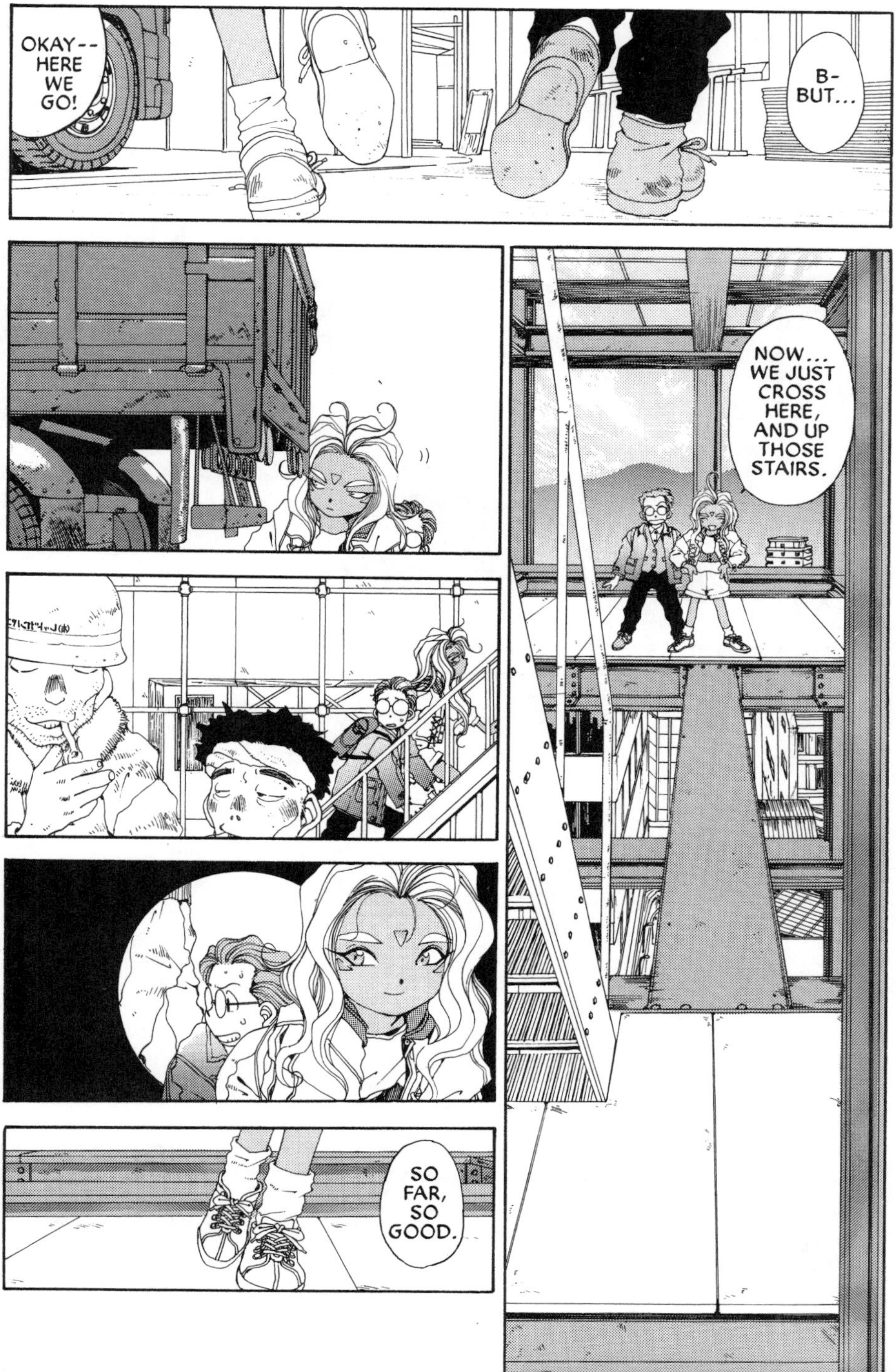
OKAY-- HERE WE GO!
B- BUT...
SO FAR, SO GOOD.
NOW... WE JUST CROSS HERE, AND UP THOSE STAIRS.

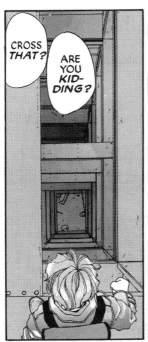

CROSS *THAT?*

ARE YOU *KIDDING?*

WHSSSH

EEP!

N-NO. I CAN'T.

IF I FALL, I'LL BE *KILLED!*

SHOHEI... IF YOU *THINK* YOU CAN'T DO SOMETHING...

...YOU WON'T BE *ABLE* TO DO IT.

EVEN THE *EASIEST* THING!

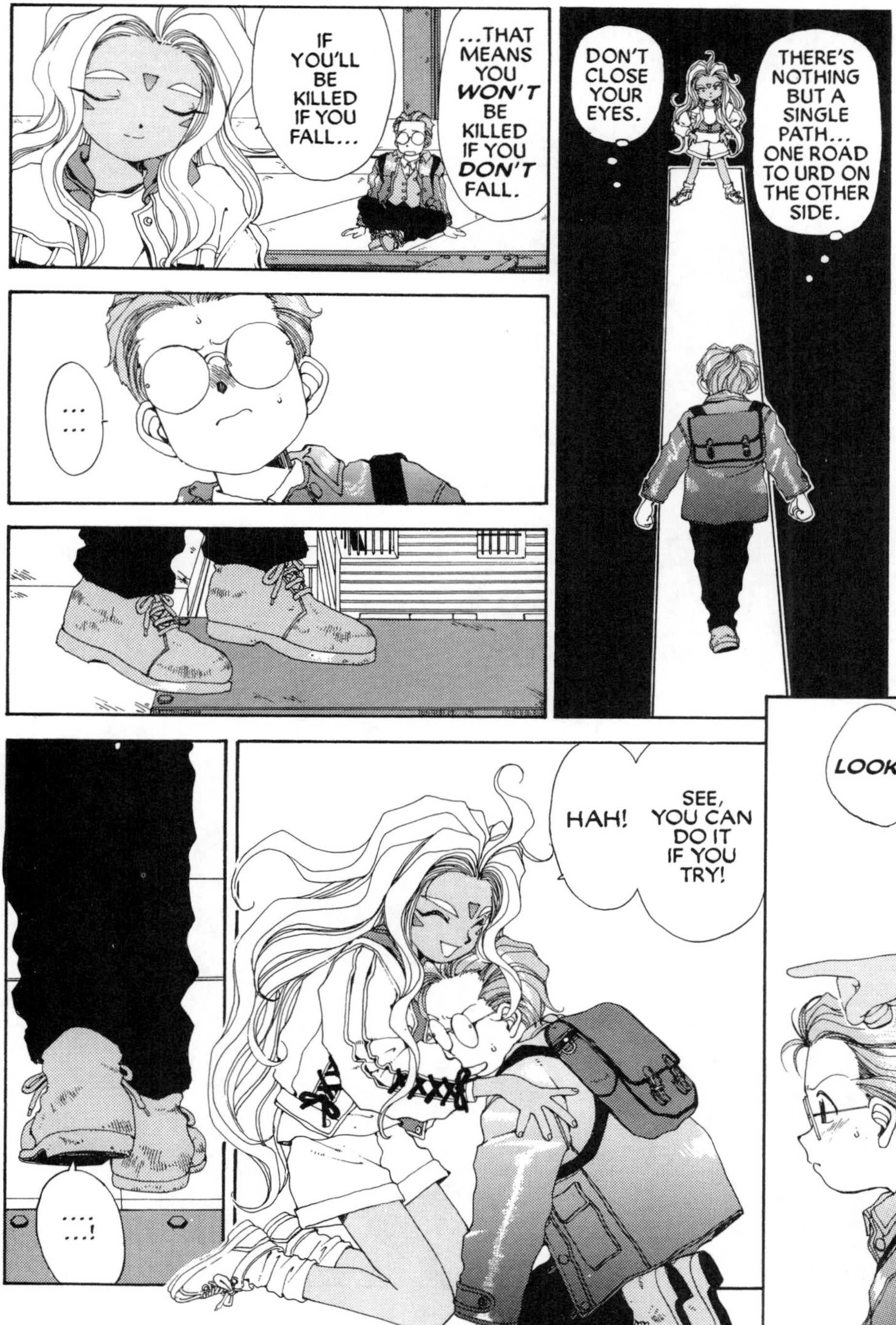
IF YOU'LL BE KILLED IF YOU FALL...
...THAT MEANS YOU WON'T BE KILLED IF YOU DON'T FALL.
......
DON'T CLOSE YOUR EYES.
THERE'S NOTHING BUT A SINGLE PATH... ONE ROAD TO URD ON THE OTHER SIDE.
......!
HAH!
SEE, YOU CAN DO IT IF YOU TRY!
LOOK!

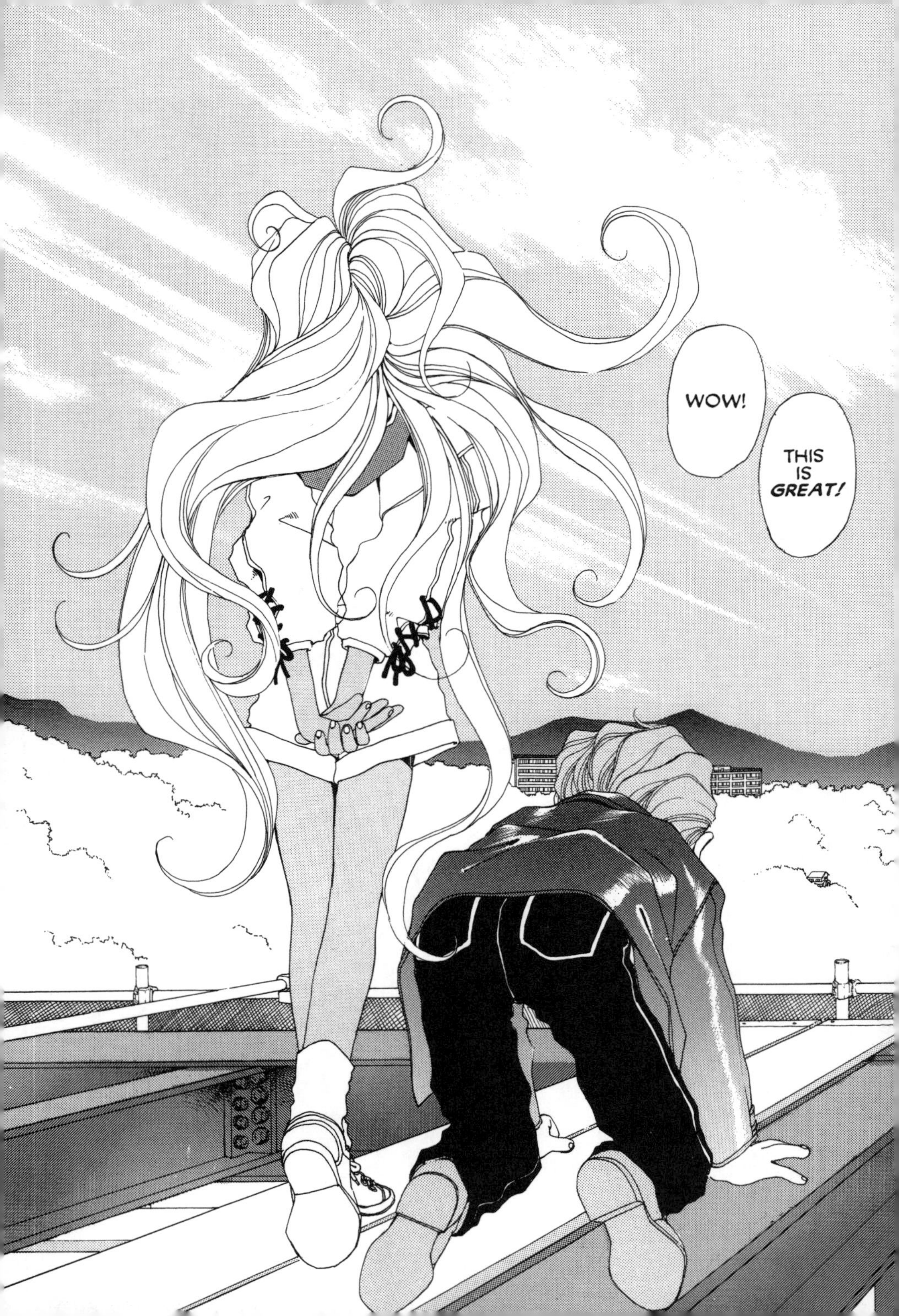
WOW!
THIS IS *GREAT!*

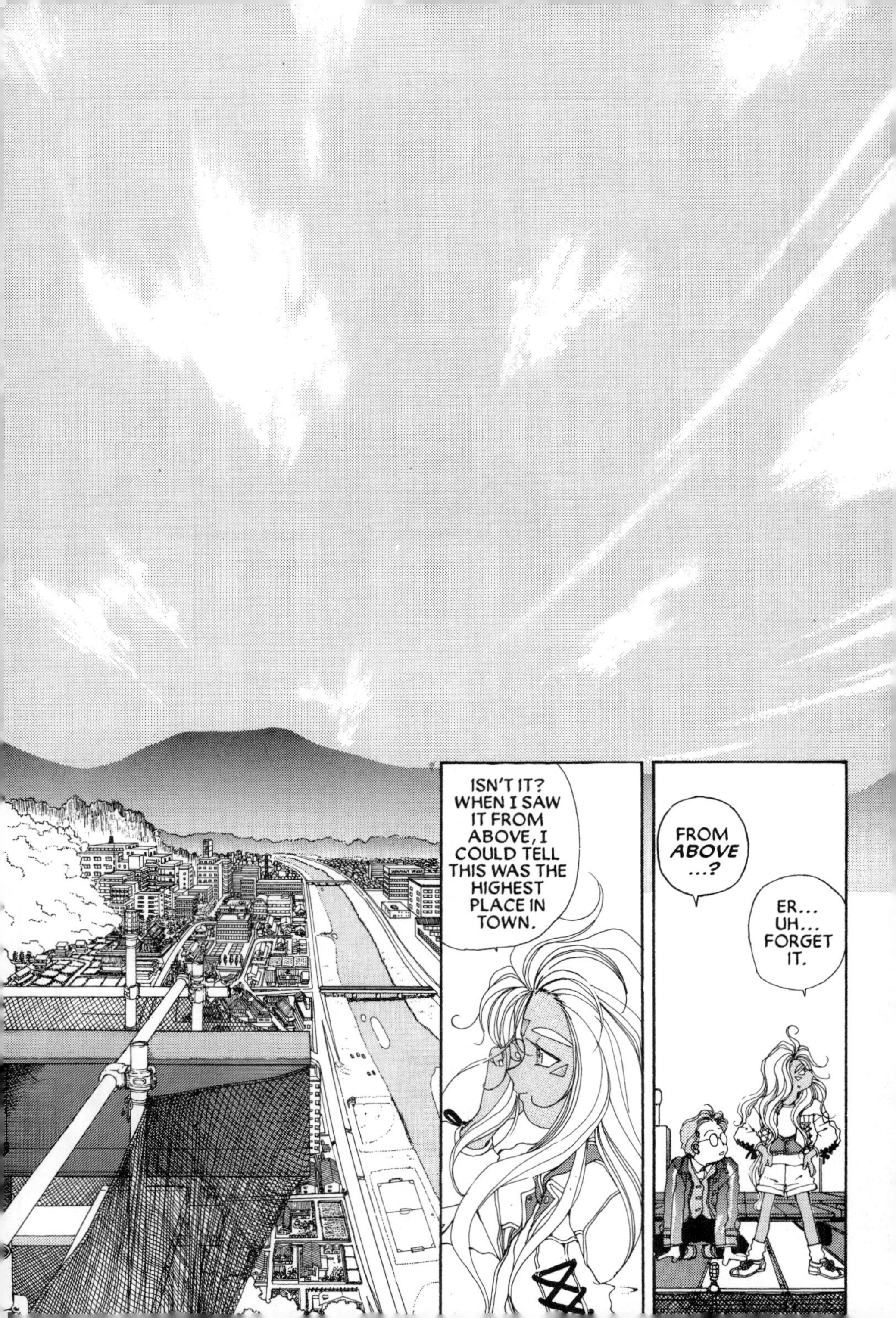
ISN'T IT? WHEN I SAW IT FROM ABOVE, I COULD TELL THIS WAS THE HIGHEST PLACE IN TOWN.
FROM *ABOVE* ...?
ER... UH... FORGET IT.

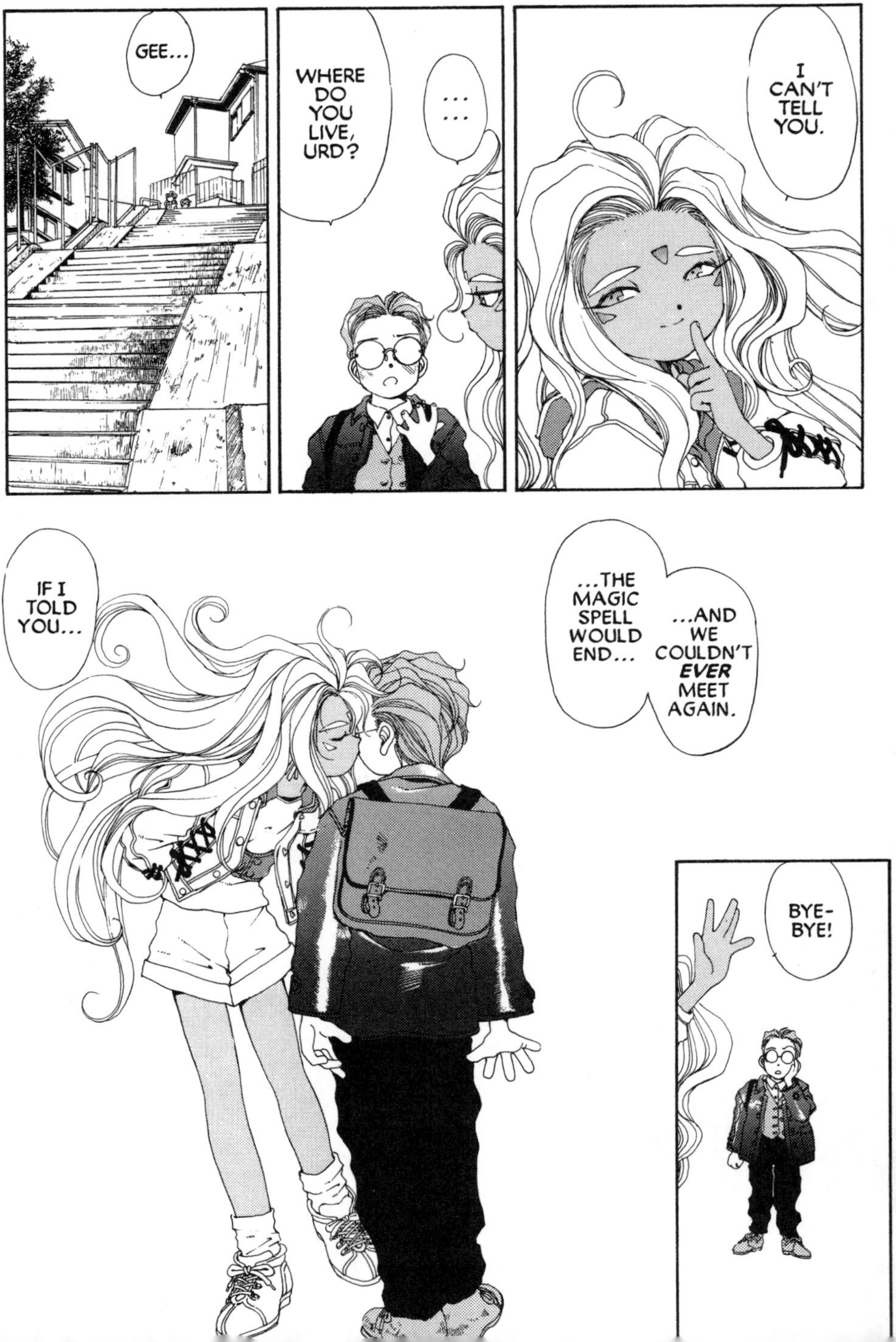
GEE...
WHERE DO YOU LIVE, URD?
... ...
I CAN'T TELL YOU.
IF I TOLD YOU...
...THE MAGIC SPELL WOULD END...
...AND WE COULDN'T *EVER* MEET AGAIN.
BYE-BYE!

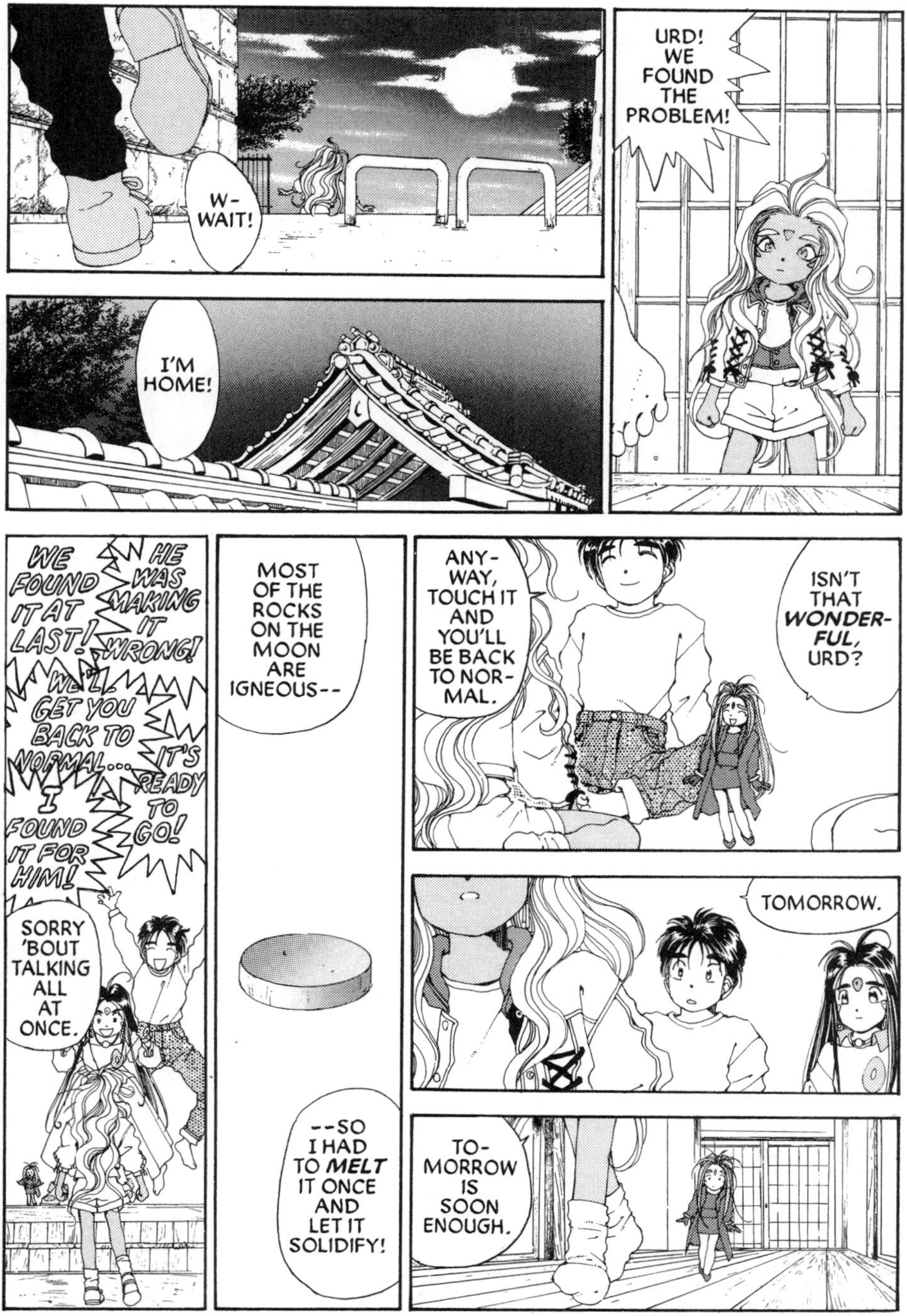
W-WAIT!
I'M HOME!
URD! WE FOUND THE PROBLEM!
WE FOUND IT AT LAST!
HE WAS MAKING IT WRONG!
WE'LL GET YOU BACK TO NORMAL...
IT'S READY TO GO!
I FOUND IT FOR HIM!
SORRY 'BOUT TALKING ALL AT ONCE.
MOST OF THE ROCKS ON THE MOON ARE IGNEOUS--
--SO I HAD TO MELT IT ONCE AND LET IT SOLIDIFY!
ANY-WAY, TOUCH IT AND YOU'LL BE BACK TO NOR-MAL.
ISN'T THAT WONDER-FUL, URD?
TOMORROW.
TO-MORROW IS SOON ENOUGH.

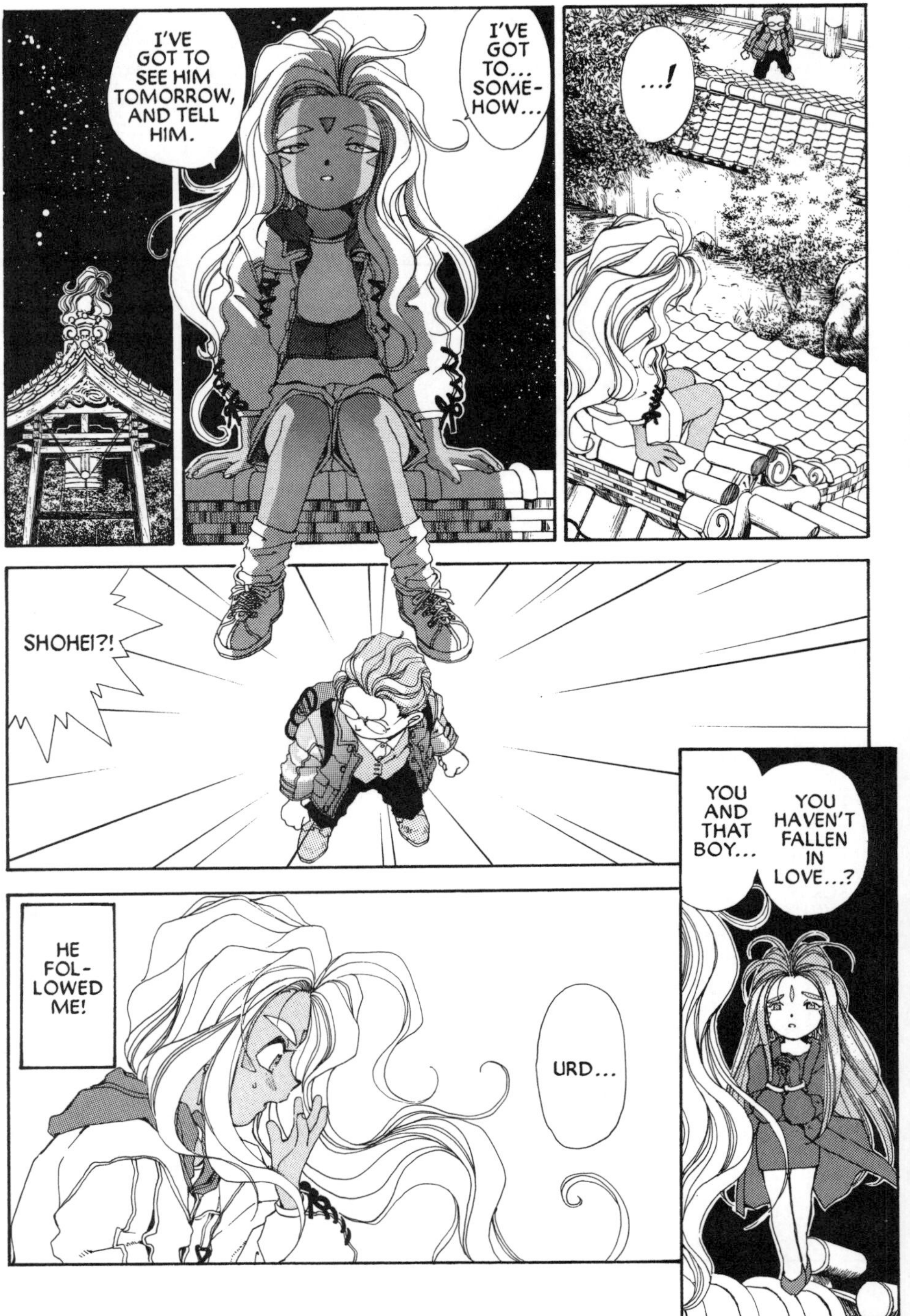

I'VE GOT TO SEE HIM TOMORROW, AND TELL HIM.
I'VE GOT TO... SOMEHOW...
...!
SHOHEI?!
HE FOLLOWED ME!
URD...
YOU AND THAT BOY...
YOU HAVEN'T FALLEN IN LOVE...?

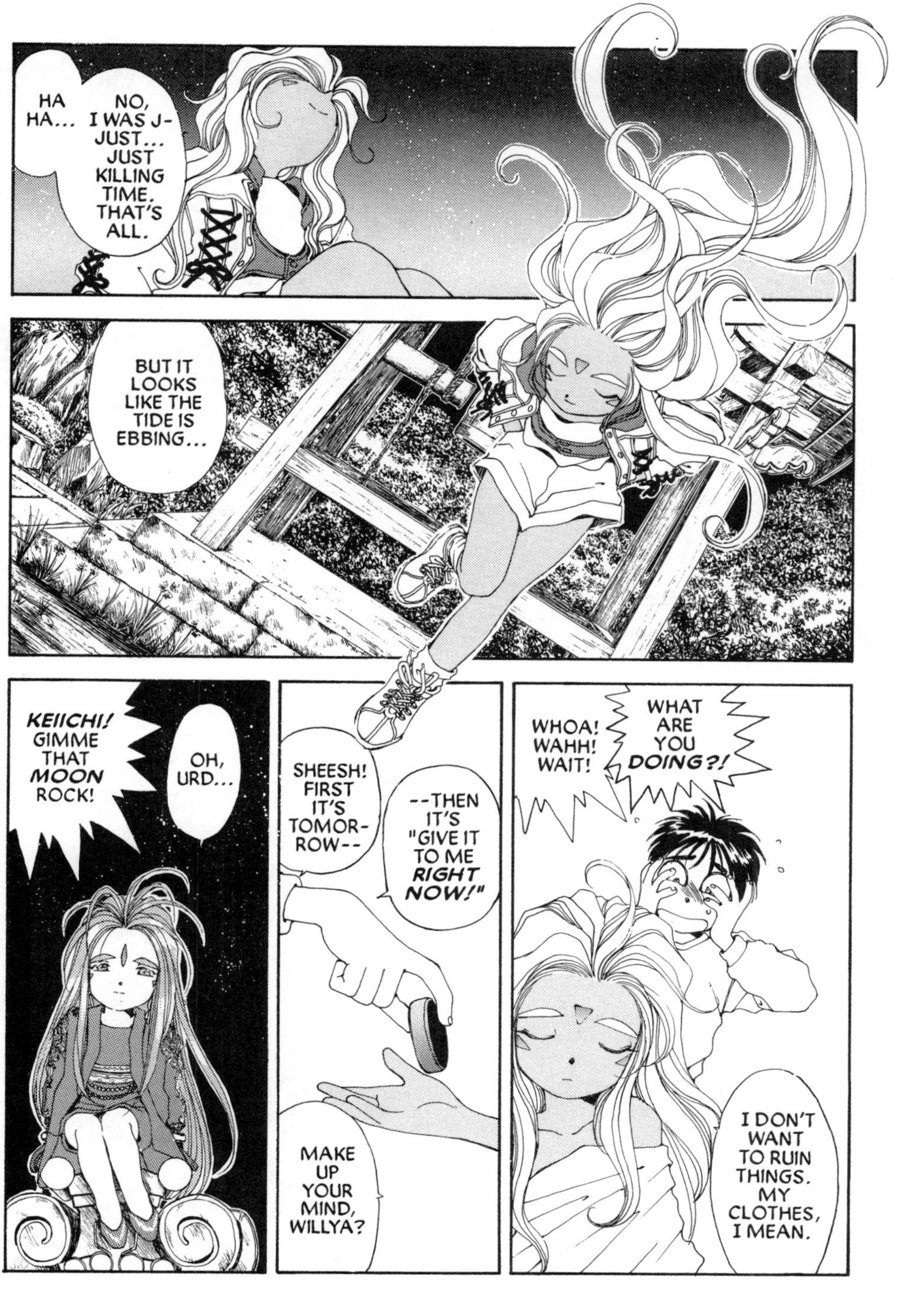
HA HA...
NO, I WAS J- JUST... JUST KILLING TIME. THAT'S ALL.
BUT IT LOOKS LIKE THE TIDE IS EBBING...
KEIICHI! GIMME THAT MOON ROCK!
OH, URD...
SHEESH! FIRST IT'S TOMORROW--
--THEN IT'S "GIVE IT TO ME RIGHT NOW!"
MAKE UP YOUR MIND, WILLYA?
WHOA! WAHH! WAIT!
WHAT ARE YOU DOING?!
I DON'T WANT TO RUIN THINGS. MY CLOTHES, I MEAN.

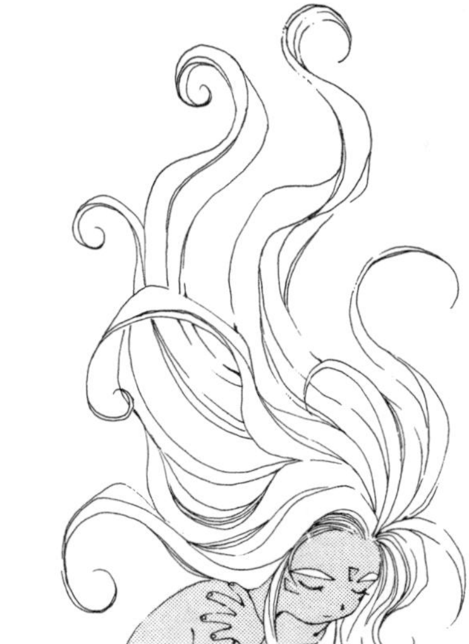

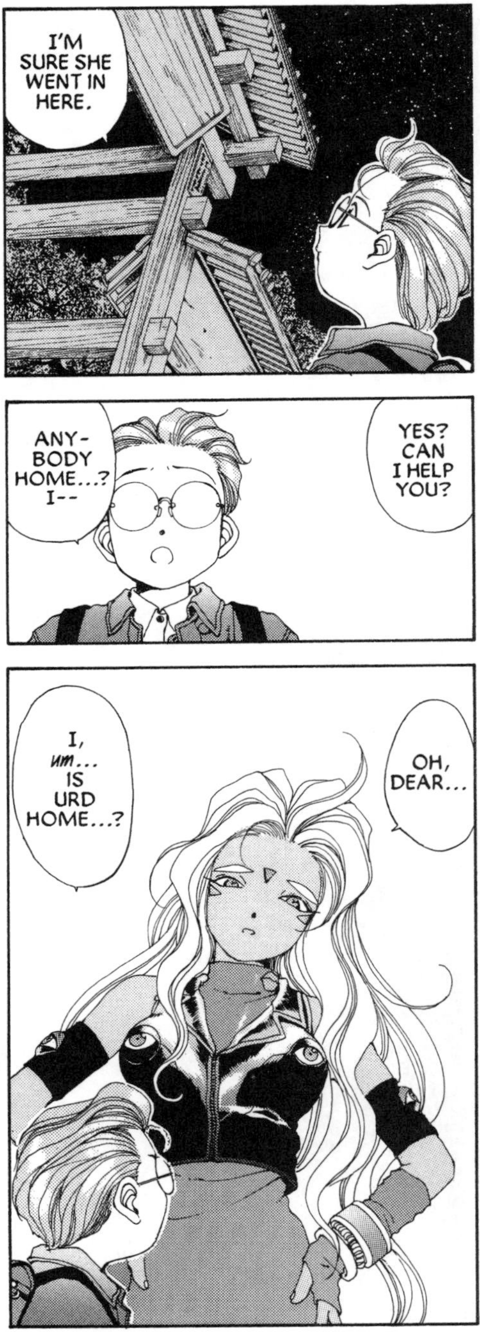
I'M SURE SHE WENT IN HERE.
ANY-BODY HOME...? I--
YES? CAN I HELP YOU?
I, *um*... IS URD HOME...?
OH, DEAR...

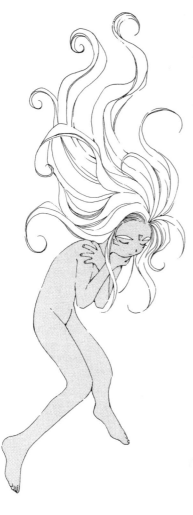

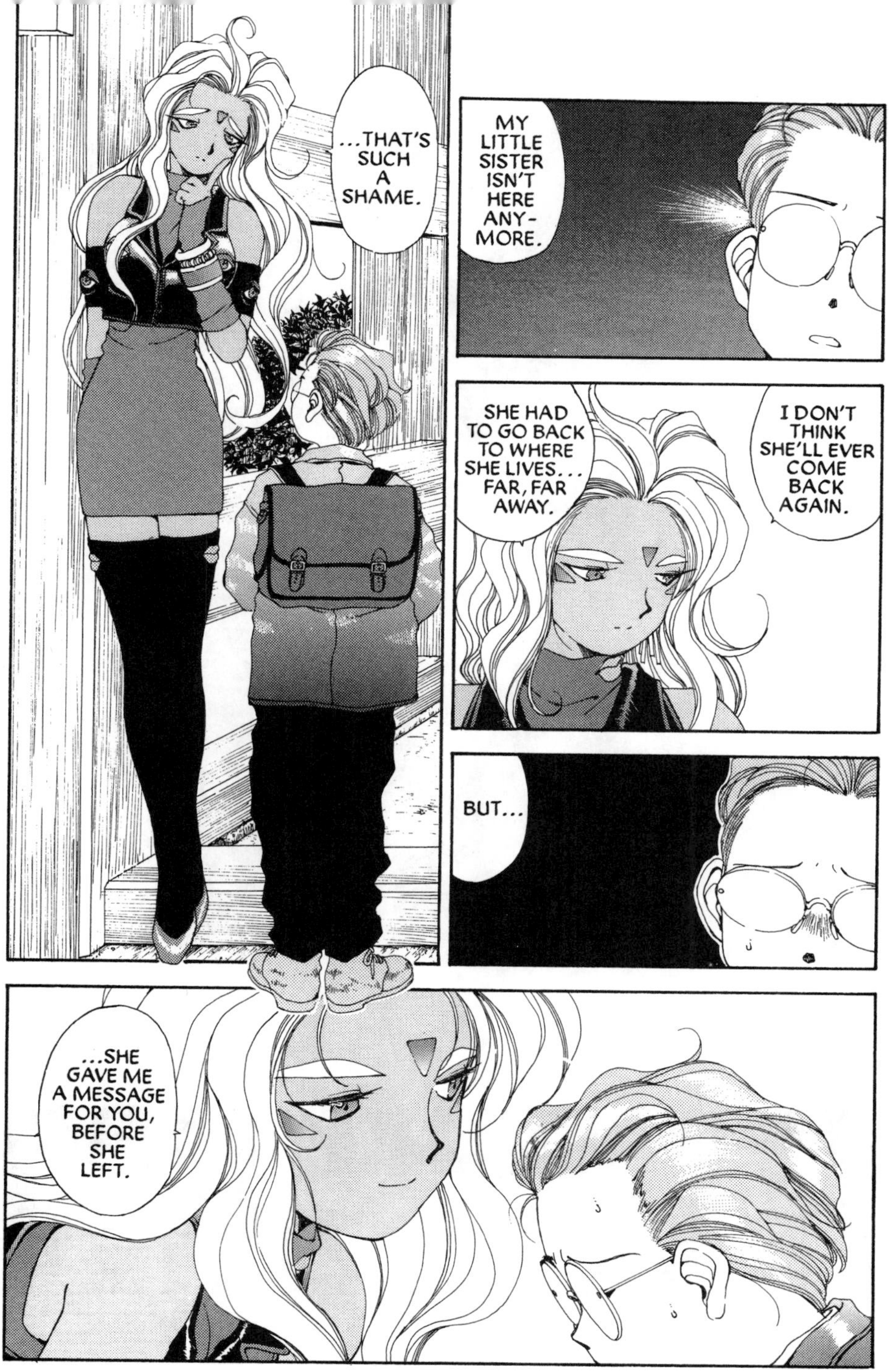
...THAT'S SUCH A SHAME.
MY LITTLE SISTER ISN'T HERE ANY-MORE.
SHE HAD TO GO BACK TO WHERE SHE LIVES... FAR, FAR AWAY.
I DON'T THINK SHE'LL EVER COME BACK AGAIN.
BUT...
...SHE GAVE ME A MESSAGE FOR YOU, BEFORE SHE LEFT.

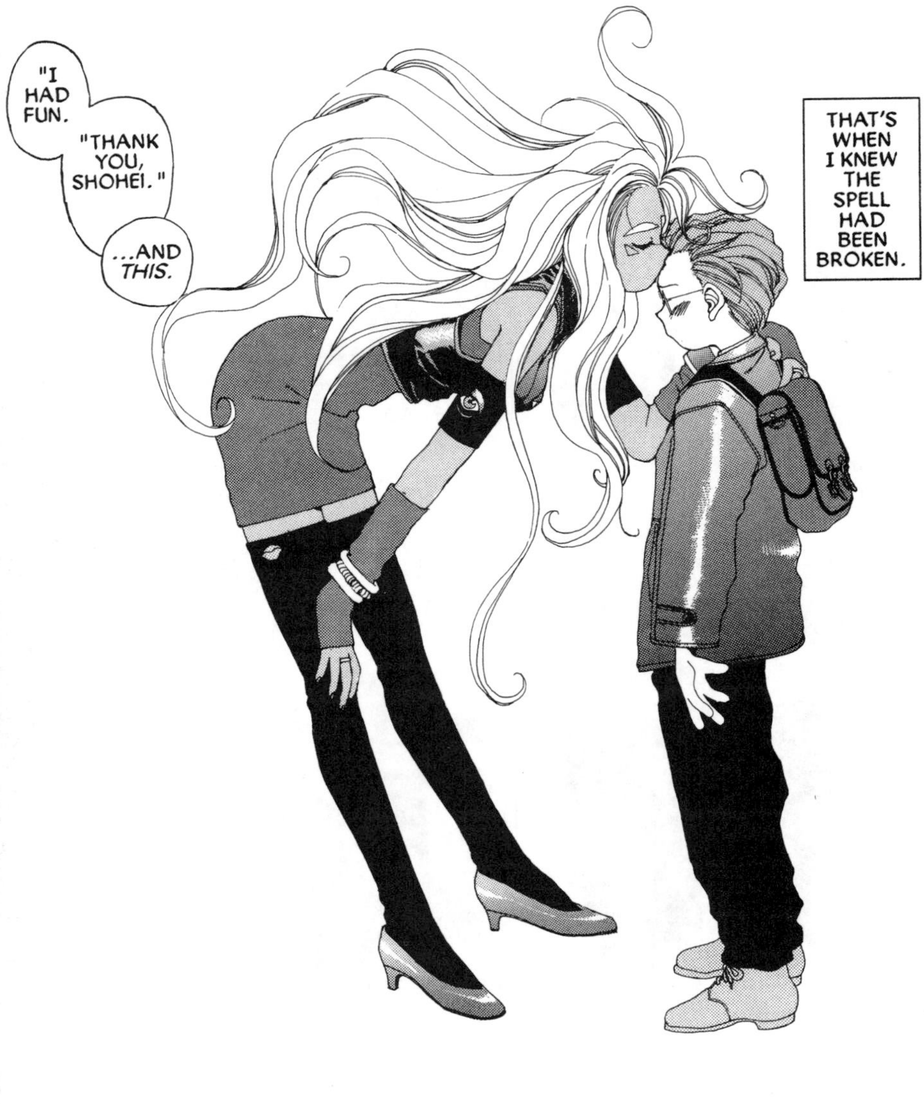
"I HAD FUN.
"THANK YOU, SHOHEI."
...AND *THIS.*
THAT'S WHEN I KNEW THE SPELL HAD BEEN BROKEN.

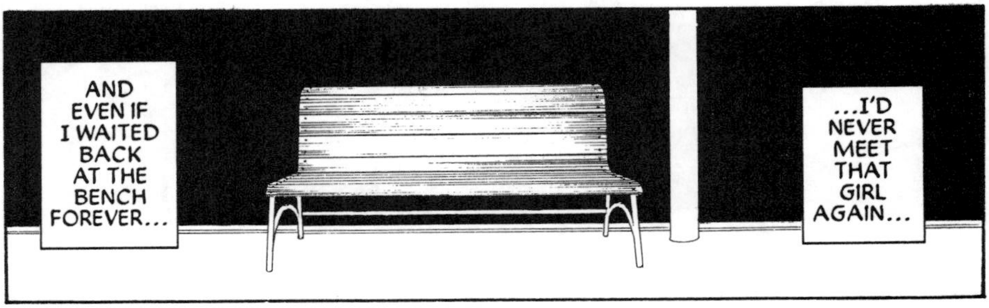
AND EVEN IF I WAITED BACK AT THE BENCH FOREVER...
...I'D NEVER MEET THAT GIRL AGAIN...

The Trials of Morisato, part 3

Belldandy's Tempestuous Heart

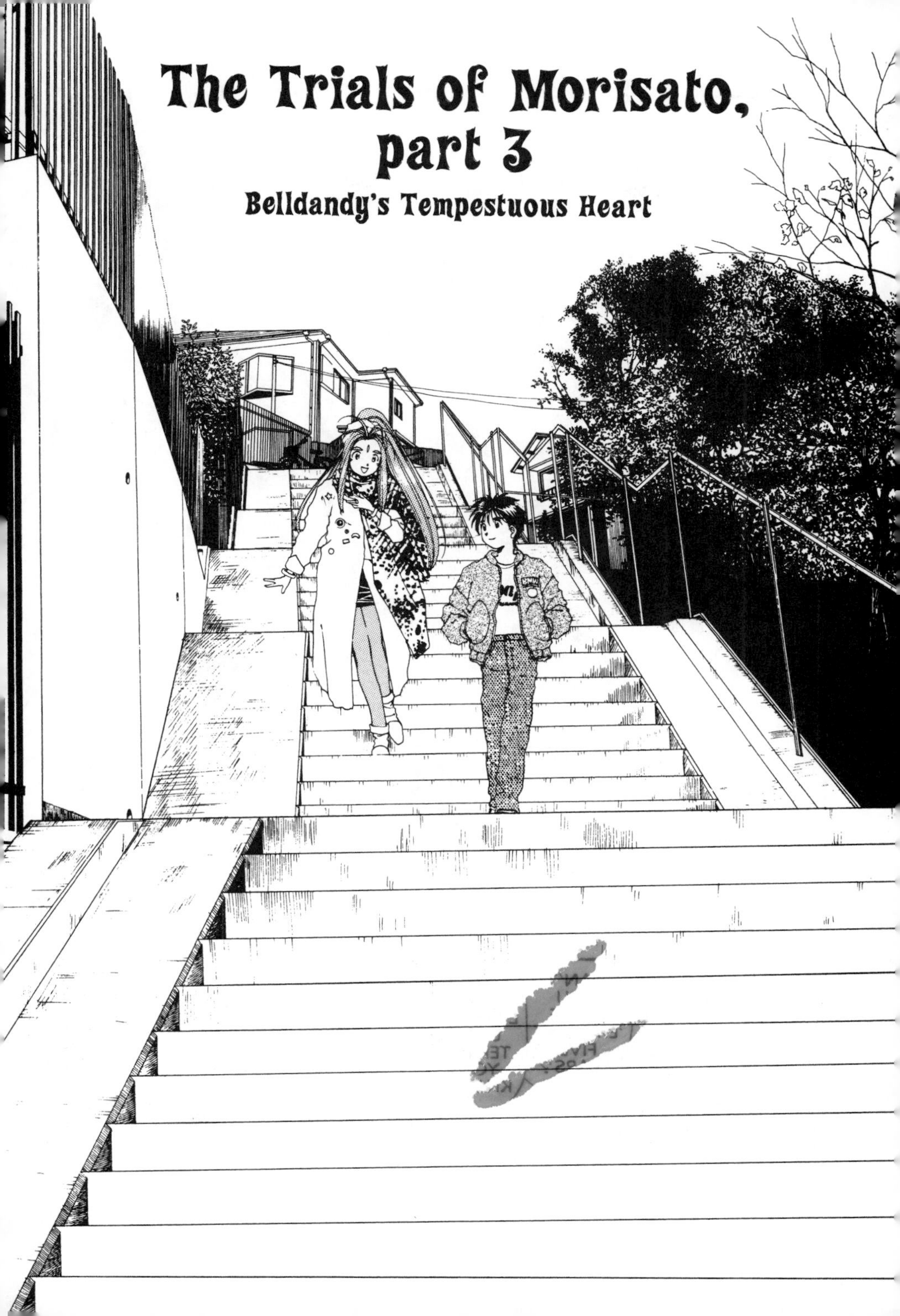

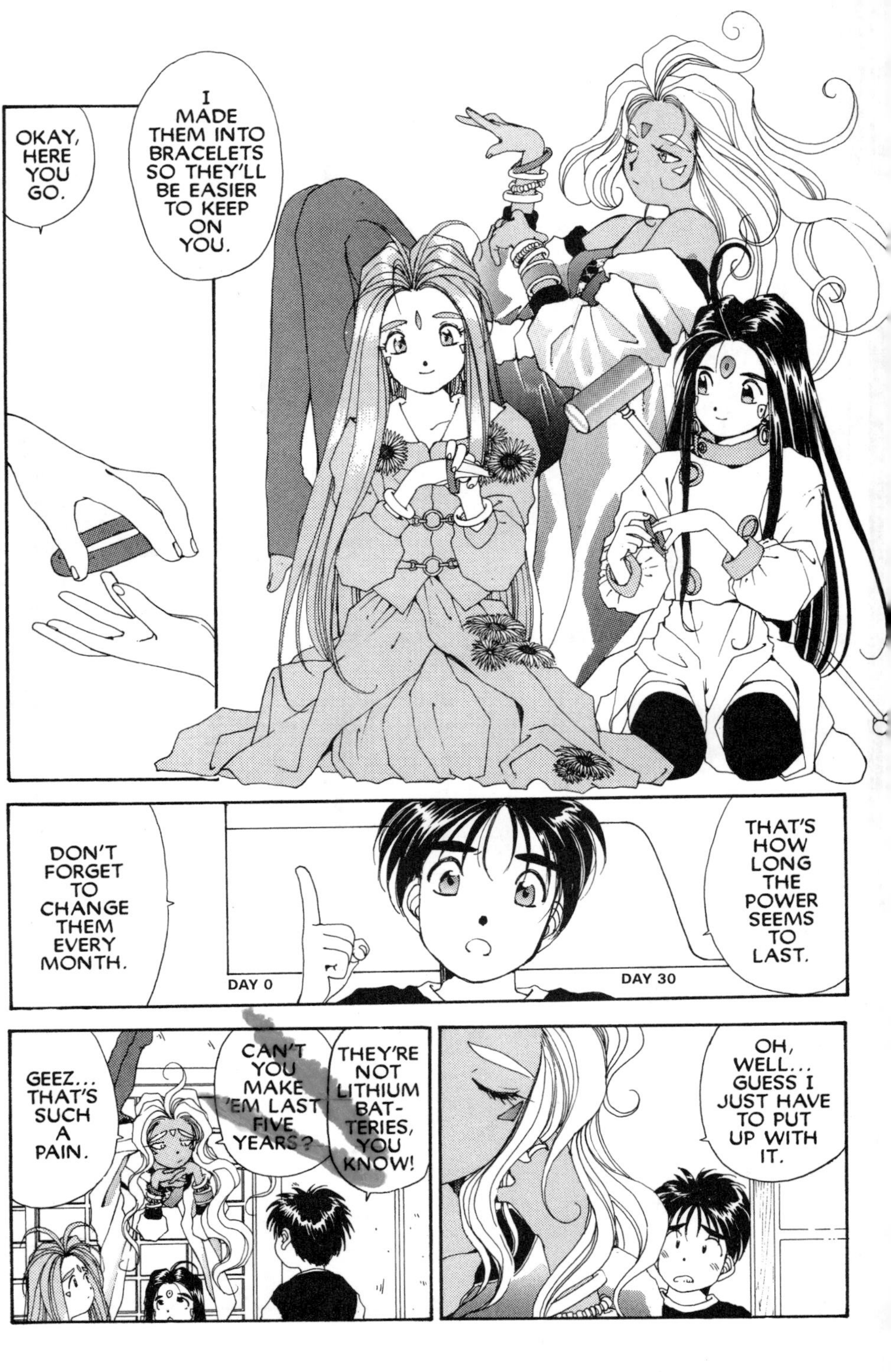
OKAY, HERE YOU GO.
I MADE THEM INTO BRACELETS SO THEY'LL BE EASIER TO KEEP ON YOU.
DON'T FORGET TO CHANGE THEM EVERY MONTH.
DAY 0
DAY 30
THAT'S HOW LONG THE POWER SEEMS TO LAST.
GEEZ... THAT'S SUCH A PAIN.
CAN'T YOU MAKE 'EM LAST FIVE YEARS?
THEY'RE NOT LITHIUM BAT-TERIES, YOU KNOW!
OH, WELL... GUESS I JUST HAVE TO PUT UP WITH IT.

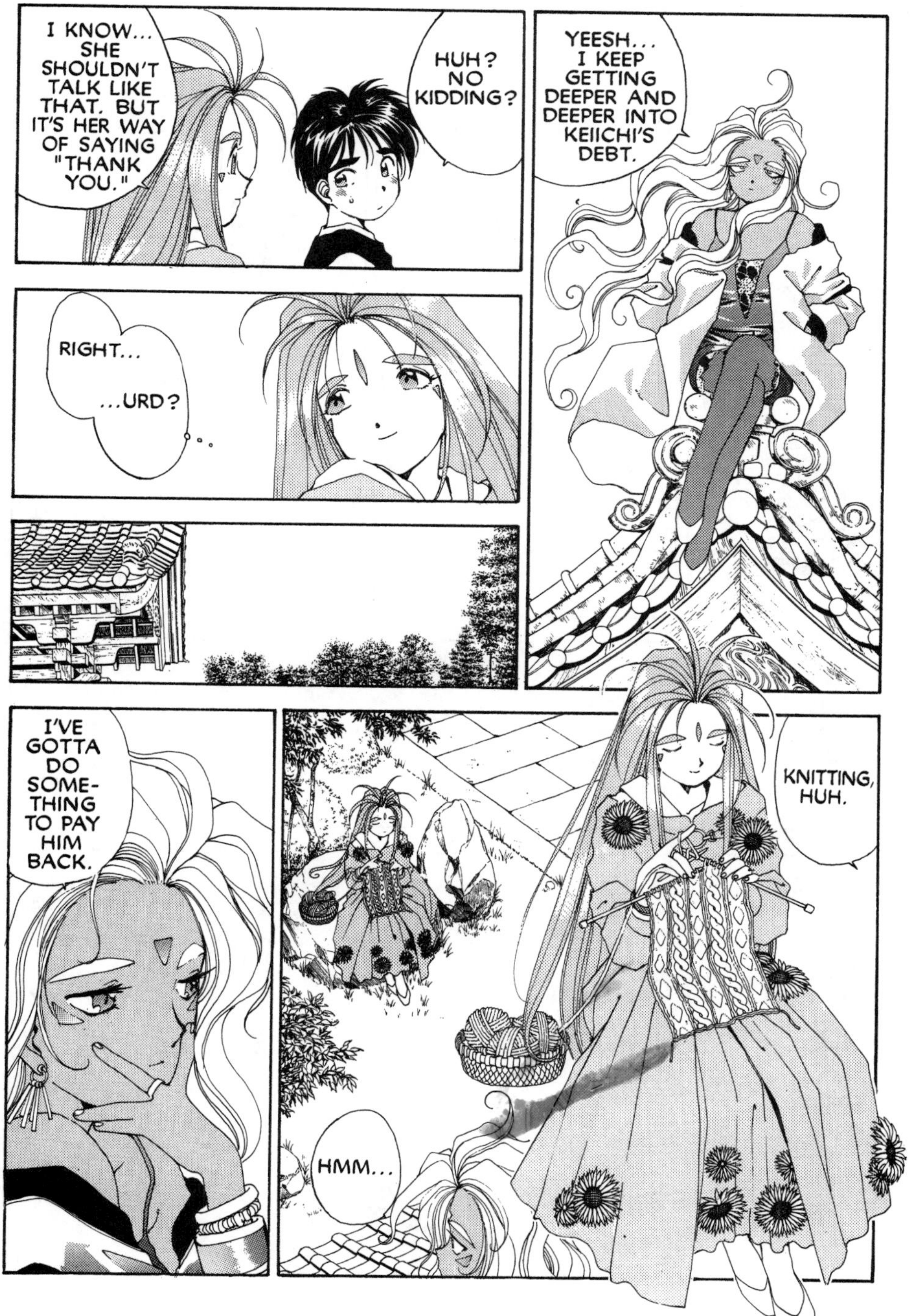
I KNOW... SHE SHOULDN'T TALK LIKE THAT. BUT IT'S HER WAY OF SAYING "THANK YOU."
HUH? NO KIDDING?
YEESH... I KEEP GETTING DEEPER AND DEEPER INTO KEIICHI'S DEBT.
RIGHT...
...URD?
I'VE GOTTA DO SOME-THING TO PAY HIM BACK.
KNITTING, HUH.
HMM...

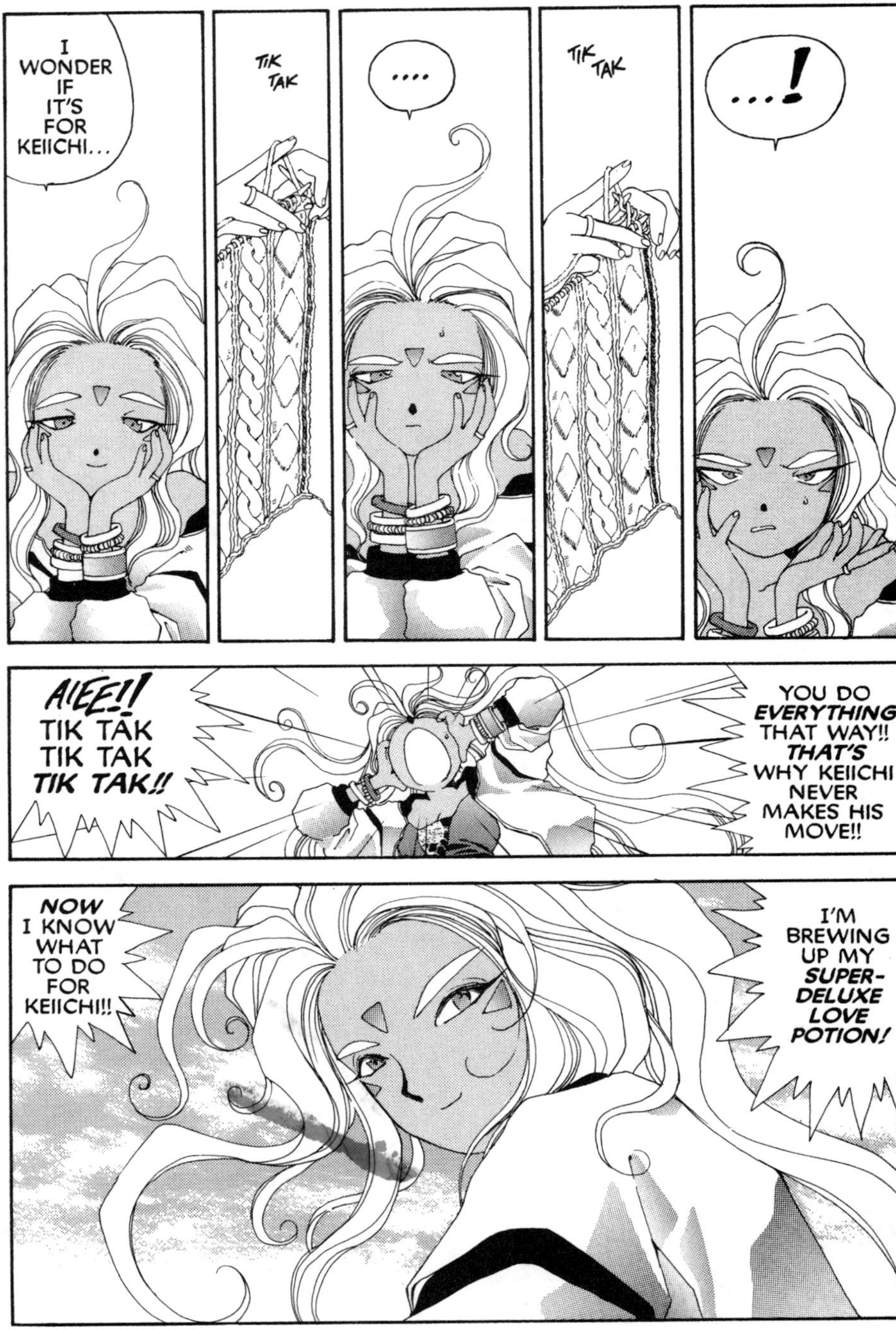
I WONDER IF IT'S FOR KEIICHI...
TIK TAK
....
TIK TAK
...!
AIEE!! TIK TAK TIK TAK TIK TAK!!
YOU DO EVERYTHING THAT WAY!! THAT'S WHY KEIICHI NEVER MAKES HIS MOVE!!
NOW I KNOW WHAT TO DO FOR KEIICHI!!
I'M BREWING UP MY SUPER-DELUXE LOVE POTION!

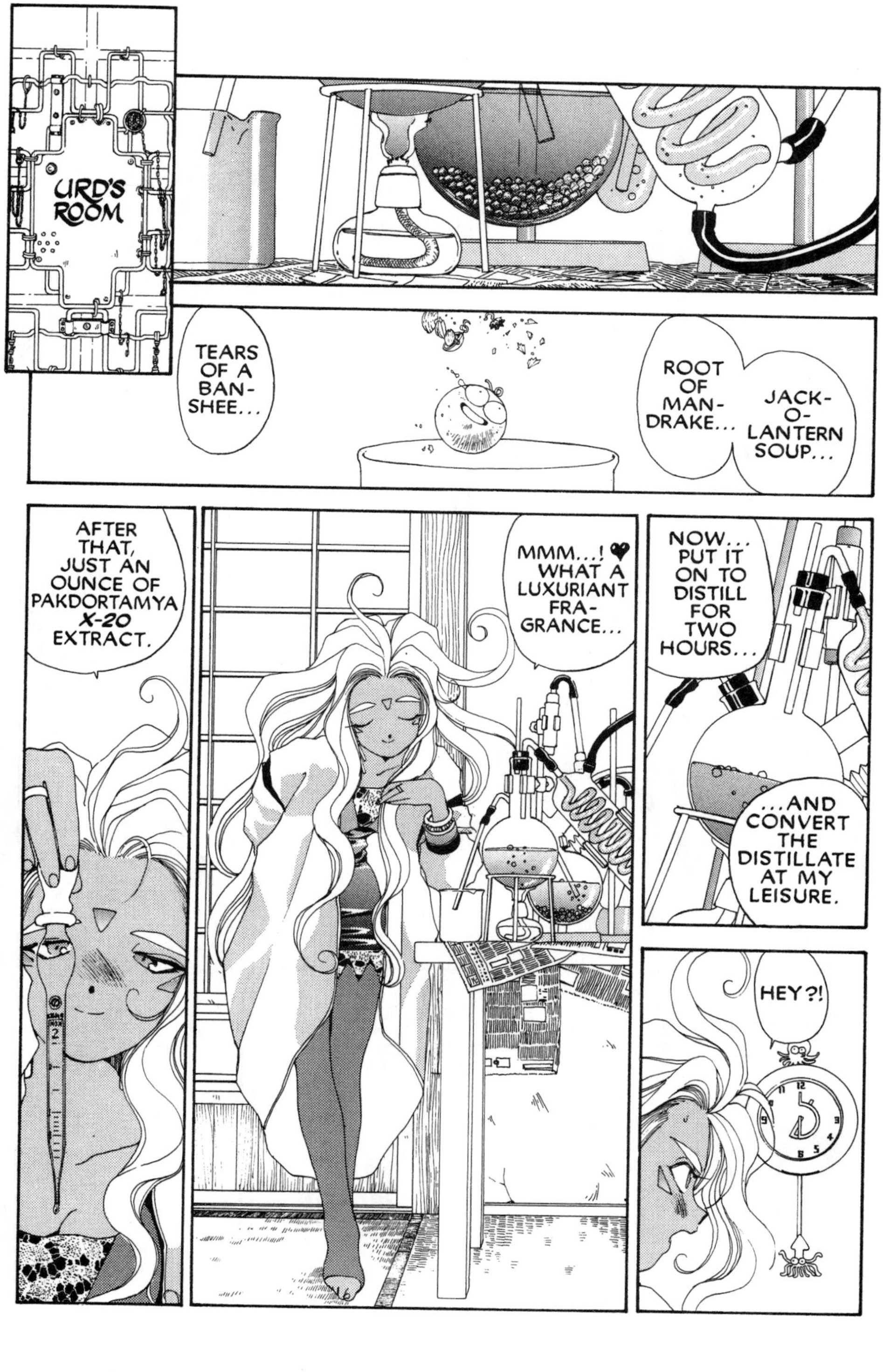
URD'S ROOM
TEARS OF A BANSHEE...
ROOT OF MANDRAKE...
JACK-O-LANTERN SOUP...
AFTER THAT, JUST AN OUNCE OF PAKDORTAMYA X-20 EXTRACT.
MMM...! ❤ WHAT A LUXURIANT FRAGRANCE...
NOW... PUT IT ON TO DISTILL FOR TWO HOURS...
...AND CONVERT THE DISTILLATE AT MY LEISURE.
HEY?!

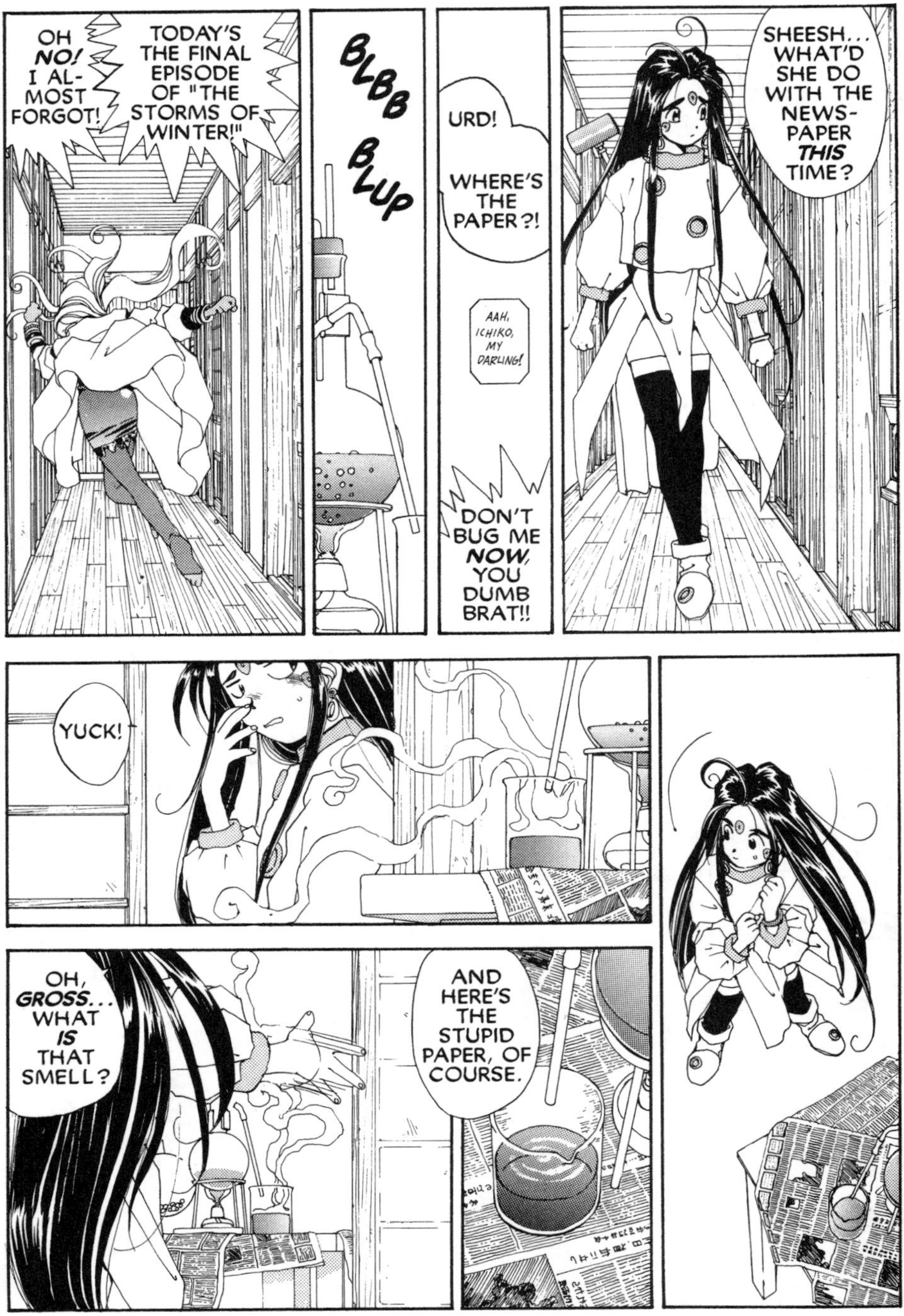
OH NO! I ALMOST FORGOT!
TODAY'S THE FINAL EPISODE OF "THE STORMS OF WINTER!"
BLBB
BLUP
URD!
WHERE'S THE PAPER?!
AAH, ICHIKO, MY DARLING!
DON'T BUG ME NOW, YOU DUMB BRAT!!
SHEESH... WHAT'D SHE DO WITH THE NEWSPAPER THIS TIME?
YUCK!
OH, GROSS... WHAT IS THAT SMELL?
AND HERE'S THE STUPID PAPER, OF COURSE.

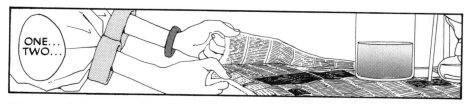

ONE...
TWO...

THREE!!

SKULD MAGIC SUPREME!

FWHAP

BLRSSH

?!

MAGNIFICENT!

...IF I MAY SAY SO MYSELF.

GACK!

N-N-
NOW WHAT DO I DO?

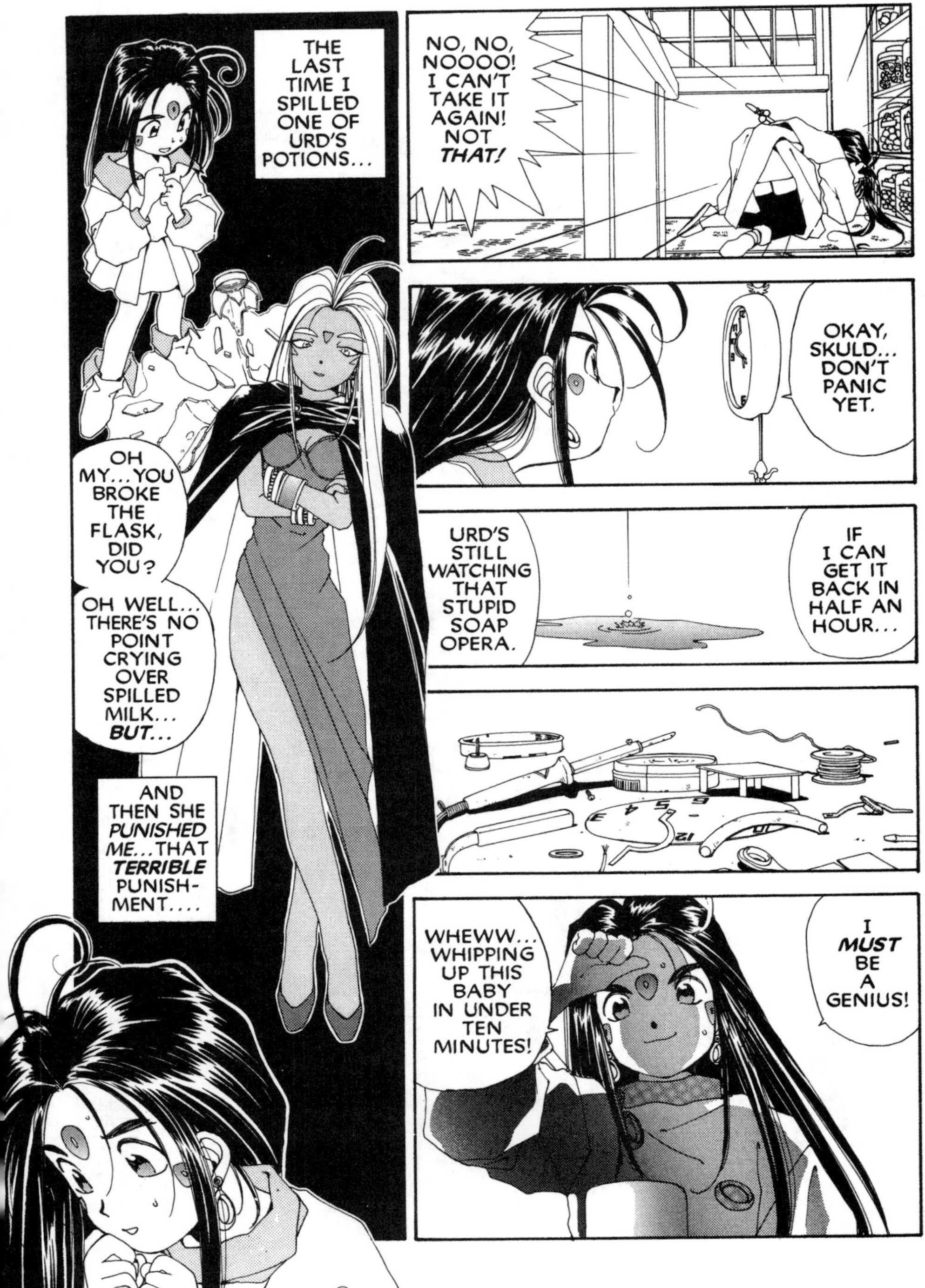
THE LAST TIME I SPILLED ONE OF URD'S POTIONS...
OH MY... YOU BROKE THE FLASK, DID YOU?
OH WELL... THERE'S NO POINT CRYING OVER SPILLED MILK... *BUT...*
AND THEN SHE *PUNISHED* ME... THAT *TERRIBLE* PUNISHMENT....
NO, NO, NOOOO! I CAN'T TAKE IT AGAIN! NOT *THAT!*
OKAY, SKULD... DON'T PANIC YET.
URD'S STILL WATCHING THAT STUPID SOAP OPERA.
IF I CAN GET IT BACK IN HALF AN HOUR...
WHEWW... WHIPPING UP THIS BABY IN UNDER TEN MINUTES!
I *MUST* BE A GENIUS!

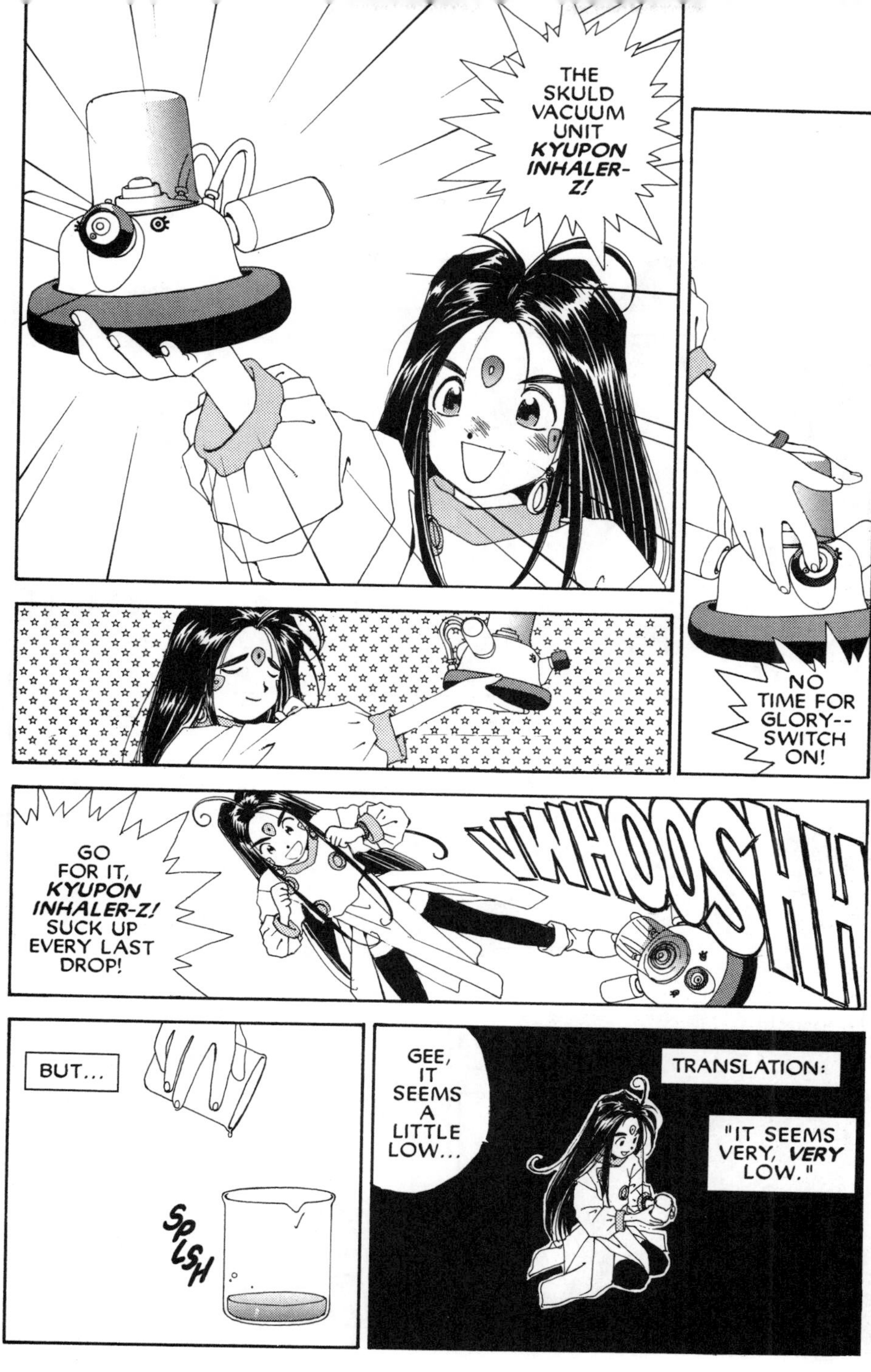
THE SKULD VACUUM UNIT *KYUPON INHALER-Z!*
NO TIME FOR GLORY-- SWITCH ON!
GO FOR IT, *KYUPON INHALER-Z!* SUCK UP EVERY LAST DROP!
VWHOOOSHH
BUT...
SPLSH
GEE, IT SEEMS A LITTLE LOW...
TRANSLATION:
"IT SEEMS VERY, *VERY* LOW."

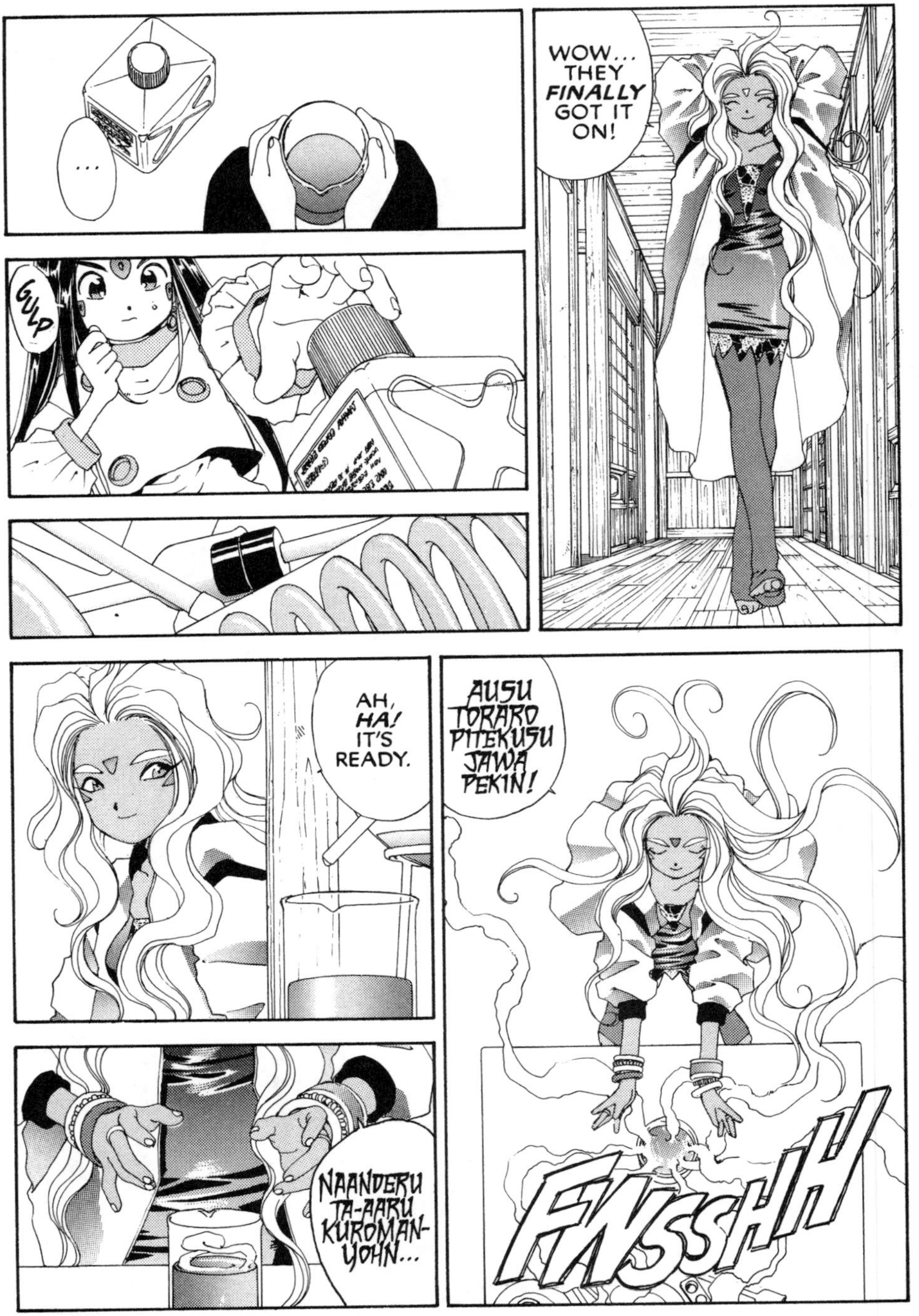
...
GULP
WOW... THEY *FINALLY* GOT IT ON!
AH, *HA!* IT'S READY.
NAANDERU TA-AARU KUROMAN-YOHN...
AUSU TORARO PITEKUSU JAWA PEKIN!
FWSSHH

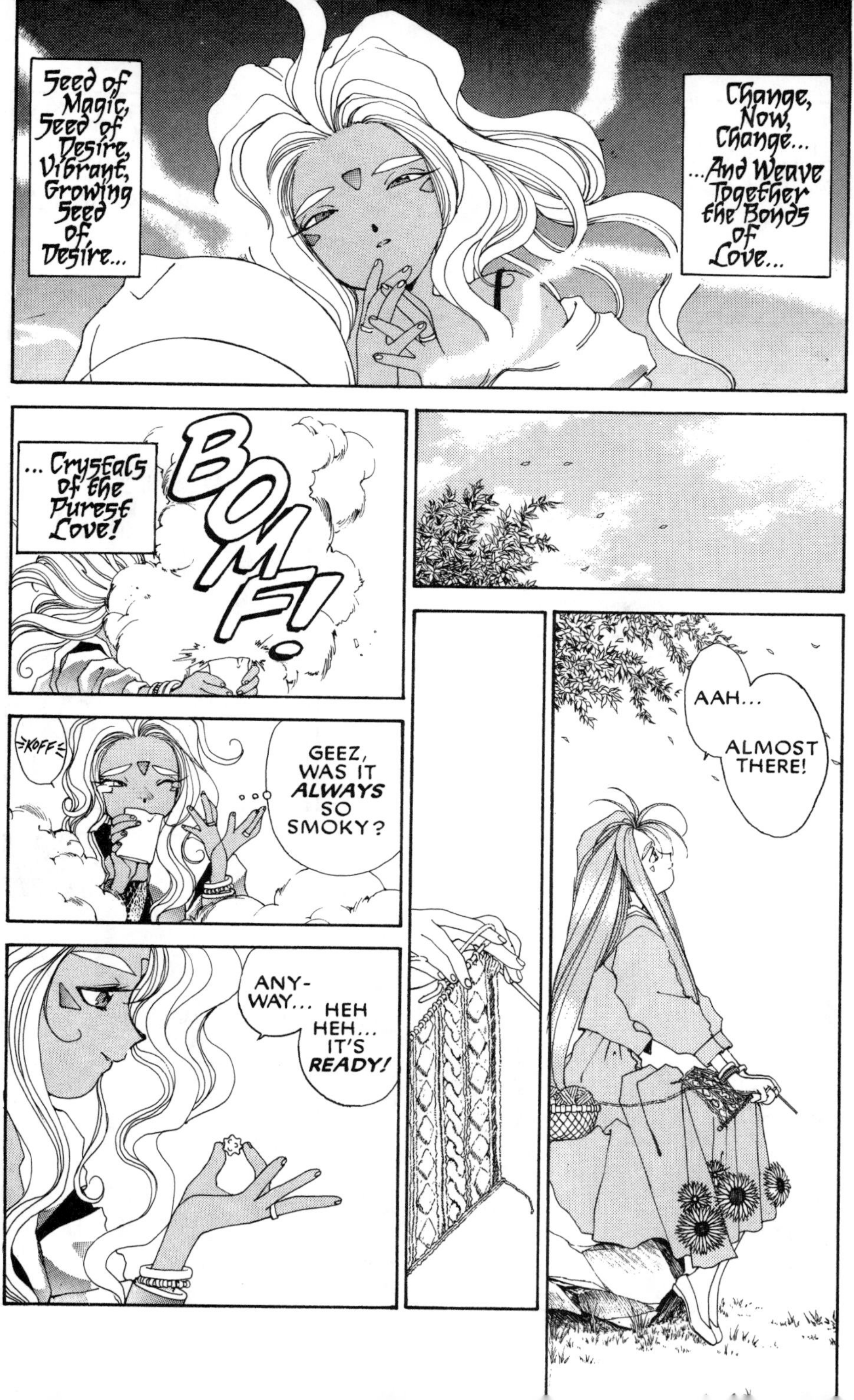

Seed of Magic, Seed of Desire, Vibrant, Growing Seed of Desire...
Change, Now, Change... ...And Weave Together the Bonds of Love...
...Crystals of the Purest Love!
BOMF!
KOFF
GEEZ, WAS IT ALWAYS SO SMOKY?
ANY-WAY...
HEH HEH... IT'S READY!
AAH... ALMOST THERE!

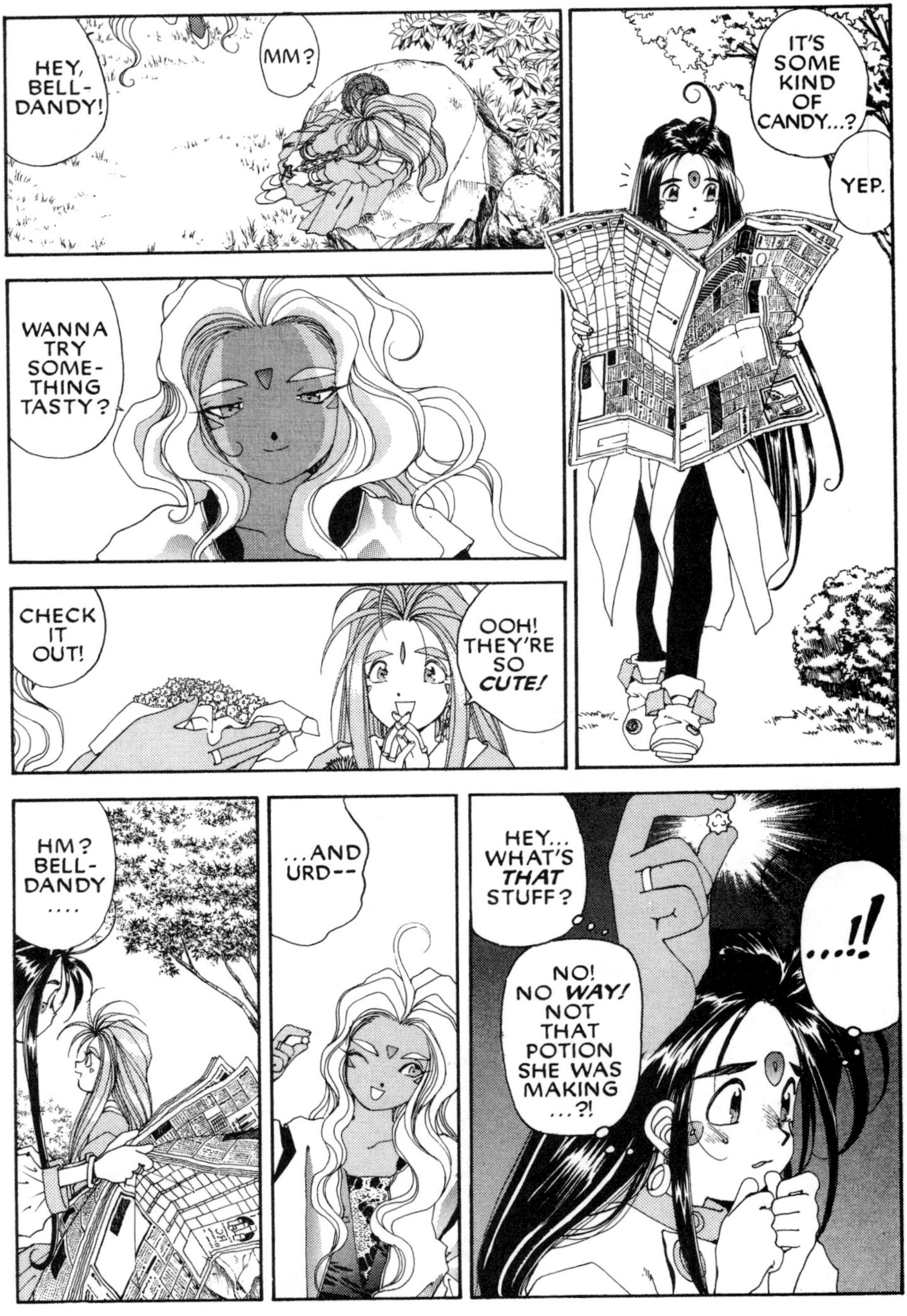
HEY, BELL-DANDY!
MM?
WANNA TRY SOME-THING TASTY?
CHECK IT OUT!
OOH! THEY'RE SO *CUTE!*
IT'S SOME KIND OF CANDY...?
YEP.
HM? BELL-DANDY....
...AND URD--
HEY... WHAT'S *THAT* STUFF?
...!!
NO! NO *WAY!* NOT THAT POTION SHE WAS MAKING...?!

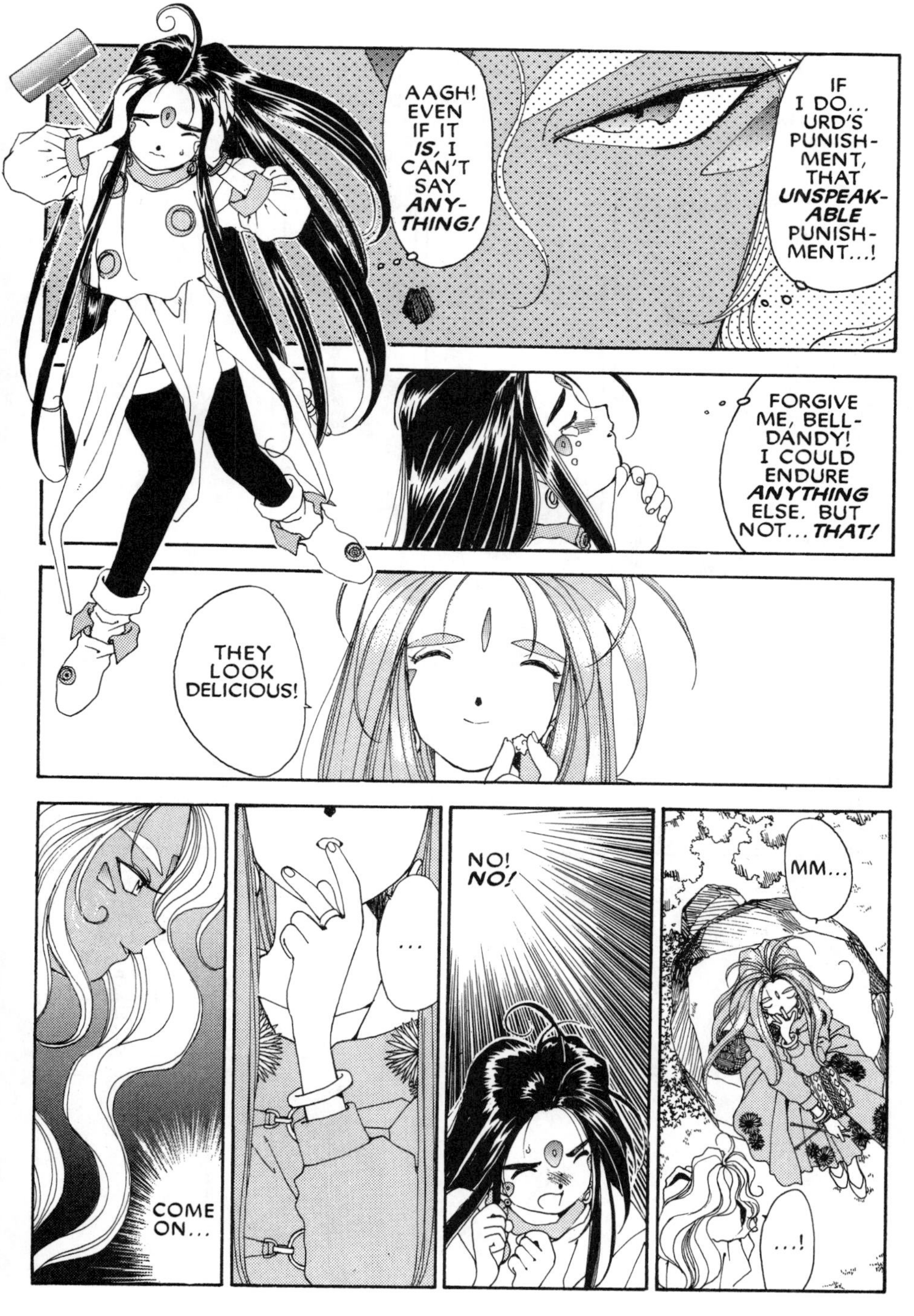
AAGH! EVEN IF IT IS, I CAN'T SAY ANYTHING!
IF I DO... URD'S PUNISHMENT, THAT UNSPEAKABLE PUNISHMENT...!
FORGIVE ME, BELLDANDY! I COULD ENDURE ANYTHING ELSE. BUT NOT... THAT!
THEY LOOK DELICIOUS!
COME ON...
...
NO! NO!
MM...
...!

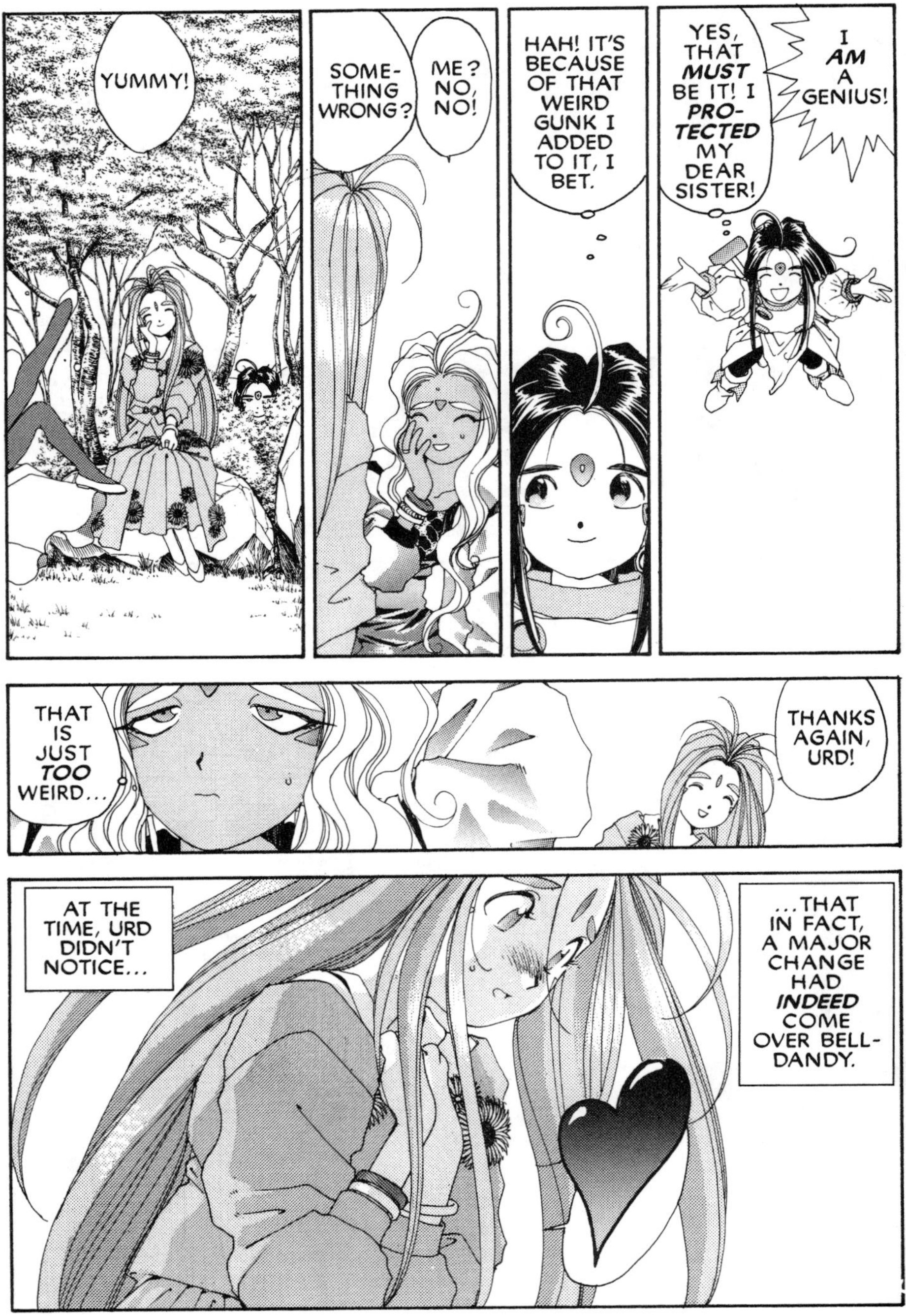
YUMMY!
SOME-THING WRONG?
ME? NO, NO!
HAH! IT'S BECAUSE OF THAT WEIRD GUNK I ADDED TO IT, I BET.
YES, THAT MUST BE IT! I PRO-TECTED MY DEAR SISTER!
I AM A GENIUS!
THAT IS JUST TOO WEIRD...
THANKS AGAIN, URD!
AT THE TIME, URD DIDN'T NOTICE...
...THAT IN FACT, A MAJOR CHANGE HAD INDEED COME OVER BELL-DANDY.

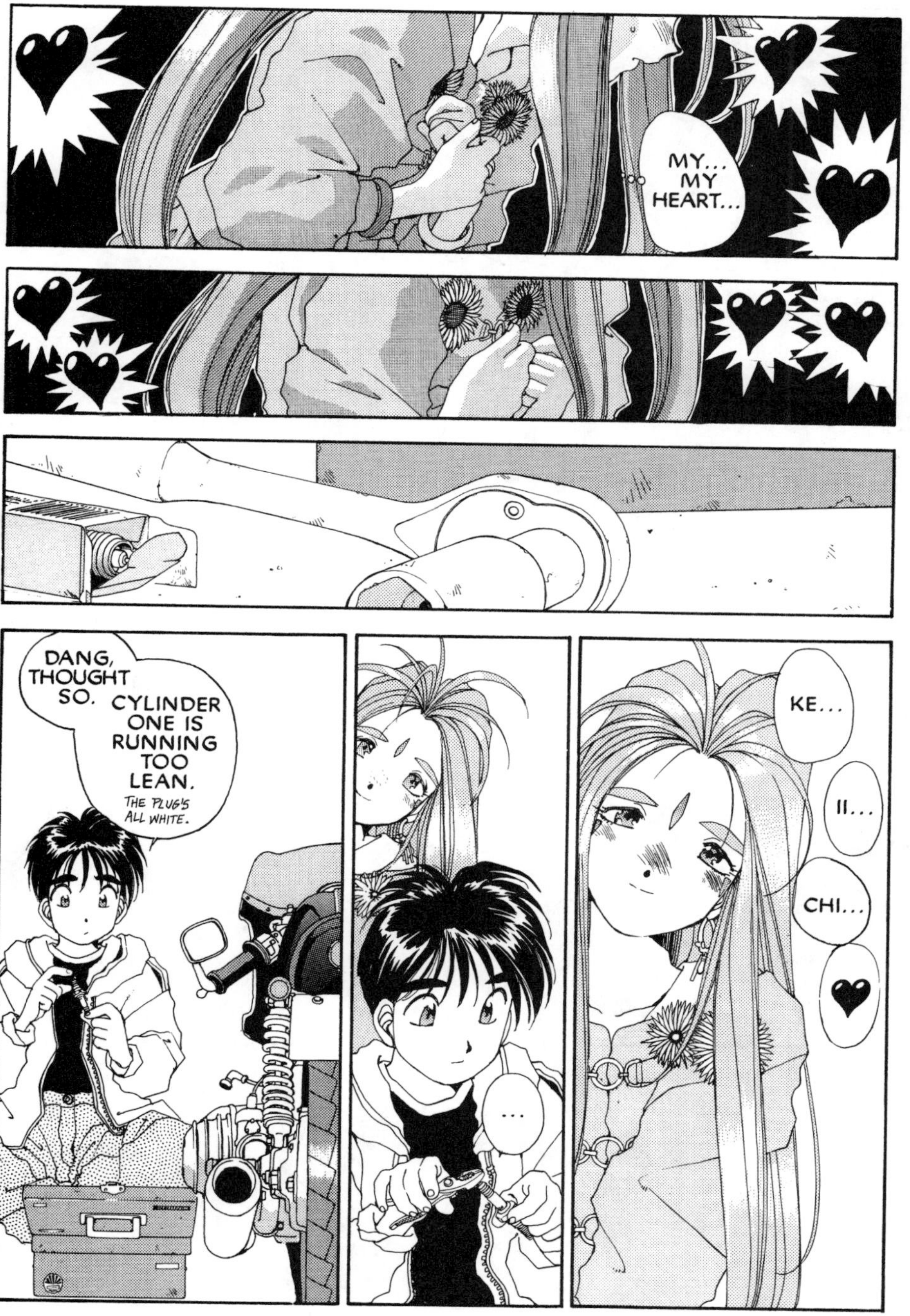
MY... MY HEART...
DANG, THOUGHT SO.
CYLINDER ONE IS RUNNING TOO LEAN.
THE PLUG'S ALL WHITE.
...
KE...
II...
CHI...
♥

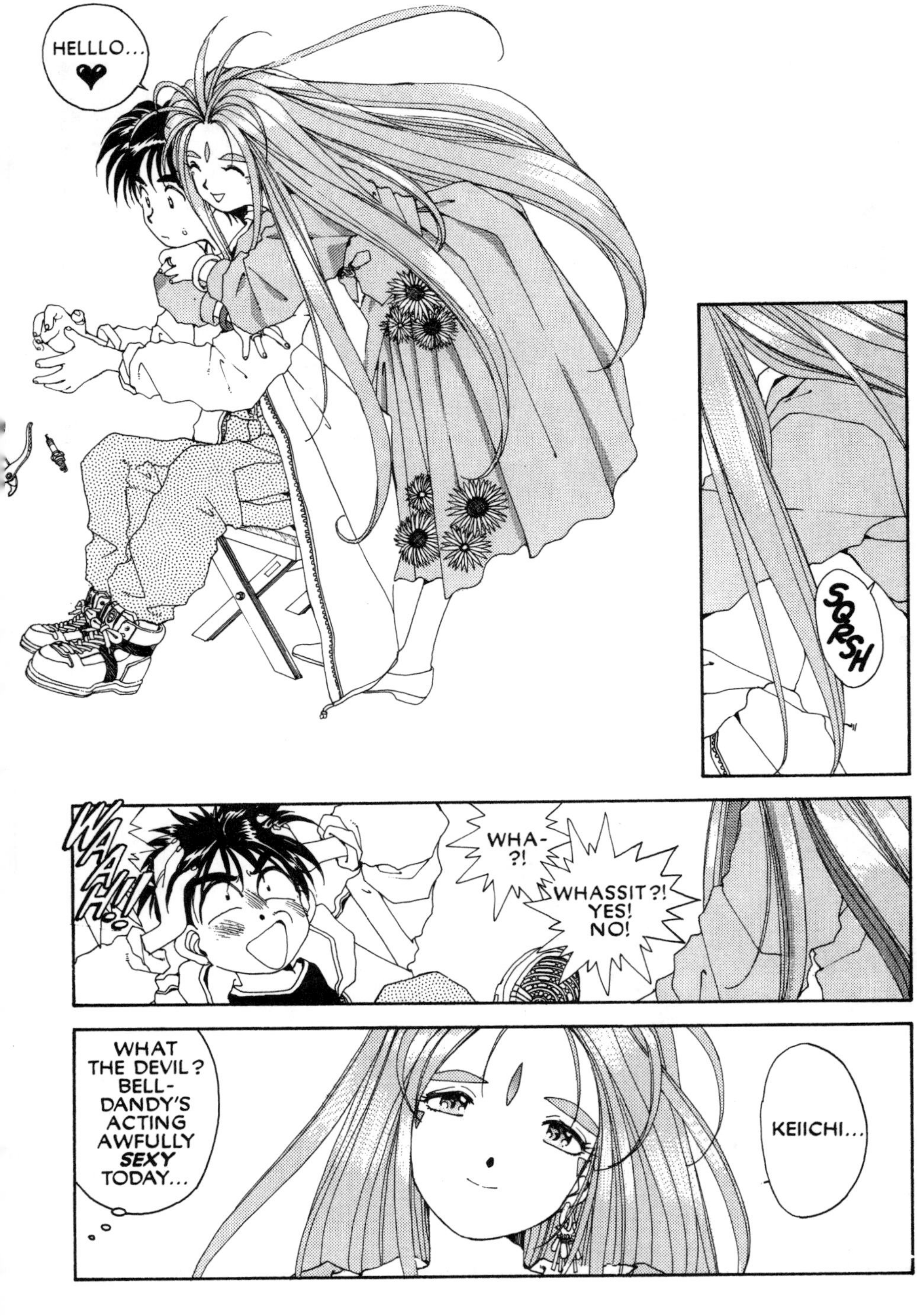
HELLLO... ♥
SORSH
WHA-?!
WHASSIT?! YES! NO!
WHAT THE DEVIL? BELL-DANDY'S ACTING AWFULLY SEXY TODAY...
KEIICHI...

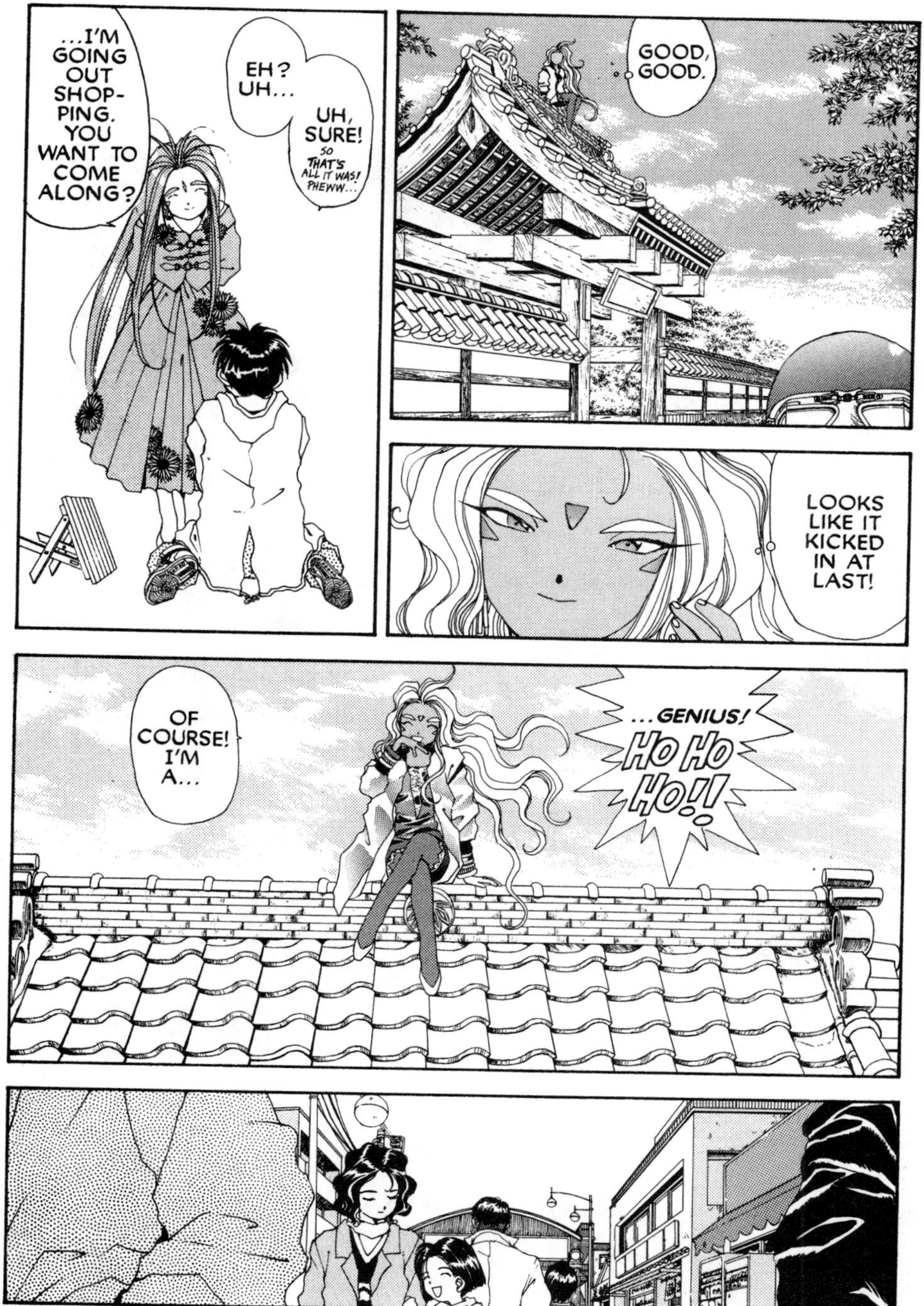
...I'M GOING OUT SHOPPING. YOU WANT TO COME ALONG?
EH? UH...
UH, SURE!
SO THAT'S ALL IT WAS! PHEWW...
GOOD, GOOD.
LOOKS LIKE IT KICKED IN AT LAST!
OF COURSE! I'M A...
...GENIUS!
HO HO HO!!

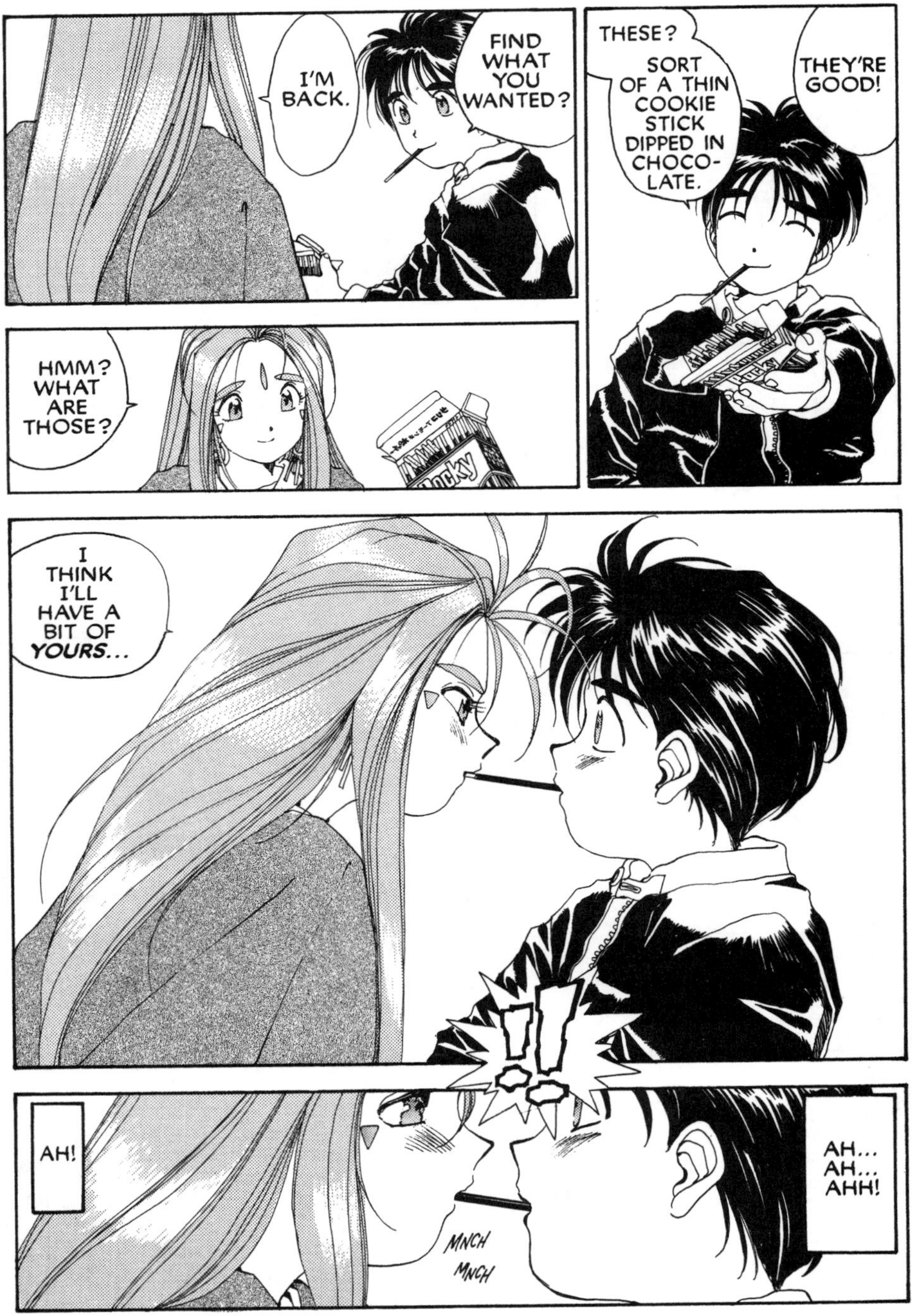
I'M BACK.
FIND WHAT YOU WANTED?
HMM? WHAT ARE THOSE?
THESE?
SORT OF A THIN COOKIE STICK DIPPED IN CHOCO-LATE.
THEY'RE GOOD!
I THINK I'LL HAVE A BIT OF *YOURS...*
!!
AH!
MNCH MNCH
AH... AH... AHH!

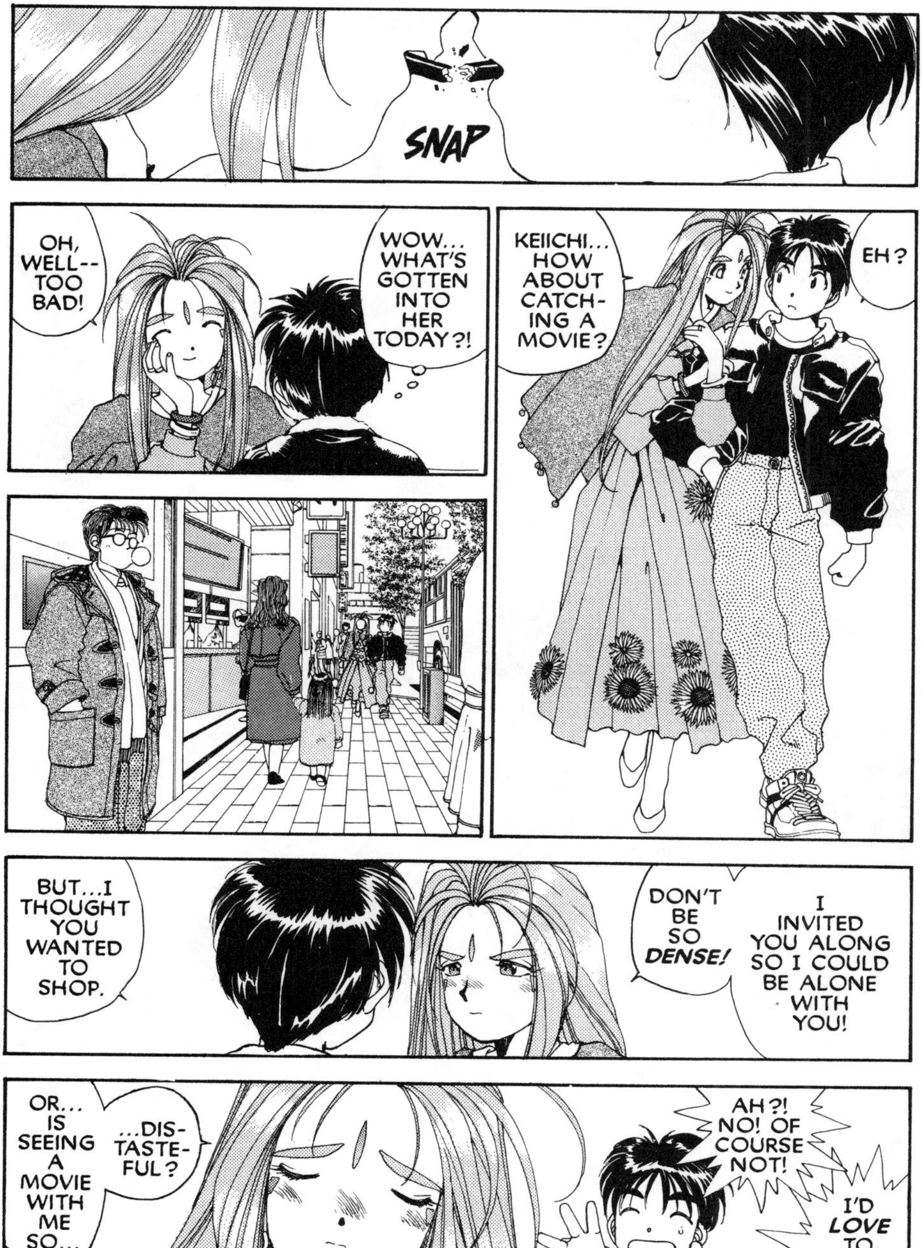
SNAP
OH, WELL-- TOO BAD!
WOW... WHAT'S GOTTEN INTO HER TODAY?!
KEIICHI... HOW ABOUT CATCHING A MOVIE?
EH?
BUT...I THOUGHT YOU WANTED TO SHOP.
DON'T BE SO DENSE!
I INVITED YOU ALONG SO I COULD BE ALONE WITH YOU!
OR... IS SEEING A MOVIE WITH ME SO...
...DISTASTEFUL?
AH?! NO! OF COURSE NOT!
I'D LOVE TO SEE A MOVIE!

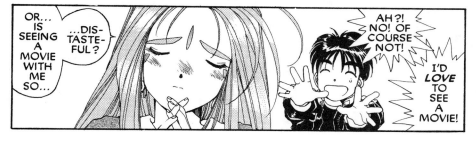

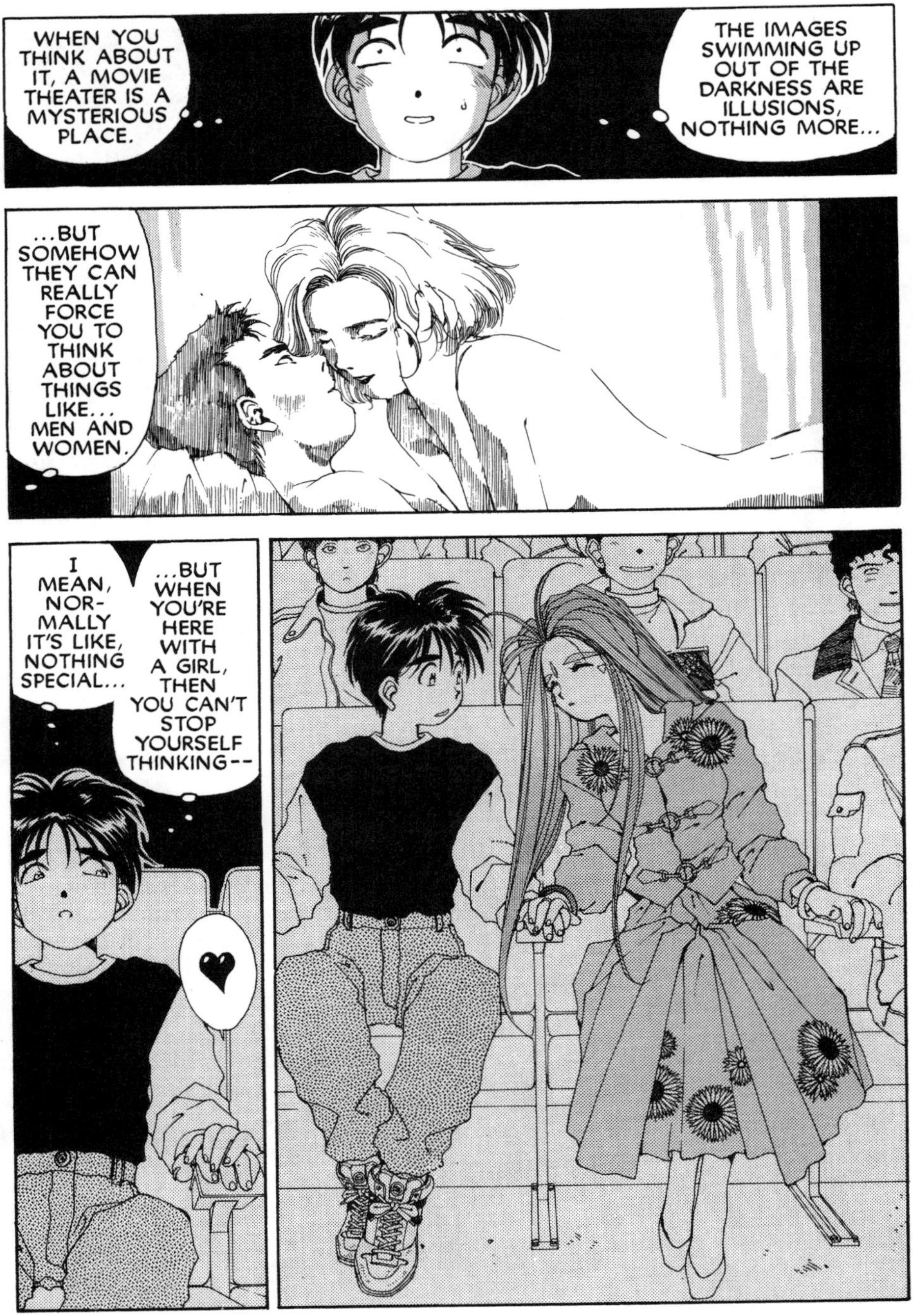
WHEN YOU THINK ABOUT IT, A MOVIE THEATER IS A MYSTERIOUS PLACE.
THE IMAGES SWIMMING UP OUT OF THE DARKNESS ARE ILLUSIONS, NOTHING MORE...
...BUT SOMEHOW THEY CAN REALLY FORCE YOU TO THINK ABOUT THINGS LIKE... MEN AND WOMEN.
I MEAN, NOR-MALLY IT'S LIKE, NOTHING SPECIAL...
...BUT WHEN YOU'RE HERE WITH A GIRL, THEN YOU CAN'T STOP YOURSELF THINKING--

WHAT'S GOING ON?! IT'S LIKE A *SETUP!*

IT'S A DREAM! I'M DREAMING! I *HAVE* TO BE!

THE PARA-LYZED KEIICHI COULD DO NO MORE.

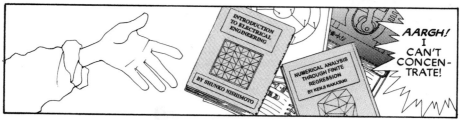

INTRODUCTION TO ELECTRICAL ENGINEERING

BY SHUNKO NISHIMOTO

NUMERICAL ANALYSIS THROUGH FINITE REGRESSION
BY KENJI NAKATANI

AARGH! I CAN'T CONCEN-TRATE!

I KEEP REMEM-BERING THE MOVIE THEATER...

CAN'T GET IT OUT OF MY HEAD!

N O K

N O K

COME IN!

HELLO, DEAR...

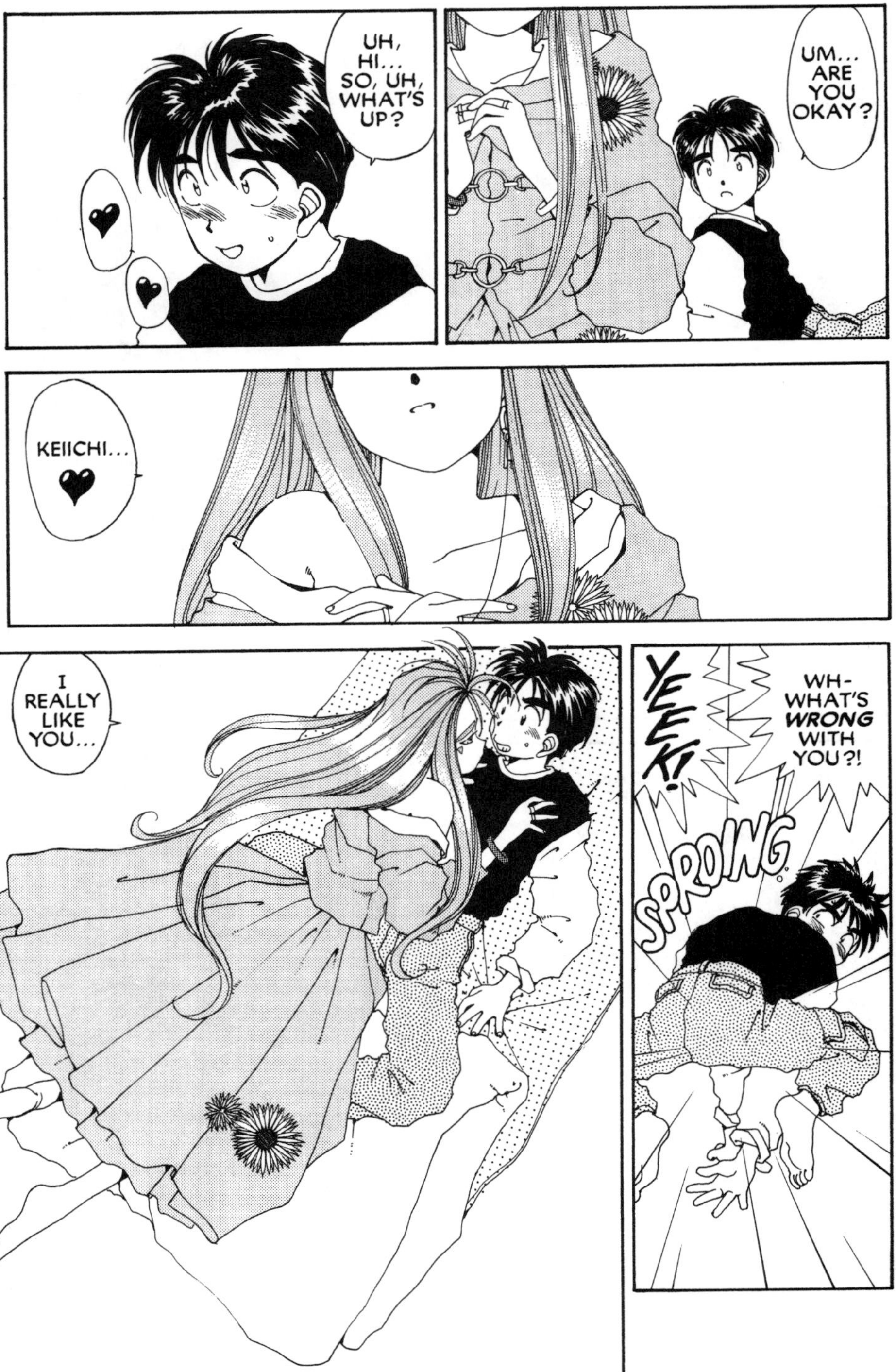
UH, HI... SO, UH, WHAT'S UP?
UM... ARE YOU OKAY?
KEIICHI...
I REALLY LIKE YOU...
YEEK!
WH-WHAT'S WRONG WITH YOU?!
SPROING

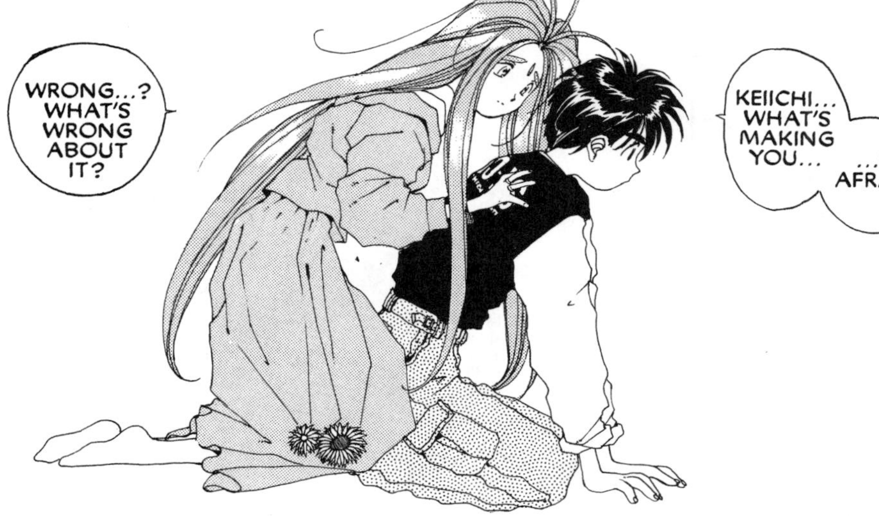
WRONG...? WHAT'S WRONG ABOUT IT?
KEIICHI... WHAT'S MAKING YOU... ...SO AFRAID?

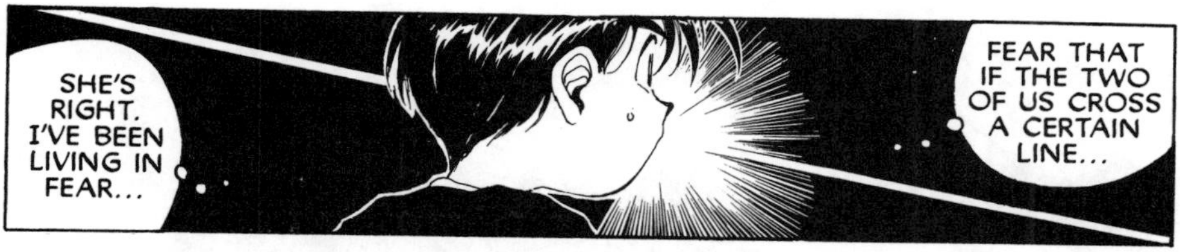
SHE'S RIGHT. I'VE BEEN LIVING IN FEAR...
FEAR THAT IF THE TWO OF US CROSS A CERTAIN LINE...

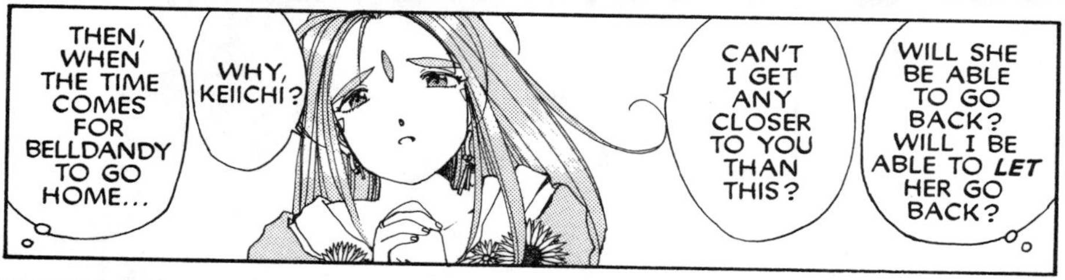
THEN, WHEN THE TIME COMES FOR BELLDANDY TO GO HOME...
WHY, KEIICHI?
CAN'T I GET ANY CLOSER TO YOU THAN THIS?
WILL SHE BE ABLE TO GO BACK? WILL I BE ABLE TO *LET* HER GO BACK?

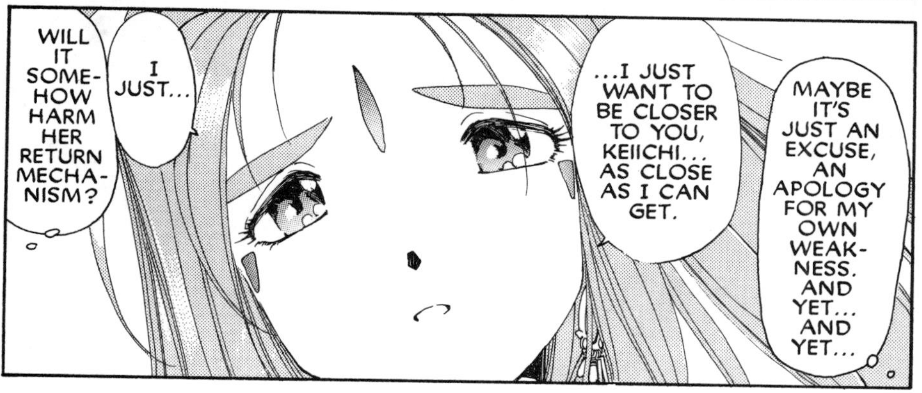
WILL IT SOMEHOW HARM HER RETURN MECHANISM?
I JUST...
...I JUST WANT TO BE CLOSER TO YOU, KEIICHI... AS CLOSE AS I CAN GET.
MAYBE IT'S JUST AN EXCUSE, AN APOLOGY FOR MY OWN WEAKNESS. AND YET... AND YET...

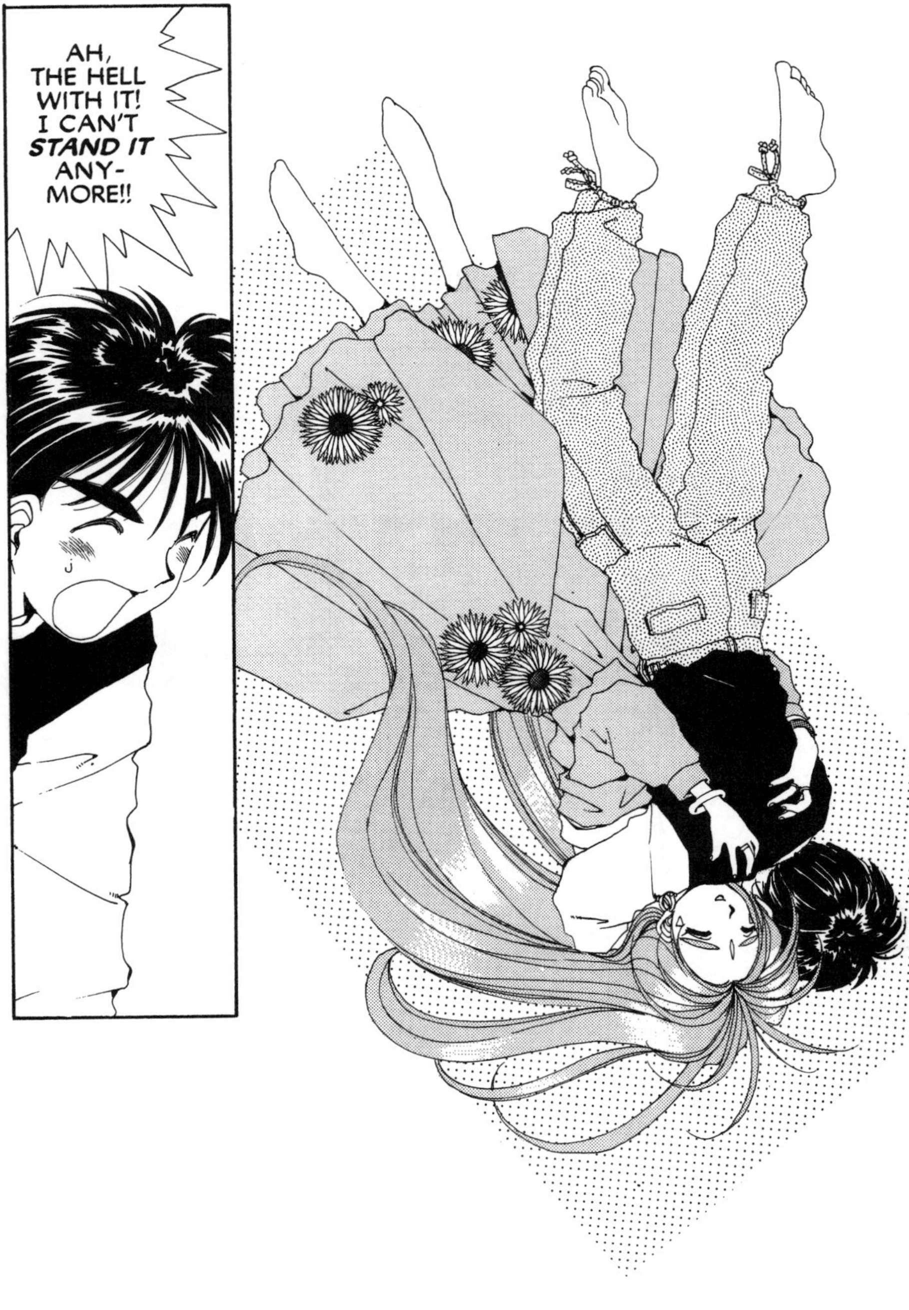
AH, THE HELL WITH IT! I CAN'T STAND IT ANY-MORE!!

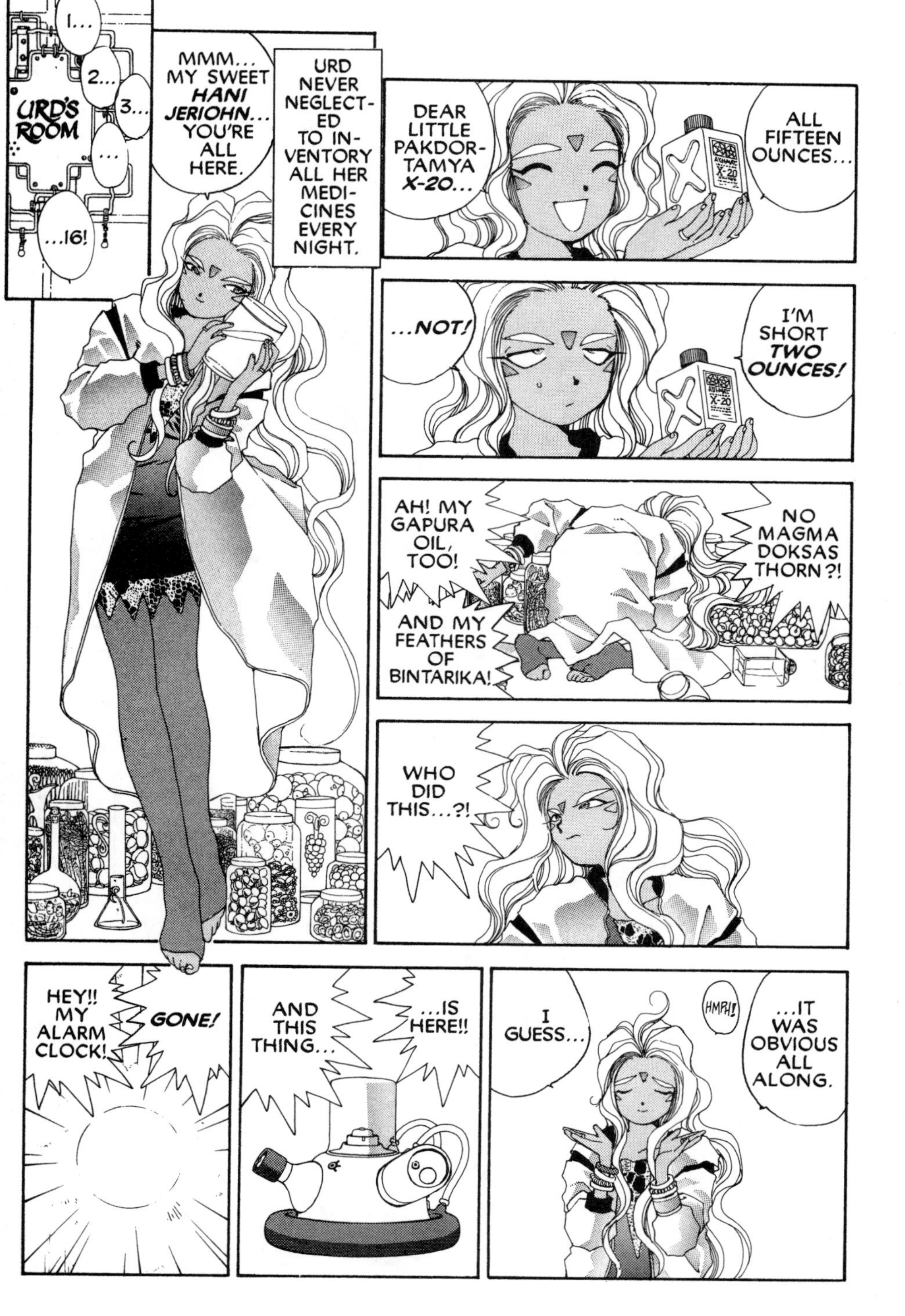
1...
2...
3...
...
...16!
URD'S ROOM
MMM... MY SWEET HANI JERIOHN... YOU'RE ALL HERE.
URD NEVER NEGLECTED TO INVENTORY ALL HER MEDICINES EVERY NIGHT.
DEAR LITTLE PAKDORTAMYA X-20...
ALL FIFTEEN OUNCES...
X-20
...NOT!
I'M SHORT TWO OUNCES!
X-20
AH! MY GAPURA OIL, TOO!
AND MY FEATHERS OF BINTARIKA!
NO MAGMA DOKSAS THORN?!
WHO DID THIS...?!
HEY!! MY ALARM CLOCK!
GONE!
AND THIS THING...
...IS HERE!!
I GUESS...
HMPH!
...IT WAS OBVIOUS ALL ALONG.

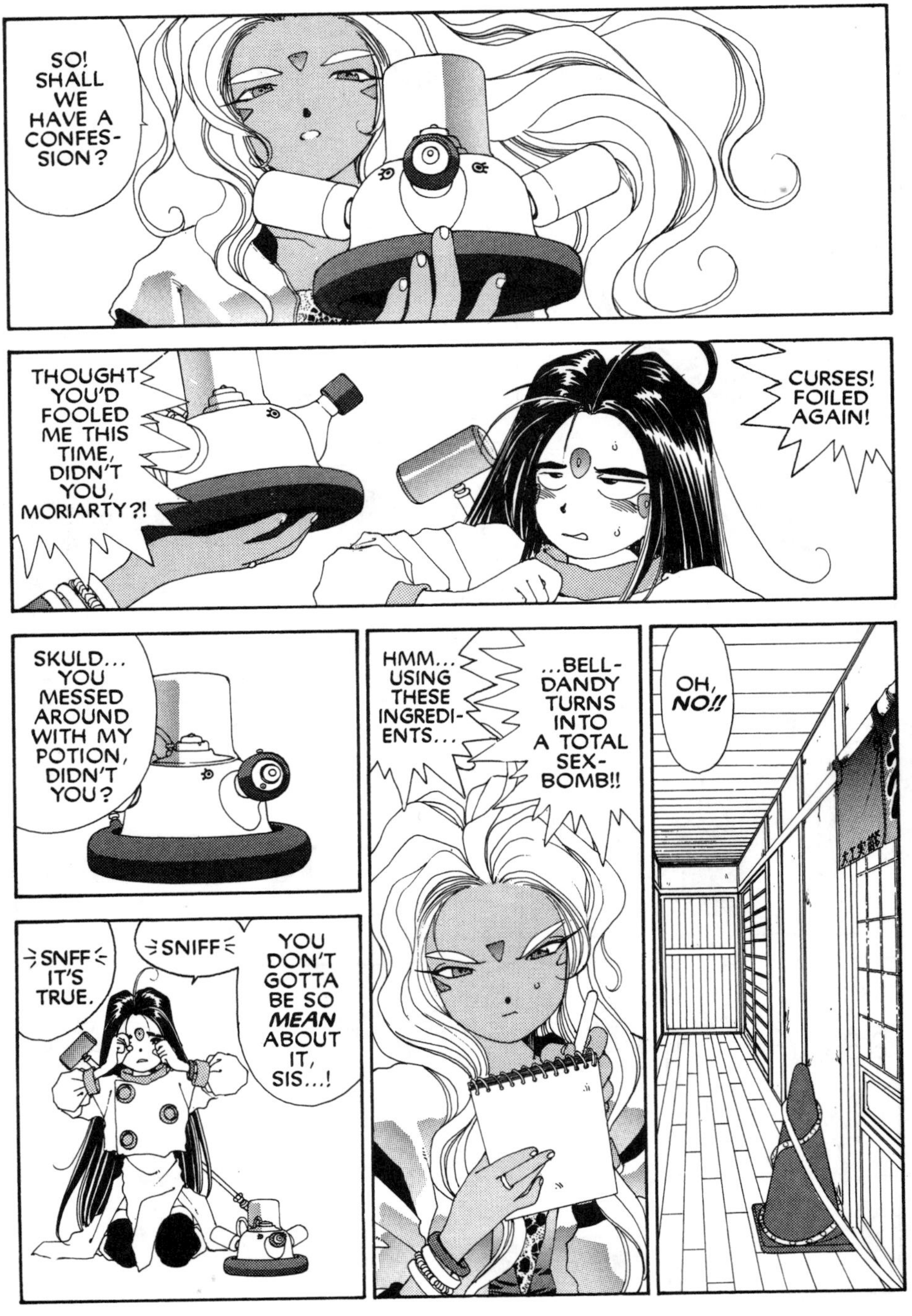
SO! SHALL WE HAVE A CONFES-SION?
THOUGHT YOU'D FOOLED ME THIS TIME, DIDN'T YOU, MORIARTY?!
CURSES! FOILED AGAIN!
SKULD... YOU MESSED AROUND WITH MY POTION, DIDN'T YOU?
SNFF IT'S TRUE.
SNIFF
YOU DON'T GOTTA BE SO *MEAN* ABOUT IT, SIS...!
HMM... USING THESE INGREDI-ENTS...
...BELL-DANDY TURNS INTO A TOTAL SEX-BOMB!!
OH, *NO!!*

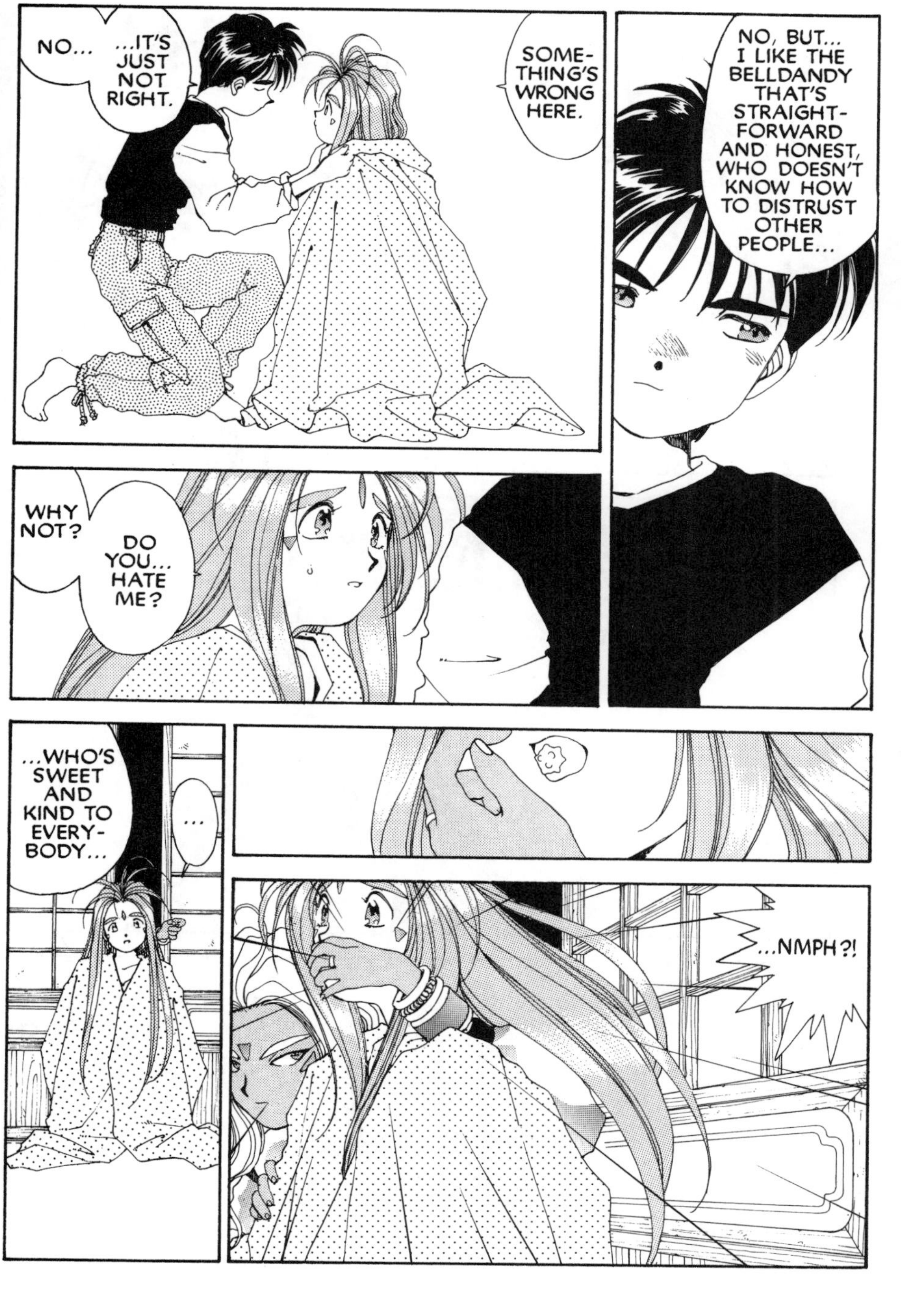
NO... ...IT'S JUST NOT RIGHT.
SOME-THING'S WRONG HERE.
WHY NOT?
DO YOU... HATE ME?
NO, BUT... I LIKE THE BELLDANDY THAT'S STRAIGHT-FORWARD AND HONEST, WHO DOESN'T KNOW HOW TO DISTRUST OTHER PEOPLE...
...WHO'S SWEET AND KIND TO EVERY-BODY...
...
...NMPH?!

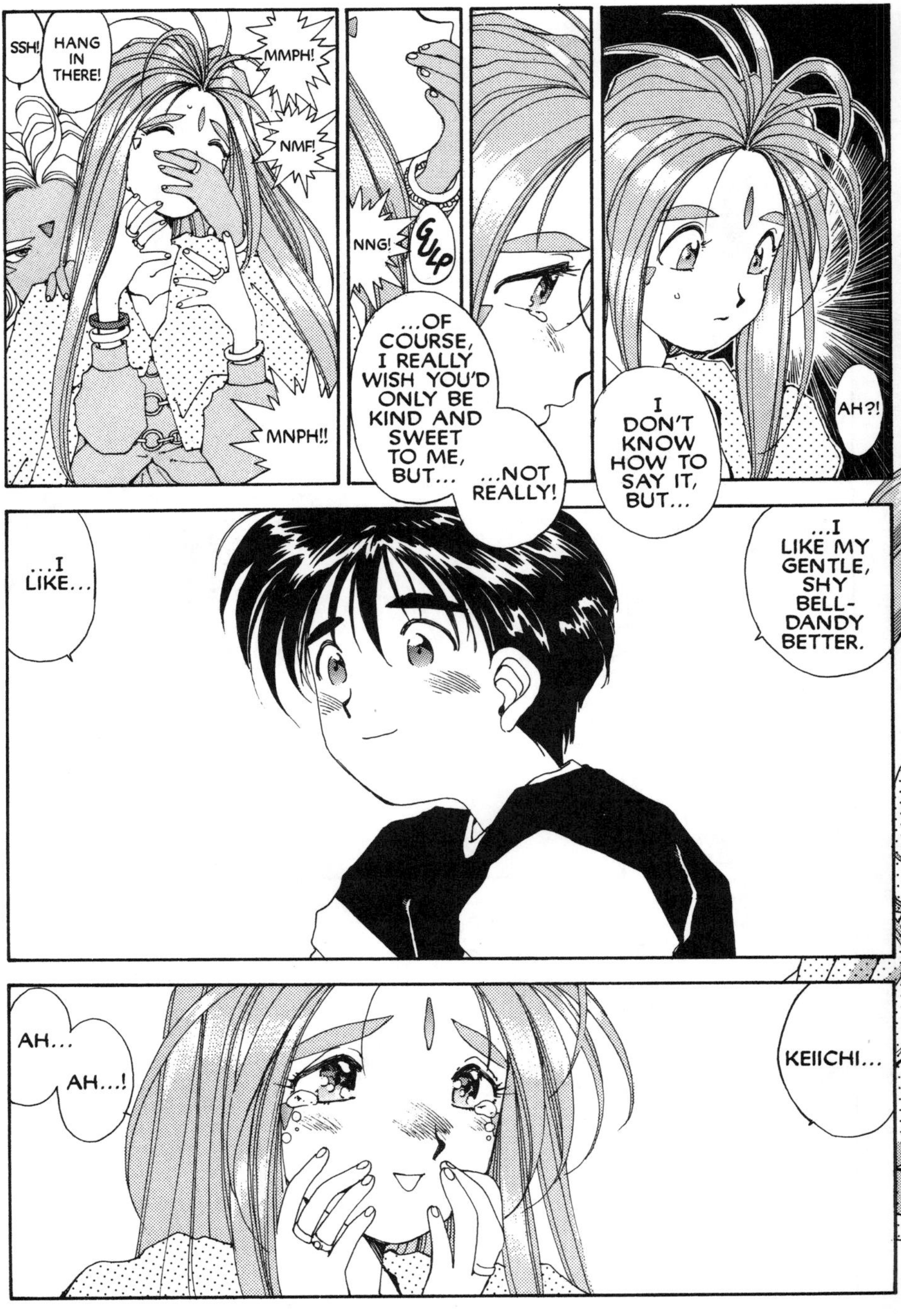
SSH!
HANG IN THERE!
MMPH!
NMF!
MNPH!!
NNG!
GULP
...OF COURSE, I REALLY WISH YOU'D ONLY BE KIND AND SWEET TO ME, BUT...
...NOT REALLY!
I DON'T KNOW HOW TO SAY IT, BUT...
AH?!
...I LIKE...
...I LIKE MY GENTLE, SHY BELL-DANDY BETTER.
AH... AH...!
KEIICHI...

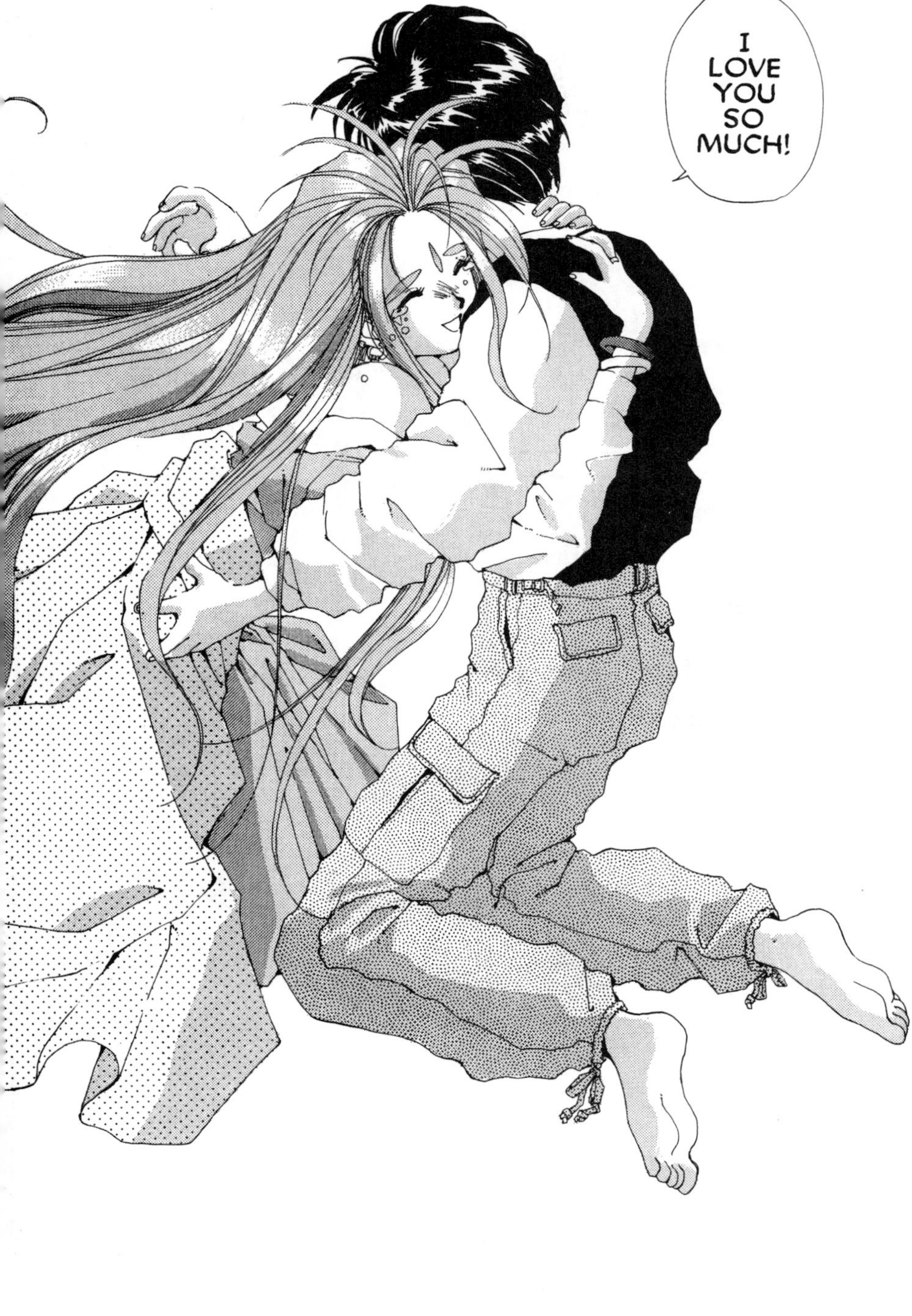
I LOVE YOU SO MUCH!

GOOD FOR YOU, BELL-DANDY!
AH, WELL... I GUESS IT WAS *MOSTLY* BECAUSE OF MY POTION...
WAAH!!
I CAN'T *STAND* IT! HE'S STEALING MY SISTER AWAY!
AND NOW... SKULD, DEAR--YOU KNOW WHAT HAP-PENS *NEXT,* DON'T YOU...?
ULP!
NO...
URD... PLEASE?
GOOD, GOOD! *NEXT!*
MAKE A MACHINE THAT DOES *NOTHING* BUT GO IN CIRCLES!
NO! NOOO! *STOP IT!!*
PLEASE DON'T MAKE ME MAKE ANY MORE MACHINES THAT DON'T DO ANY-THING USE-FUL!! *PLEEEAASE!!*

The Queen of Vengeance

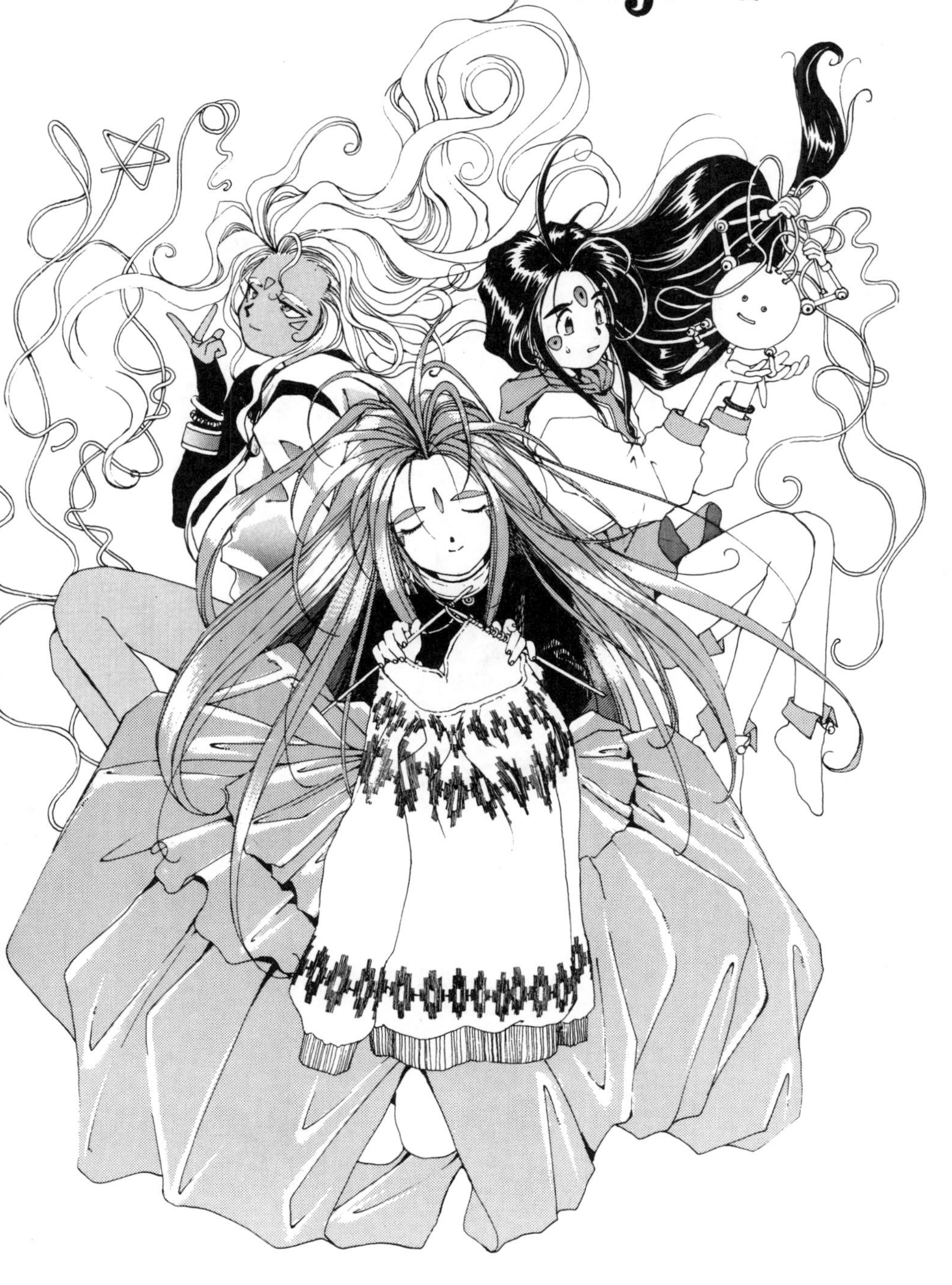

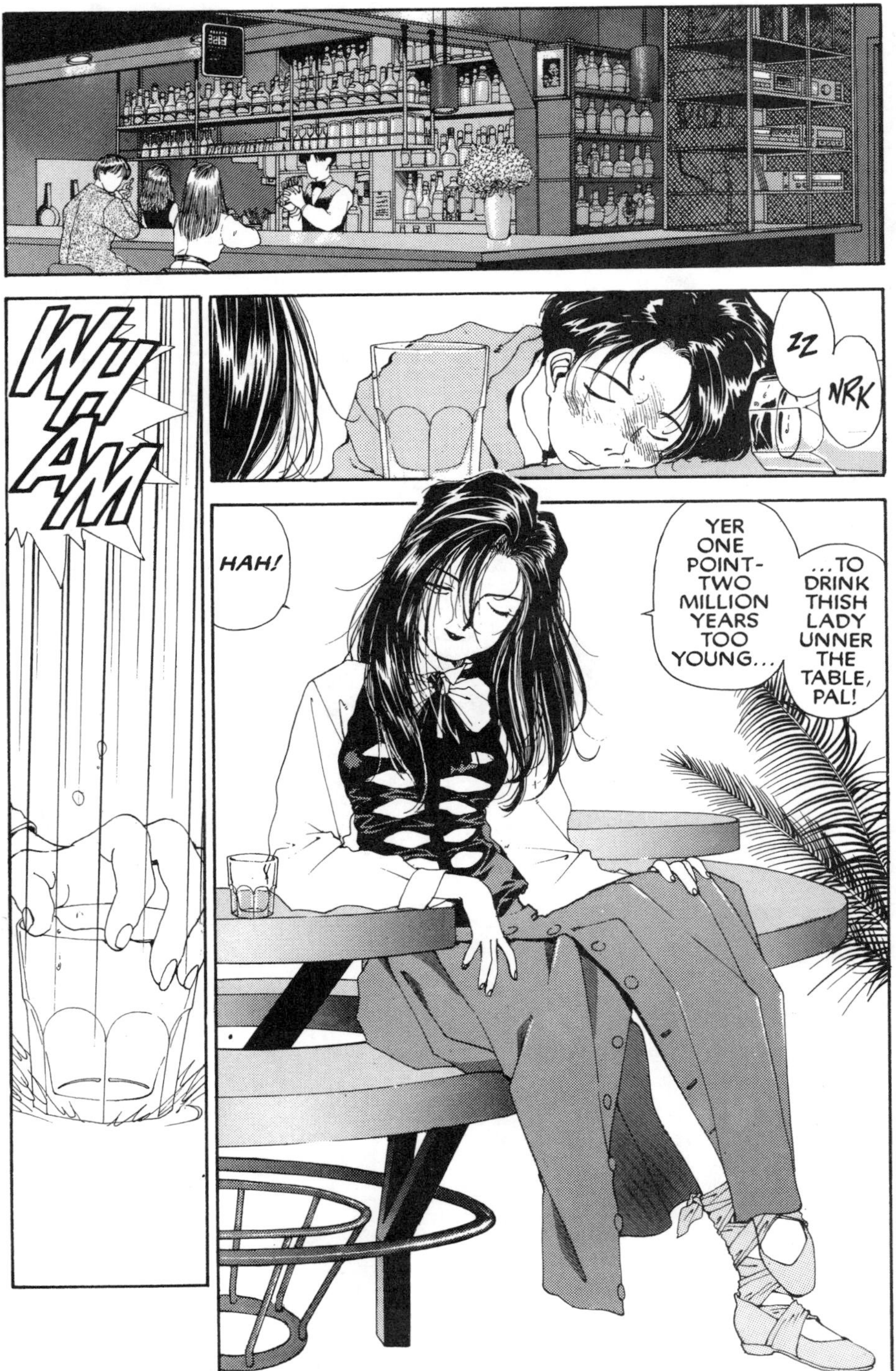
WHAM
ZZ
NRK
HAH!
YER ONE POINT-TWO MILLION YEARS TOO YOUNG...
...TO DRINK THISH LADY UNNER THE TABLE, PAL!

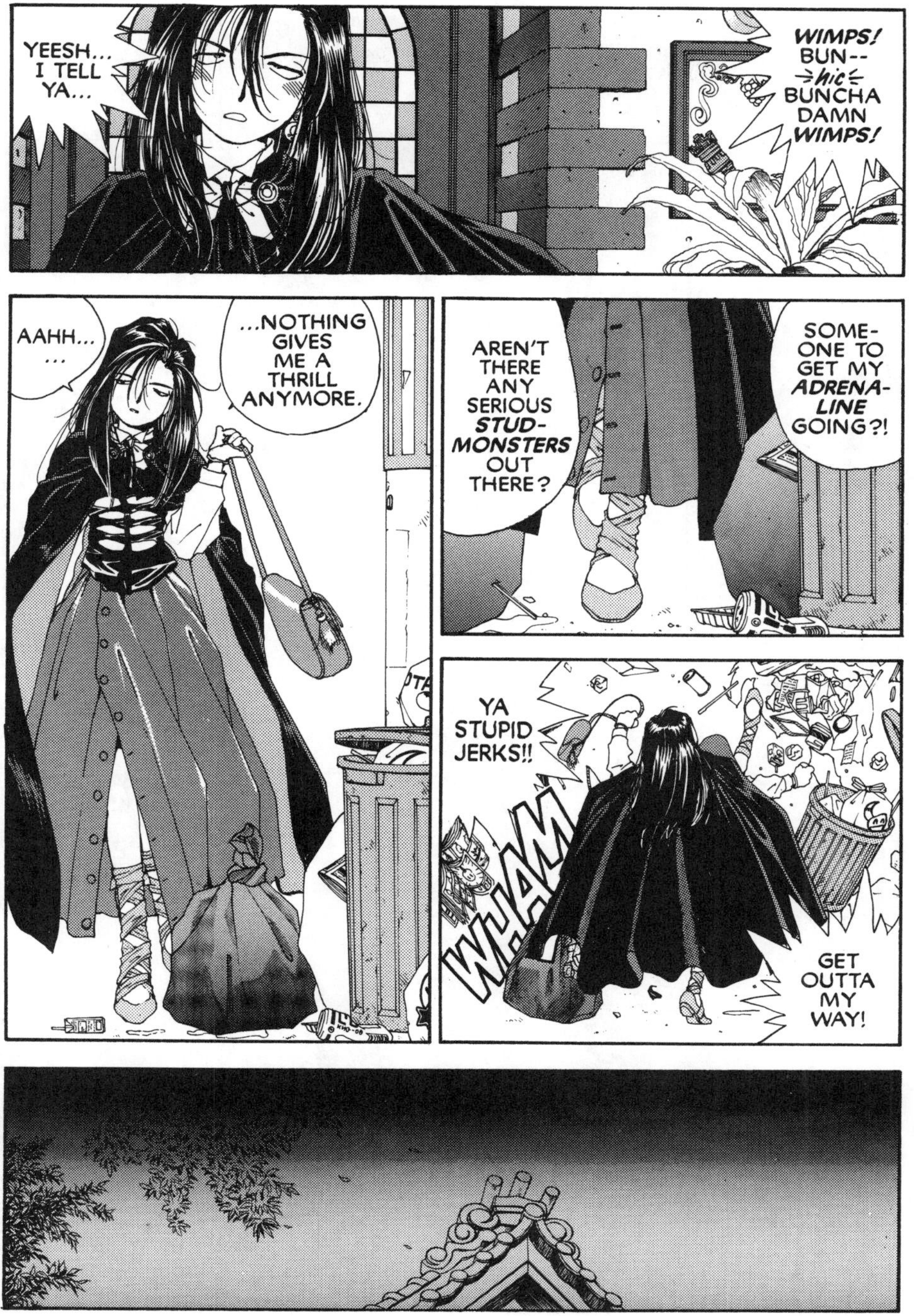
YEESH... I TELL YA...
WIMPS! BUN-- hic BUNCHA DAMN WIMPS!
AAHH... ...
...NOTHING GIVES ME A THRILL ANYMORE.
AREN'T THERE ANY SERIOUS STUD-MONSTERS OUT THERE?
SOME-ONE TO GET MY ADRENA-LINE GOING?!
YA STUPID JERKS!!
WHAM
GET OUTTA MY WAY!

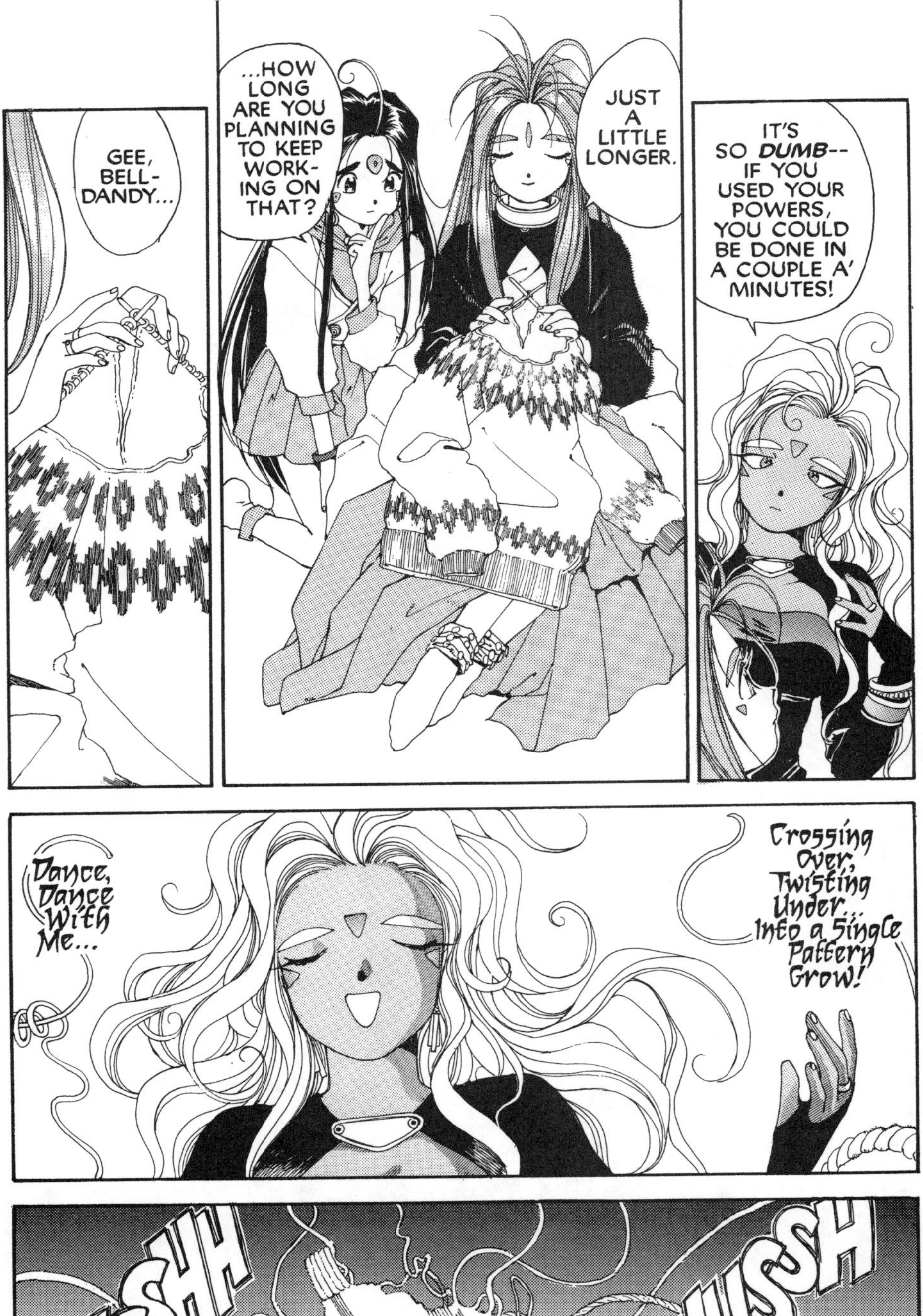
GEE, BELL-DANDY...
...HOW LONG ARE YOU PLANNING TO KEEP WORKING ON THAT?
JUST A LITTLE LONGER.
IT'S SO DUMB-- IF YOU USED YOUR POWERS, YOU COULD BE DONE IN A COUPLE A' MINUTES!
Dance, Dance With Me...
Crossing Over, Twisting Under... Into a Single Pattern Grow!
FWSSH
WHSSH

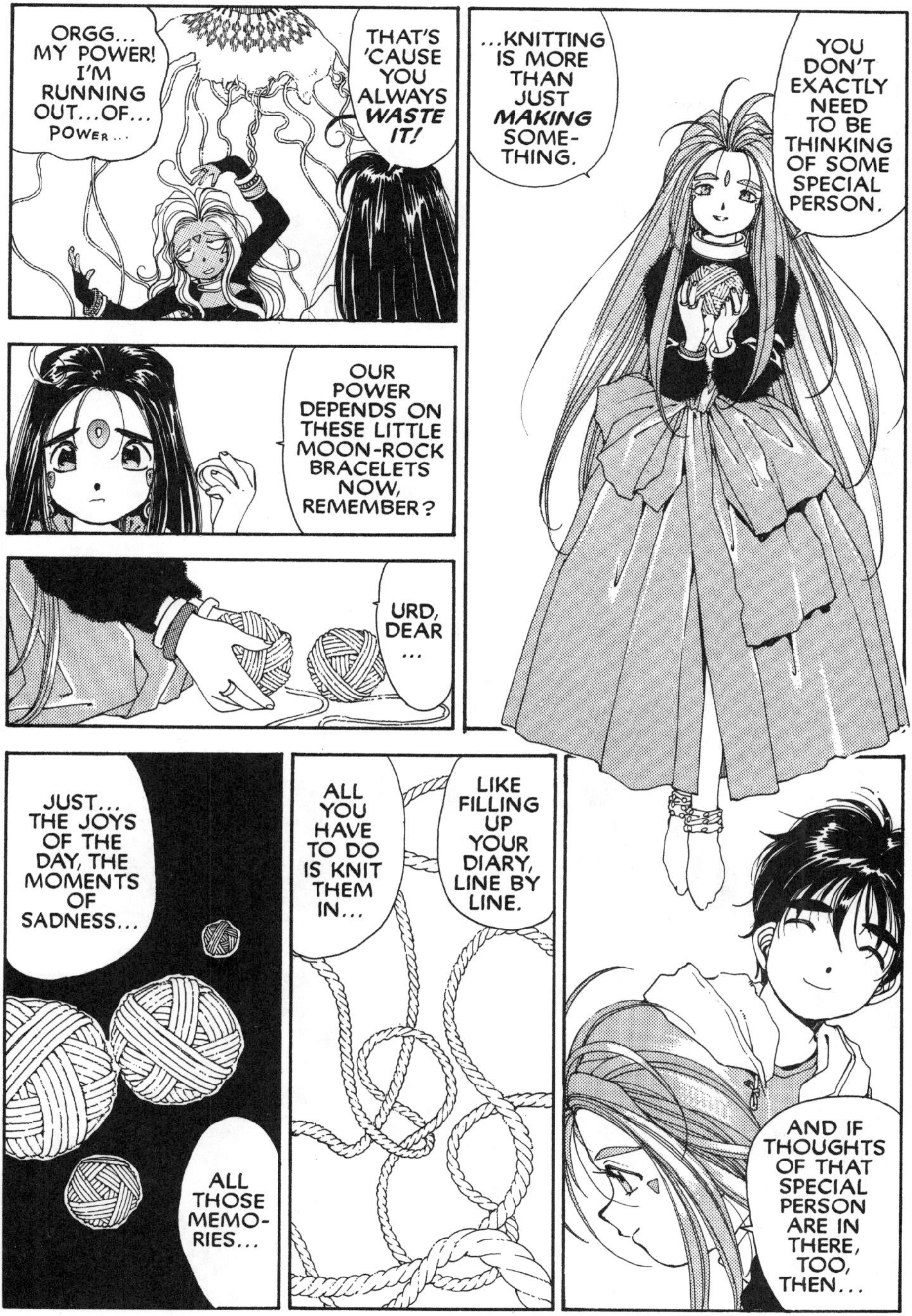
ORGG... MY POWER! I'M RUNNING OUT...OF... POWER...
THAT'S 'CAUSE YOU ALWAYS *WASTE IT!*
OUR POWER DEPENDS ON THESE LITTLE MOON-ROCK BRACELETS NOW, REMEMBER?
URD, DEAR ...
...KNITTING IS MORE THAN JUST *MAKING* SOME-THING.
YOU DON'T EXACTLY NEED TO BE THINKING OF SOME SPECIAL PERSON.
JUST... THE JOYS OF THE DAY, THE MOMENTS OF SADNESS...
ALL THOSE MEMO-RIES...
ALL YOU HAVE TO DO IS KNIT THEM IN...
LIKE FILLING UP YOUR DIARY, LINE BY LINE.
AND IF THOUGHTS OF THAT SPECIAL PERSON ARE IN THERE, TOO, THEN...

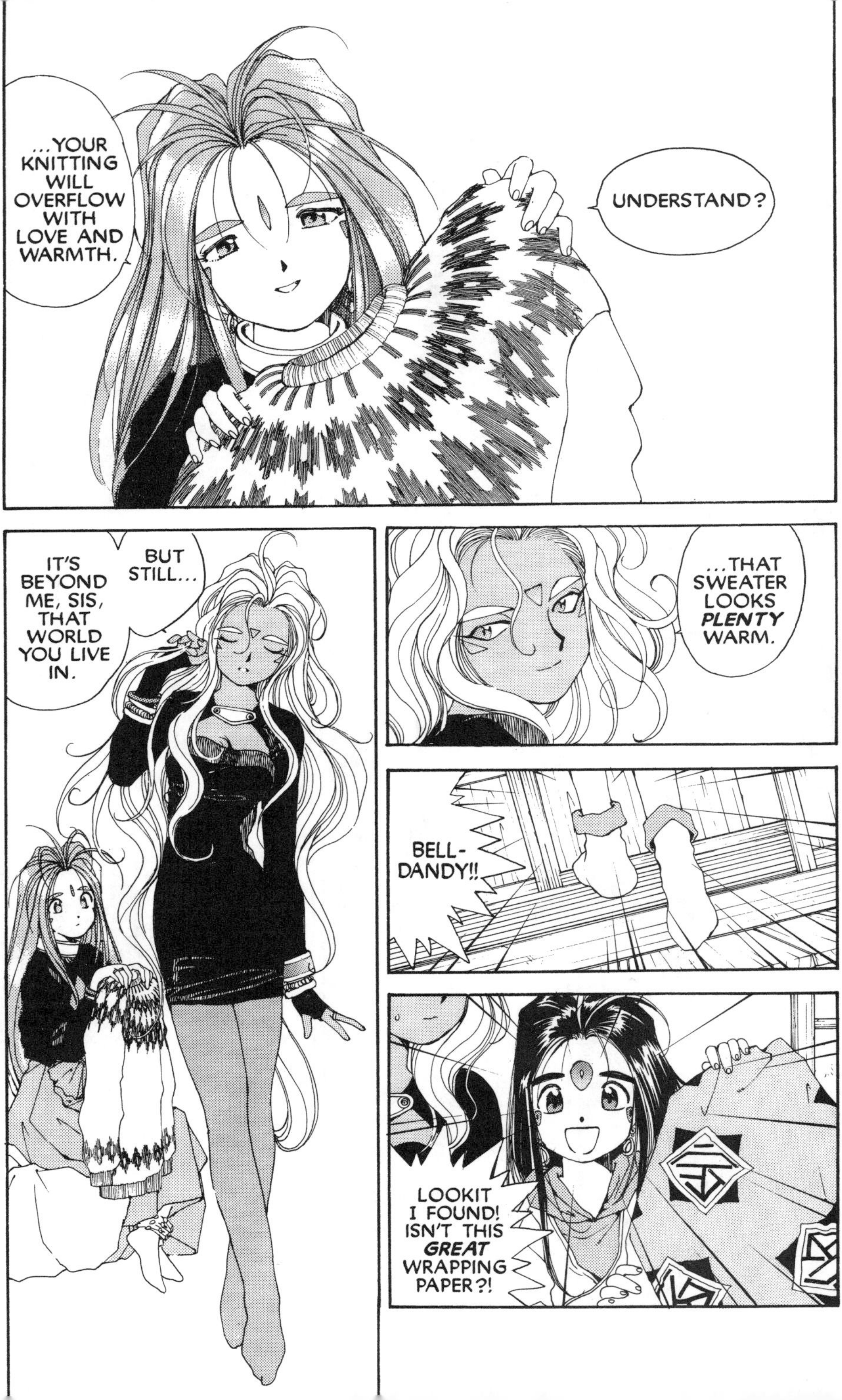
...YOUR KNITTING WILL OVERFLOW WITH LOVE AND WARMTH.
UNDERSTAND?
BUT STILL...
IT'S BEYOND ME, SIS, THAT WORLD YOU LIVE IN.
...THAT SWEATER LOOKS PLENTY WARM.
BELL-DANDY!!
LOOKIT I FOUND! ISN'T THIS GREAT WRAPPING PAPER?!

WON-DERFUL! THANK YOU SO MUCH, SKULD.

HEH HEH!

SINCE WHEN DID YOU GET SO THOUGHT-FUL, BRAT?

WHERE'D YOU FIND IT?

THERE WAS SOME THAT WAS JUST PER-FECT...

...IN THE KITCHEN CUP-BOARD.

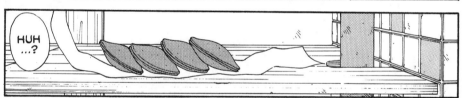

HUH ...?

WHO LEFT THESE COOKIES UN-WRAPPED LIKE THIS?

AH, WELL.

I'VE GOT OTHER THINGS TO WORRY ABOUT NOW.

LIKE THAT BIG TEST TOMOR-ROW...

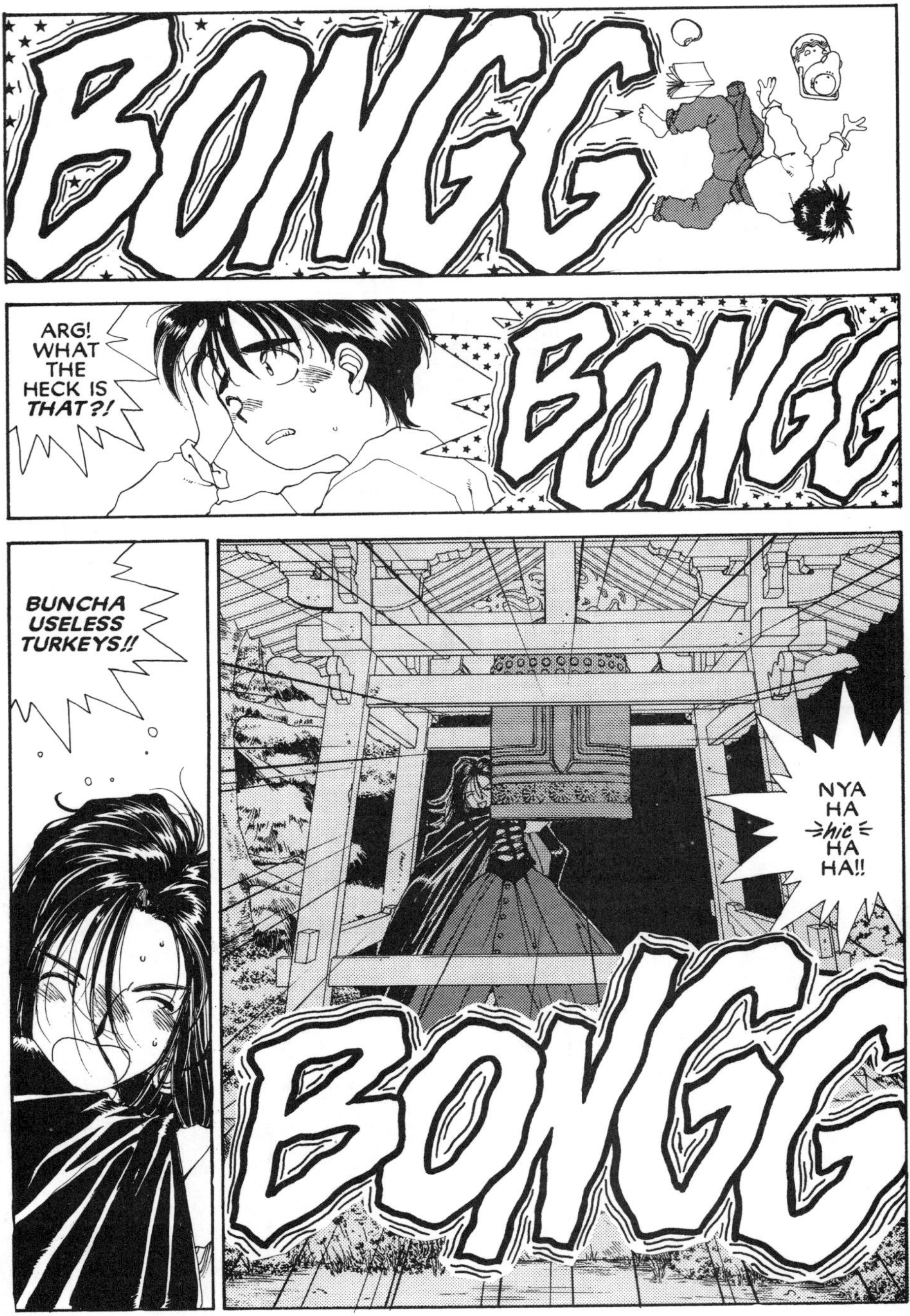
BONGG
ARG! WHAT THE HECK IS *THAT?!*
BONGG
BUNCHA USELESS TURKEYS!!
NYA HA *hic* HA HA!!
BONGG

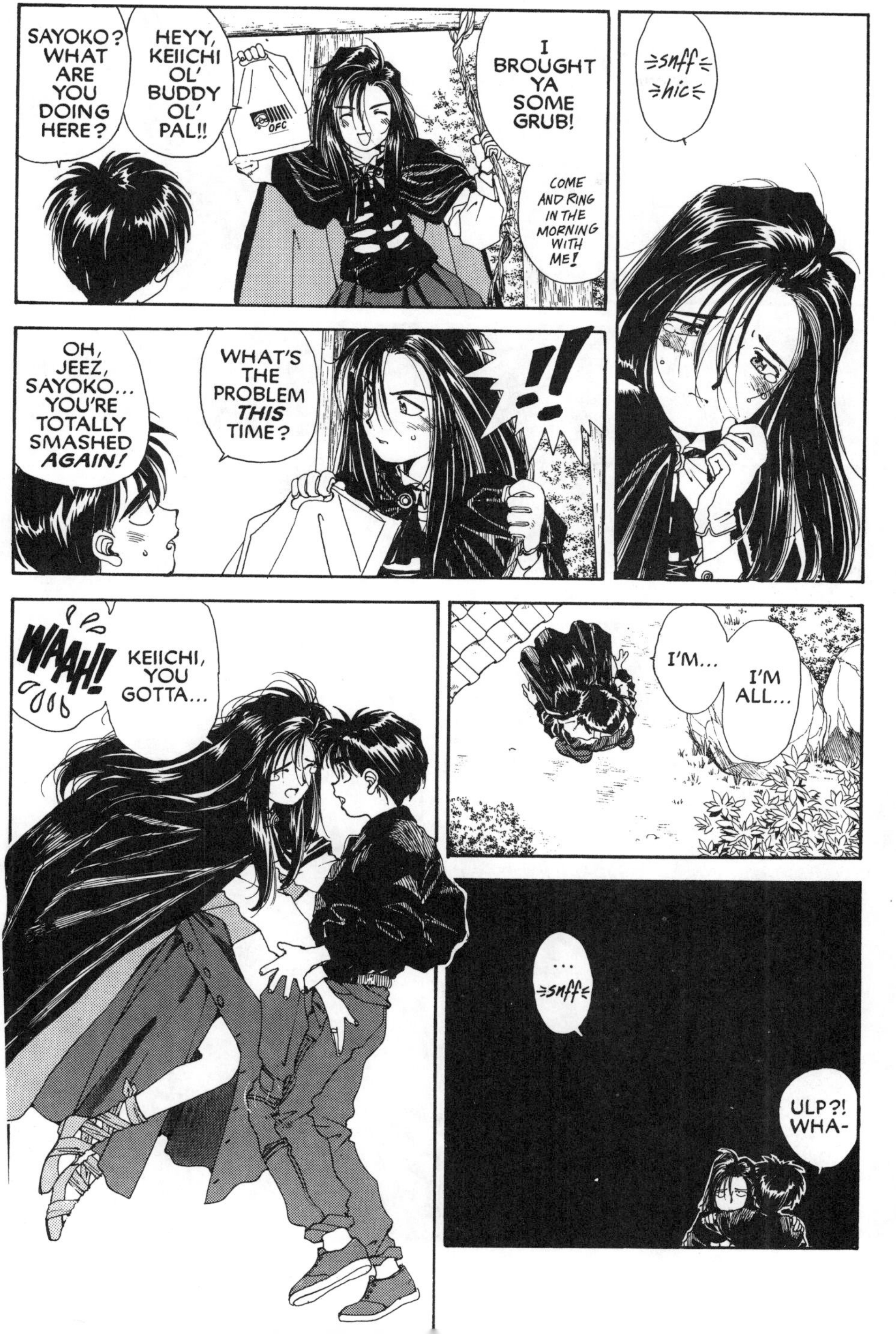
SAYOKO? WHAT ARE YOU DOING HERE?
HEYY, KEIICHI OL' BUDDY OL' PAL!!
OFC
I BROUGHT YA SOME GRUB!
COME AND RING IN THE MORNING WITH ME!
OH, JEEZ, SAYOKO... YOU'RE TOTALLY SMASHED AGAIN!
WHAT'S THE PROBLEM THIS TIME?
!!
snff hic
WAAH!
KEIICHI, YOU GOTTA...
I'M...
I'M ALL...
... snff
ULP?! WHA-

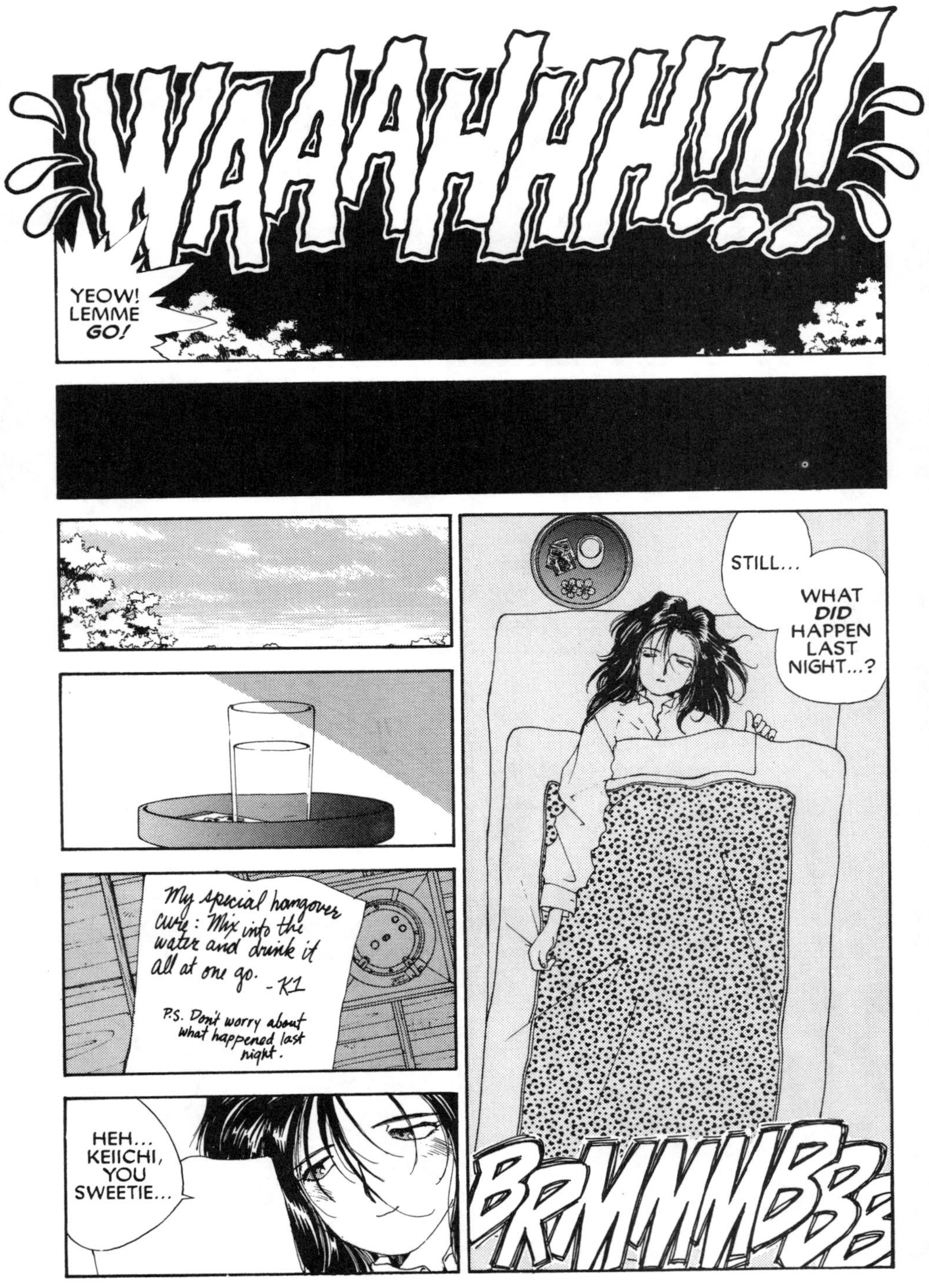
WAAAHHH!!!
YEOW! LEMME GO!
My special hangover cure: Mix into the water and drink it all at one go. -K1
P.S. Don't worry about what happened last night.
HEH... KEIICHI, YOU SWEETIE...
STILL...
WHAT DID HAPPEN LAST NIGHT...?
BRMMMBBB

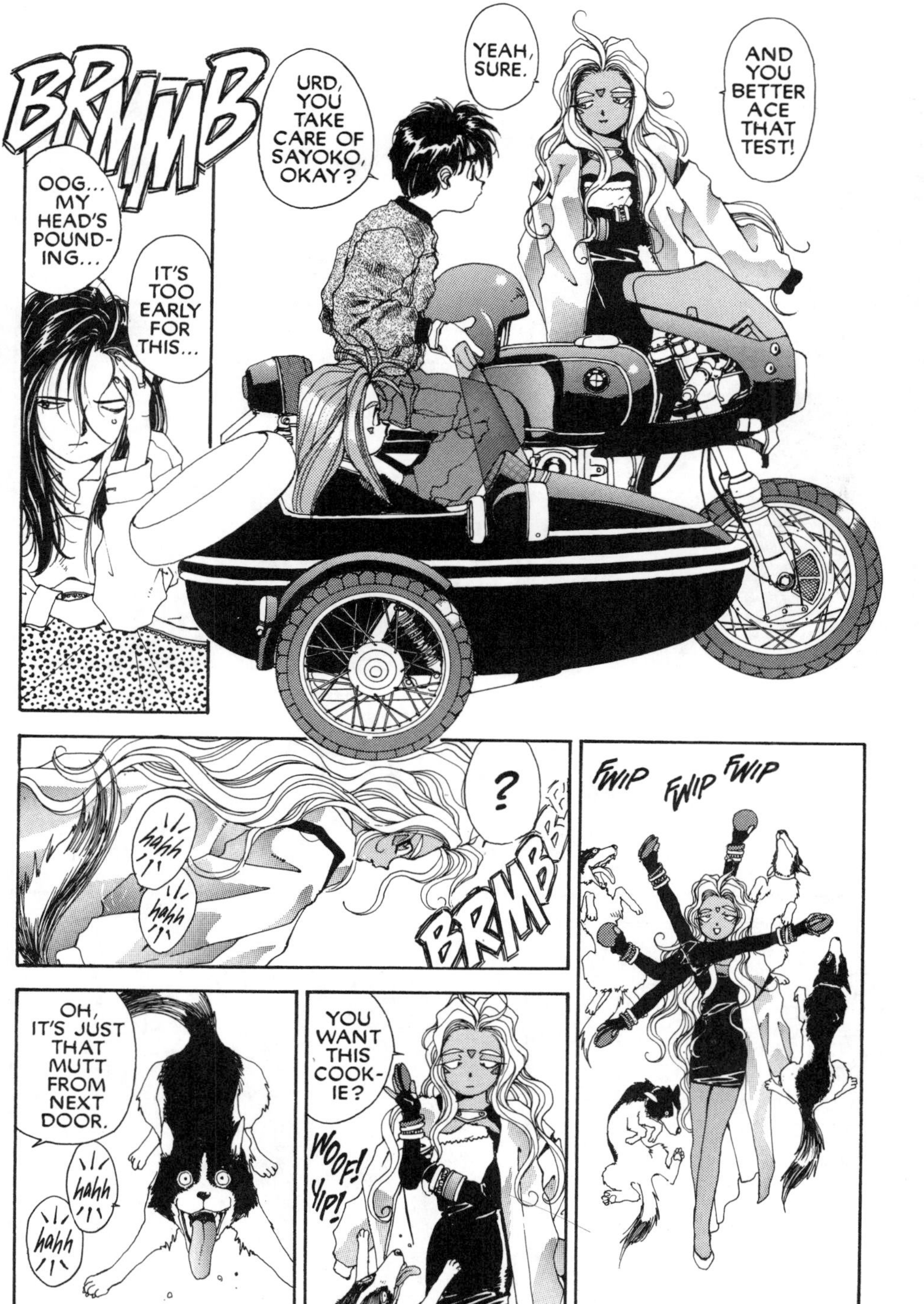
BRMMMB
OOG... MY HEAD'S POUND-ING...
IT'S TOO EARLY FOR THIS...
URD, YOU TAKE CARE OF SAYOKO, OKAY?
YEAH, SURE.
AND YOU BETTER ACE THAT TEST!
hahh
hahh
?
BRMBB
FWIP FWIP FWIP
OH, IT'S JUST THAT MUTT FROM NEXT DOOR.
hahh
hahh
YOU WANT THIS COOK-IE?
WOOF!
YIP!

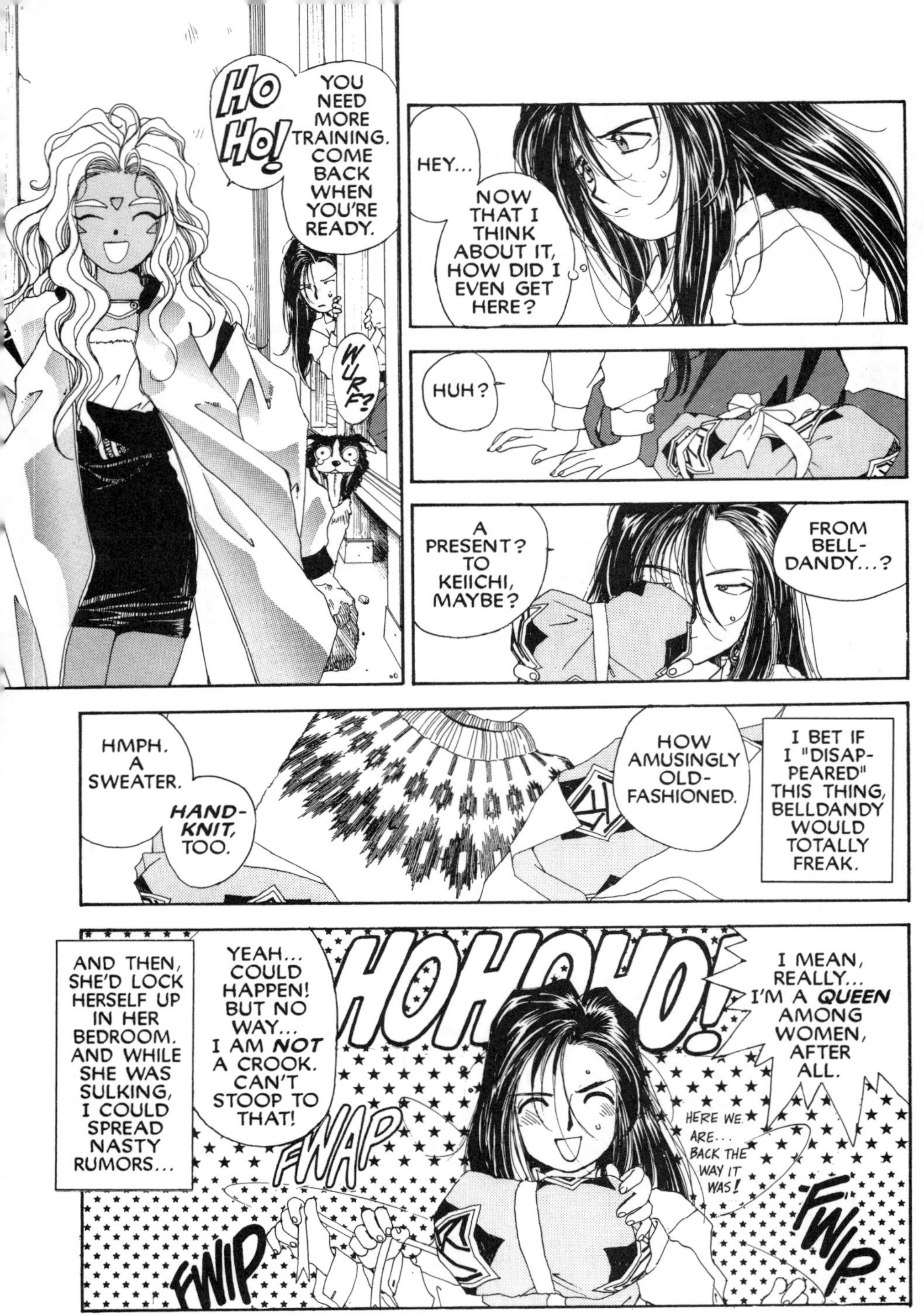
HO HO!
YOU NEED MORE TRAINING. COME BACK WHEN YOU'RE READY.
WURF?
HEY...
NOW THAT I THINK ABOUT IT, HOW DID I EVEN GET HERE?
HUH?
A PRESENT? TO KEIICHI, MAYBE?
FROM BELL-DANDY...?
HMPH. A SWEATER.
HAND-KNIT, TOO.
HOW AMUSINGLY OLD-FASHIONED.
I BET IF I "DISAP-PEARED" THIS THING, BELLDANDY WOULD TOTALLY FREAK.
AND THEN, SHE'D LOCK HERSELF UP IN HER BEDROOM, AND WHILE SHE WAS SULKING, I COULD SPREAD NASTY RUMORS...
YEAH... COULD HAPPEN! BUT NO WAY... I AM NOT A CROOK. CAN'T STOOP TO THAT!
HOHOHO!
I MEAN, REALLY... I'M A QUEEN AMONG WOMEN, AFTER ALL.
HERE WE ARE... BACK THE WAY IT WAS!
FWAP
FWIP
FWIP

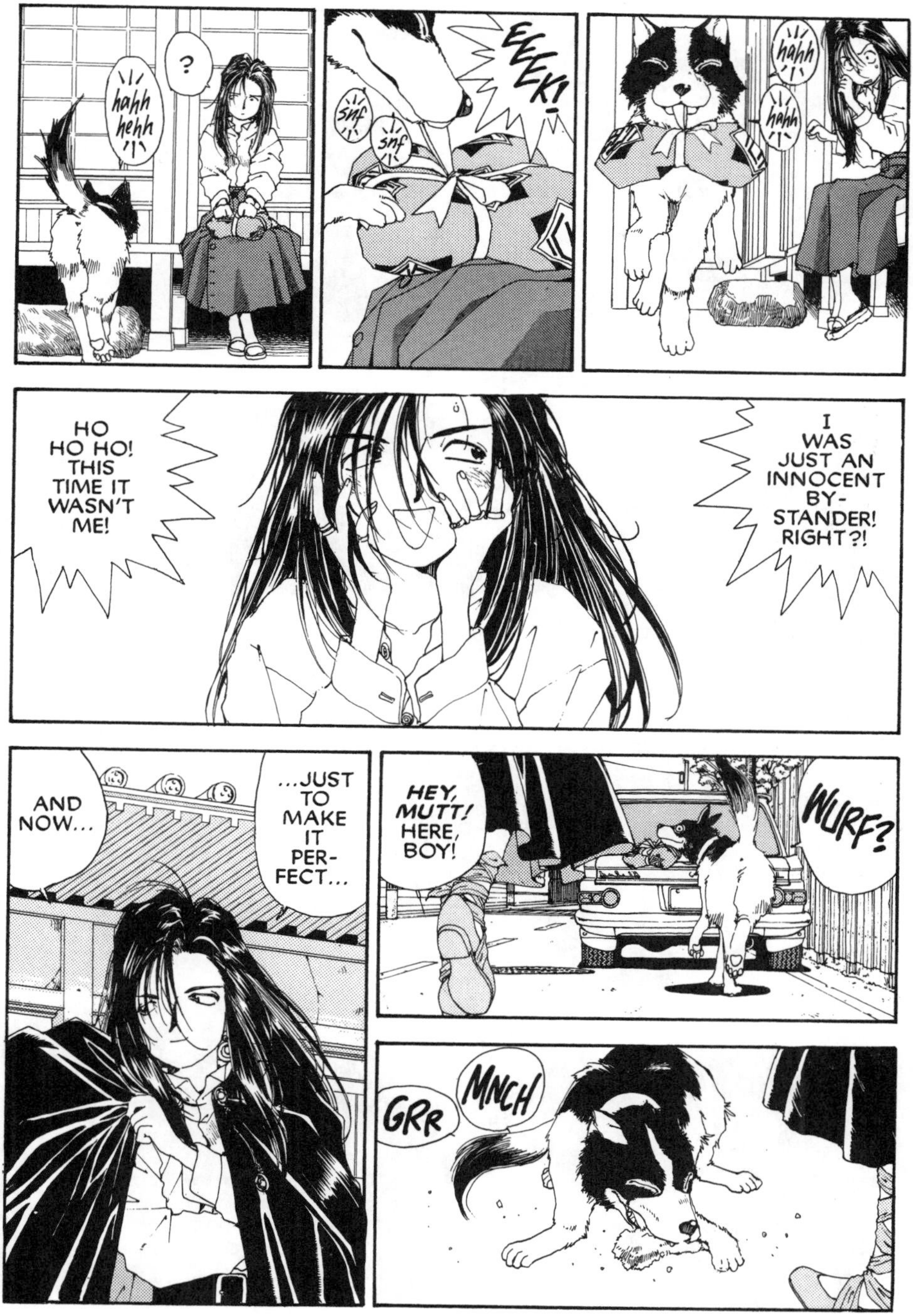
?
hahh hehh
snf
snf
EEEEK!
hahh
hahh
HO HO HO! THIS TIME IT WASN'T ME!
I WAS JUST AN INNOCENT BY-STANDER! RIGHT?!
AND NOW...
...JUST TO MAKE IT PER-FECT...
HEY, MUTT! HERE, BOY!
WURF?
GRR
MNCH

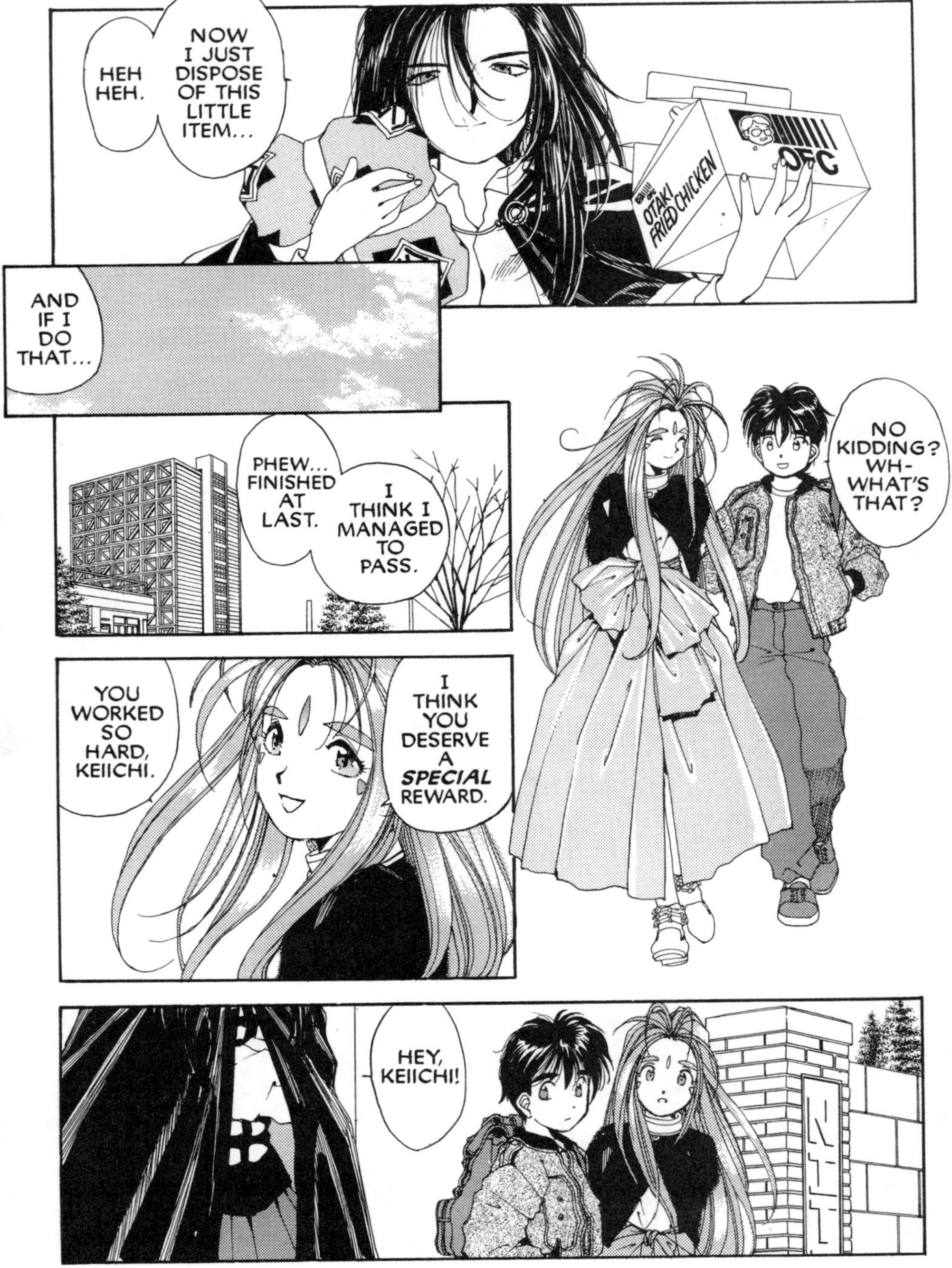
HEH HEH.
NOW I JUST DISPOSE OF THIS LITTLE ITEM...
OTAKI FRIED CHICKEN
OFC
AND IF I DO THAT...
PHEW... FINISHED AT LAST.
I THINK I MANAGED TO PASS.
YOU WORKED SO HARD, KEIICHI.
I THINK YOU DESERVE A *SPECIAL* REWARD.
NO KIDDING? WH- WHAT'S THAT?
HEY, KEIICHI!

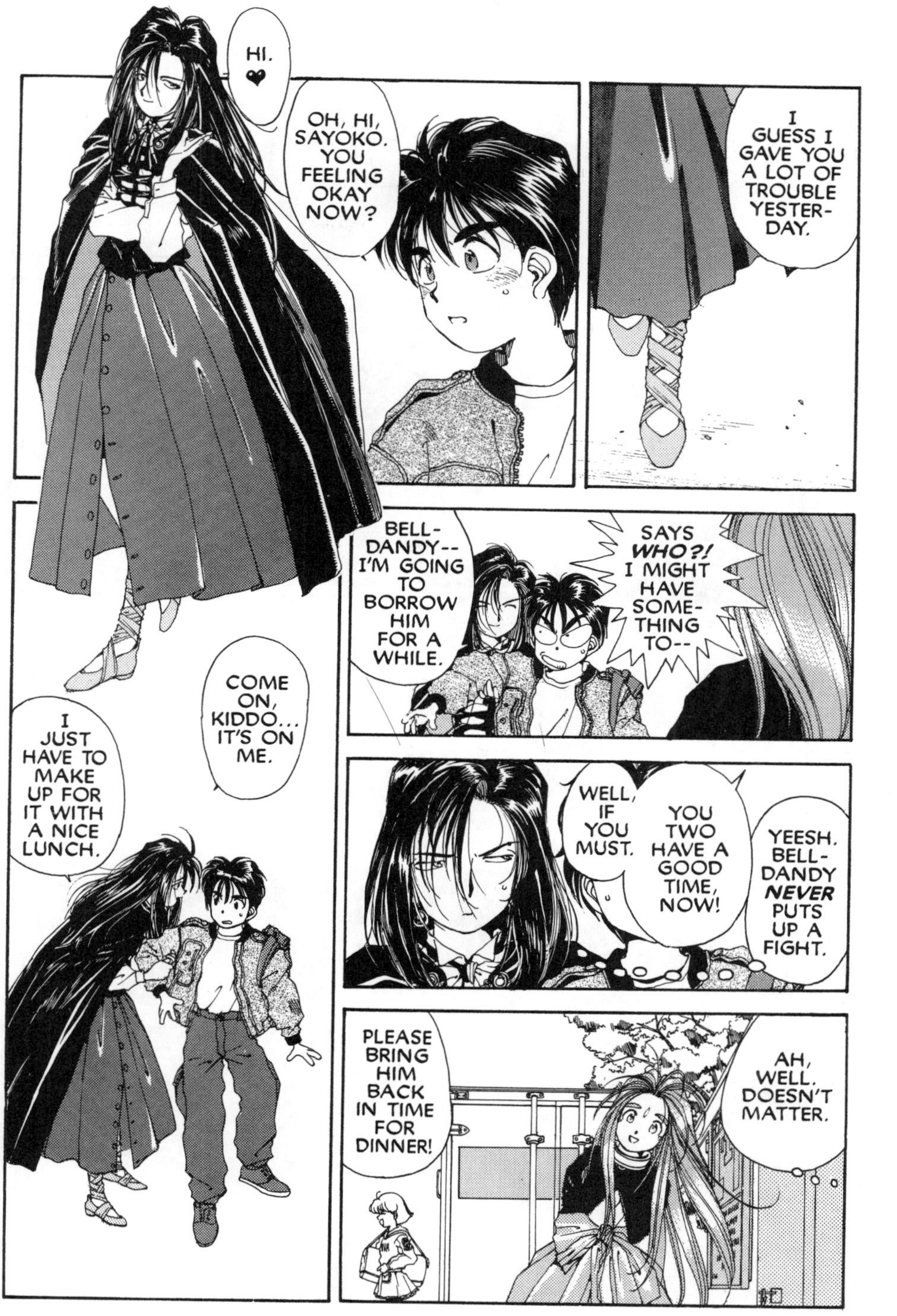
HI. ❤
OH, HI, SAYOKO. YOU FEELING OKAY NOW?
I GUESS I GAVE YOU A LOT OF TROUBLE YESTER-DAY.
I JUST HAVE TO MAKE UP FOR IT WITH A NICE LUNCH.
COME ON, KIDDO... IT'S ON ME.
BELL-DANDY-- I'M GOING TO BORROW HIM FOR A WHILE.
SAYS ***WHO?!*** I MIGHT HAVE SOME-THING TO--
WELL, IF YOU MUST.
YOU TWO HAVE A GOOD TIME, NOW!
YEESH. BELL-DANDY ***NEVER*** PUTS UP A FIGHT.
PLEASE BRING HIM BACK IN TIME FOR DINNER!
AH, WELL. DOESN'T MATTER.

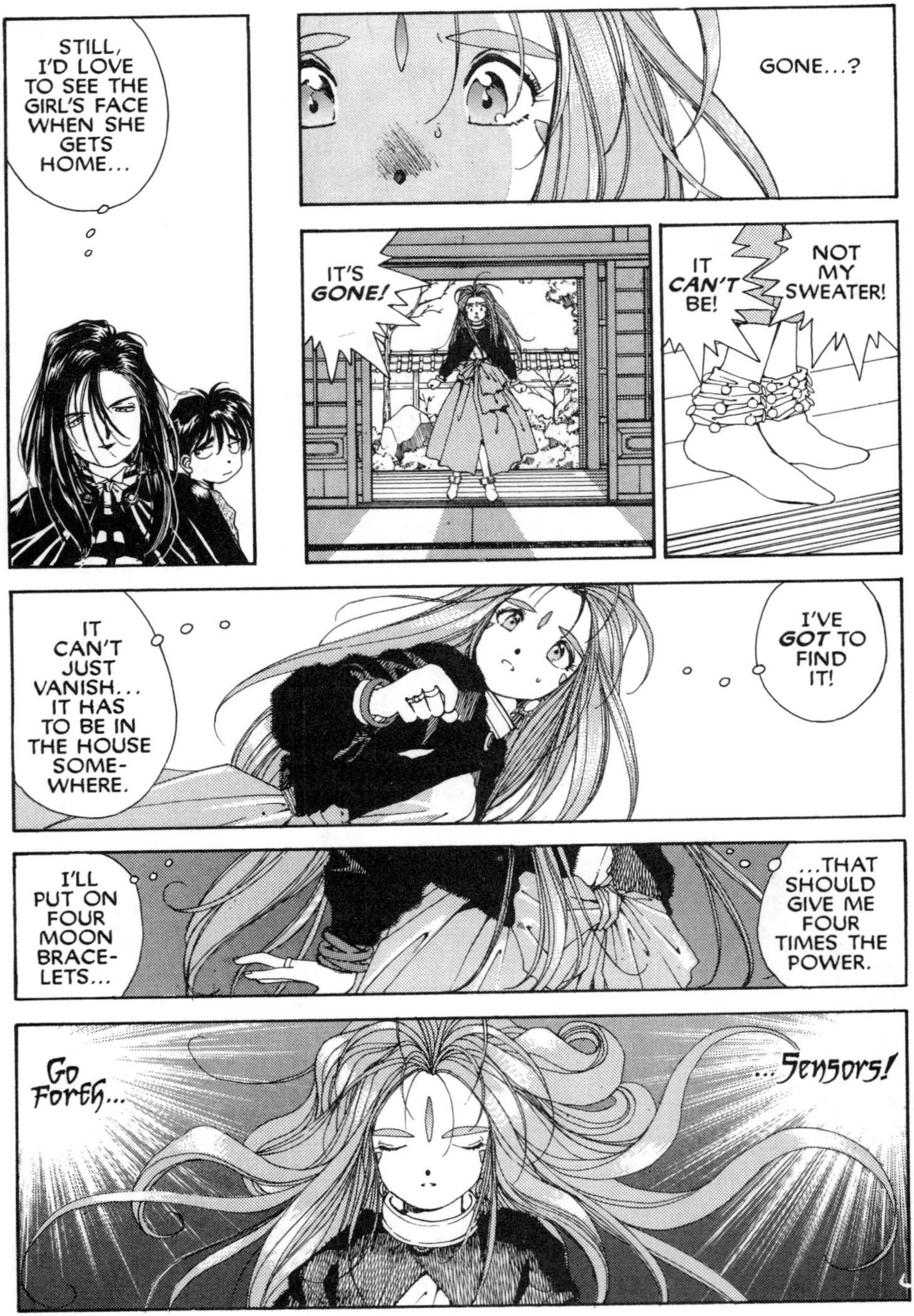
STILL, I'D LOVE TO SEE THE GIRL'S FACE WHEN SHE GETS HOME...
GONE...?
IT'S GONE!
IT CAN'T BE!
NOT MY SWEATER!
IT CAN'T JUST VANISH... IT HAS TO BE IN THE HOUSE SOME-WHERE.
I'VE GOT TO FIND IT!
I'LL PUT ON FOUR MOON BRACE-LETS...
...THAT SHOULD GIVE ME FOUR TIMES THE POWER.
Go Forth...
...Sensors!

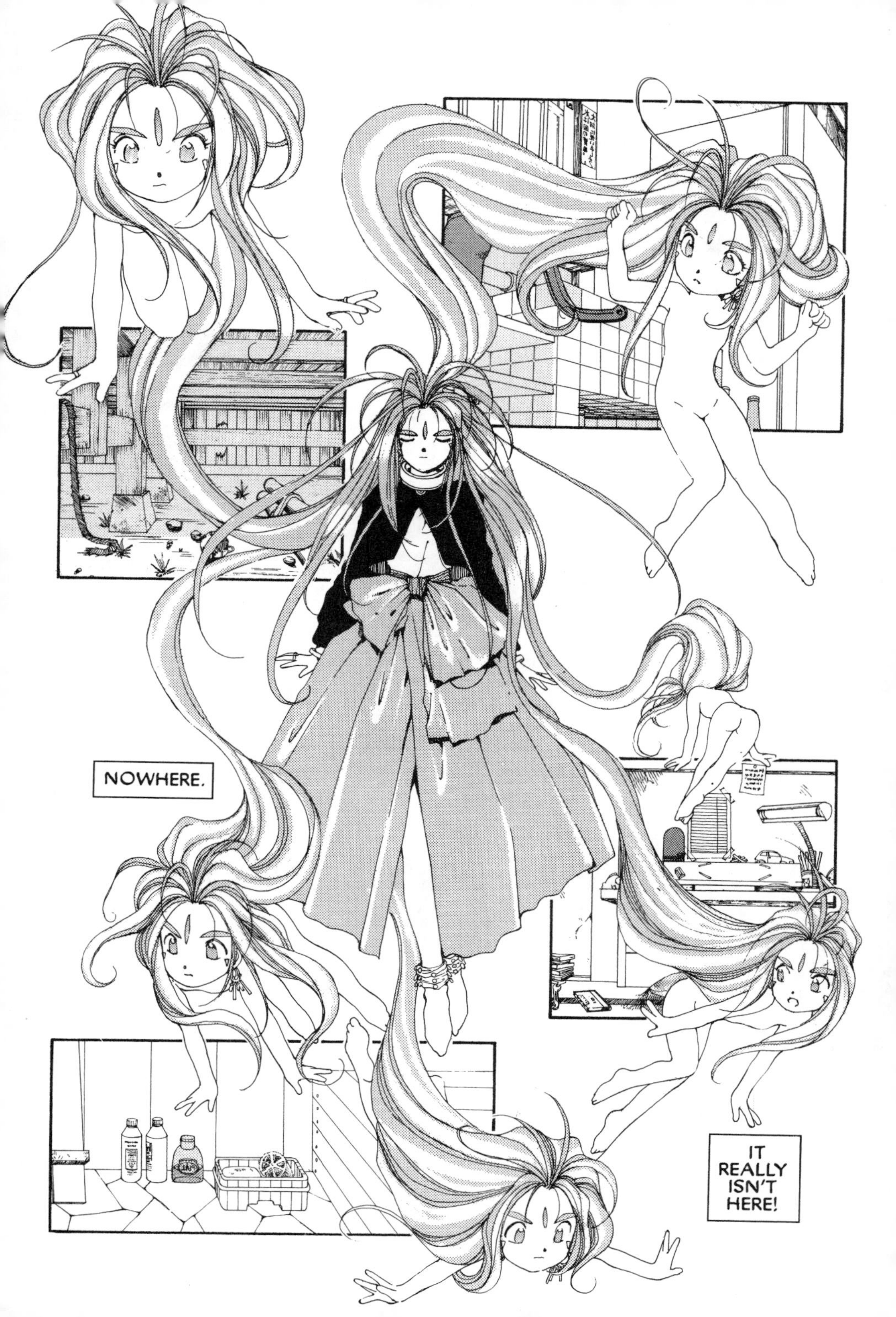
NOWHERE.
IT REALLY ISN'T HERE!

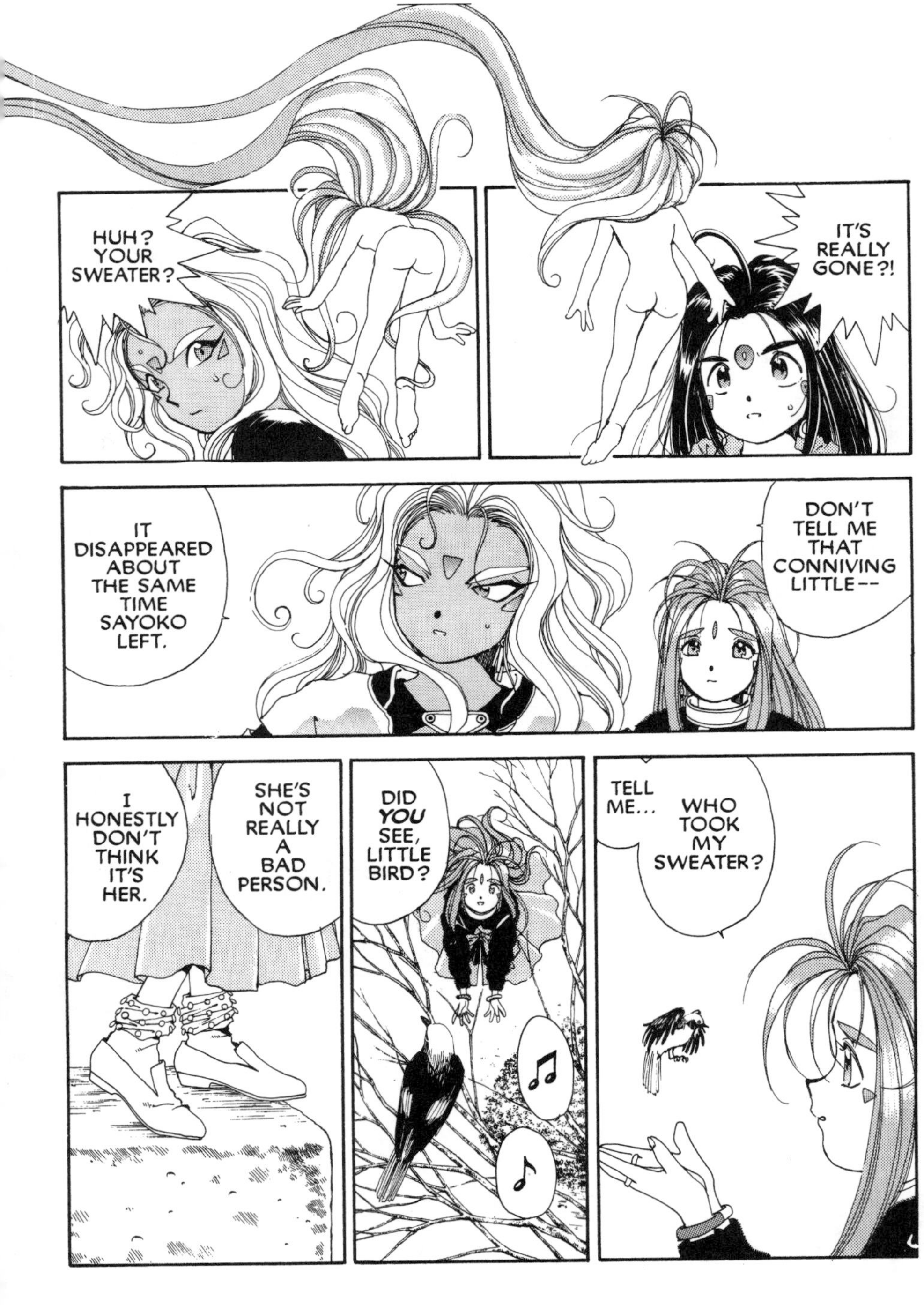
HUH? YOUR SWEATER?
IT'S REALLY GONE?!
IT DISAPPEARED ABOUT THE SAME TIME SAYOKO LEFT.
DON'T TELL ME THAT CONNIVING LITTLE--
I HONESTLY DON'T THINK IT'S HER.
SHE'S NOT REALLY A BAD PERSON.
DID *YOU* SEE, LITTLE BIRD?
TELL ME...
WHO TOOK MY SWEATER?

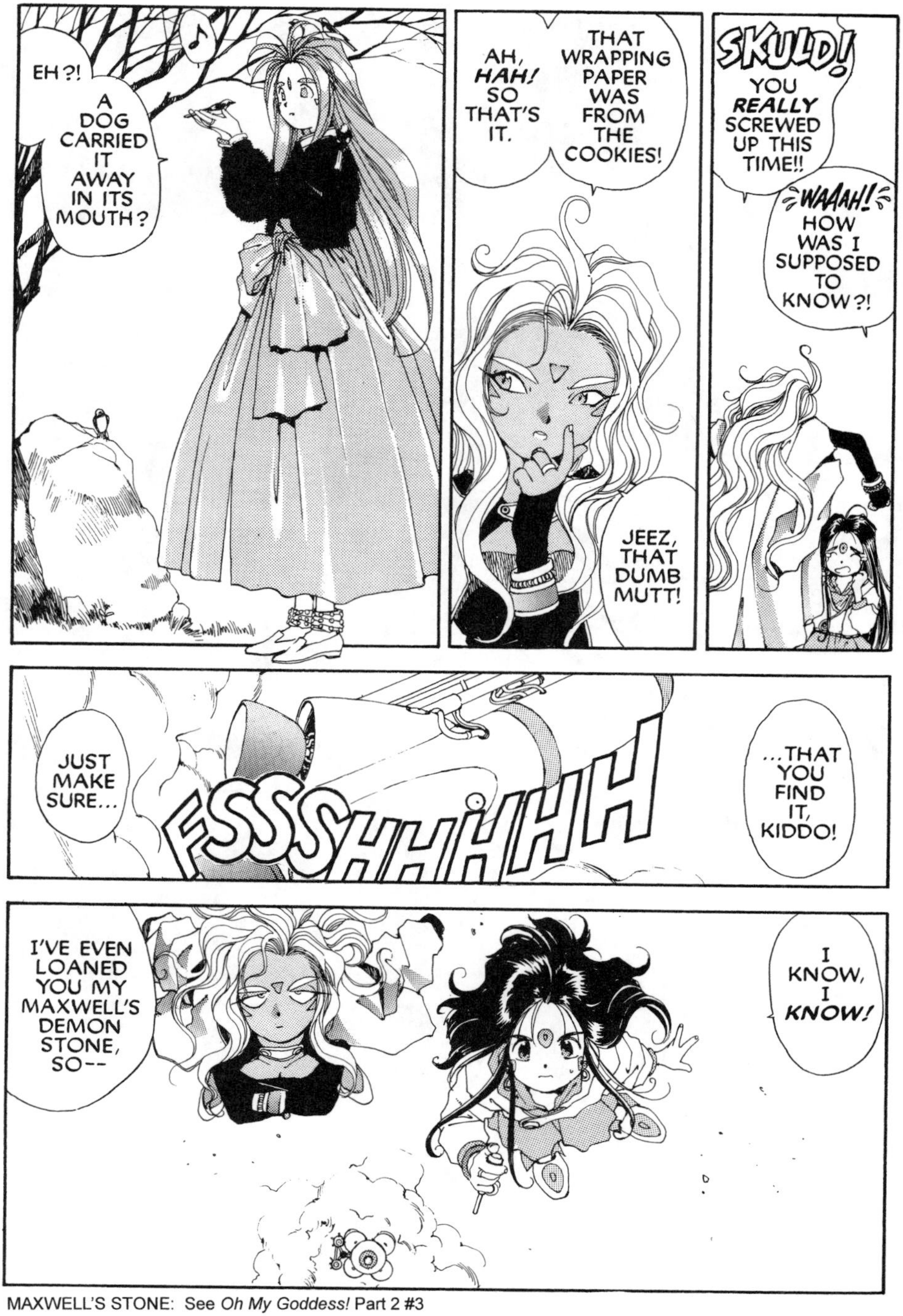
EH?!
A DOG CARRIED IT AWAY IN ITS MOUTH?
AH, *HAH!* SO THAT'S IT.
THAT WRAPPING PAPER WAS FROM THE COOKIES!
JEEZ, THAT DUMB MUTT!
SKULD!
YOU *REALLY* SCREWED UP THIS TIME!!
WAAAH!
HOW WAS I SUPPOSED TO KNOW?!
JUST MAKE SURE...
FSSSHHHHHH
...THAT YOU FIND IT, KIDDO!
I'VE EVEN LOANED YOU MY MAXWELL'S DEMON STONE, SO--
I KNOW, I *KNOW!*

MAXWELL'S STONE: See *Oh My Goddess!* Part 2 #3

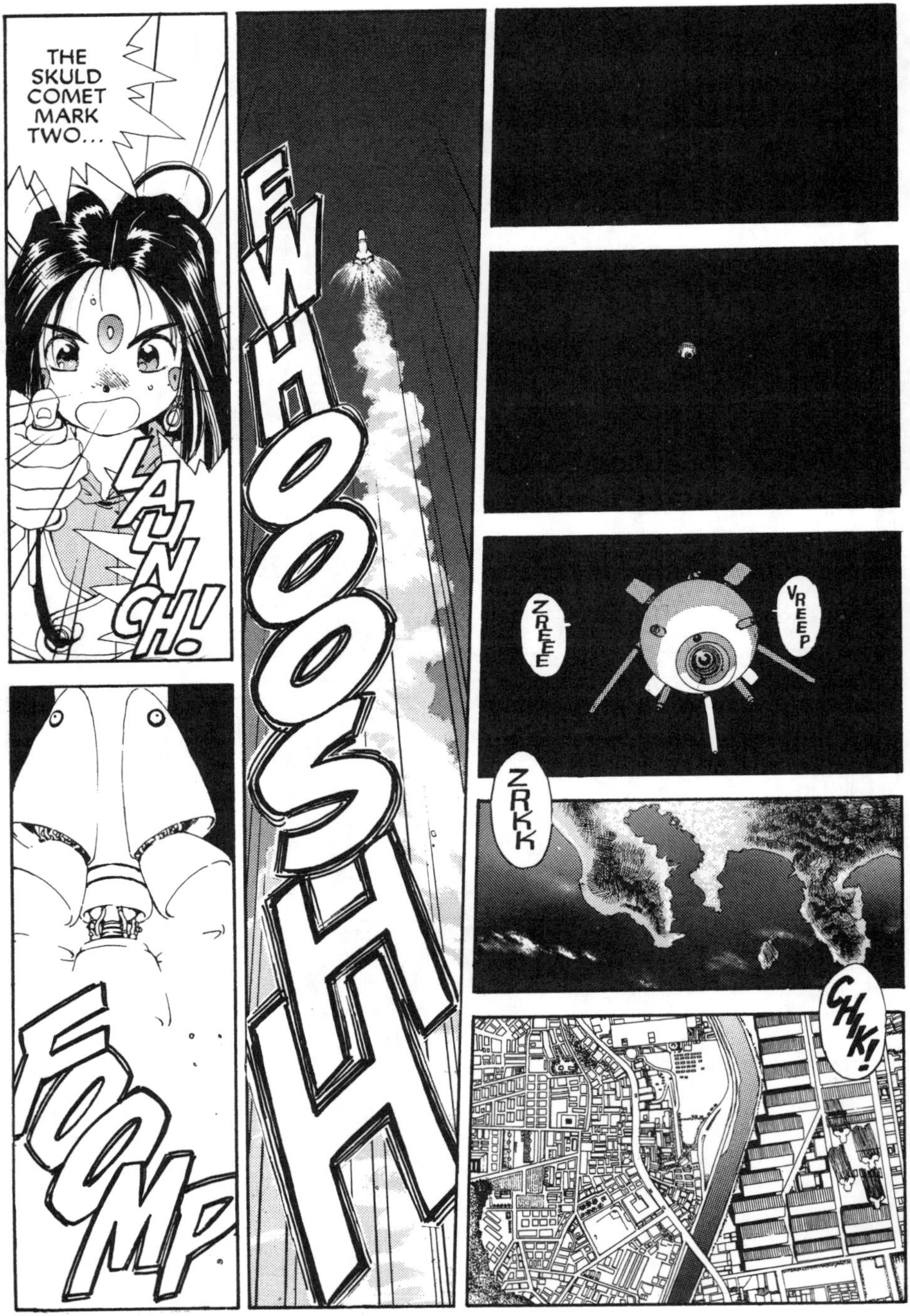
THE SKULD COMET MARK TWO...
LAUNCH!
FWHOOOOSH
VOOOMP
ZREEE
VREEP
ZRKK
CHIK!

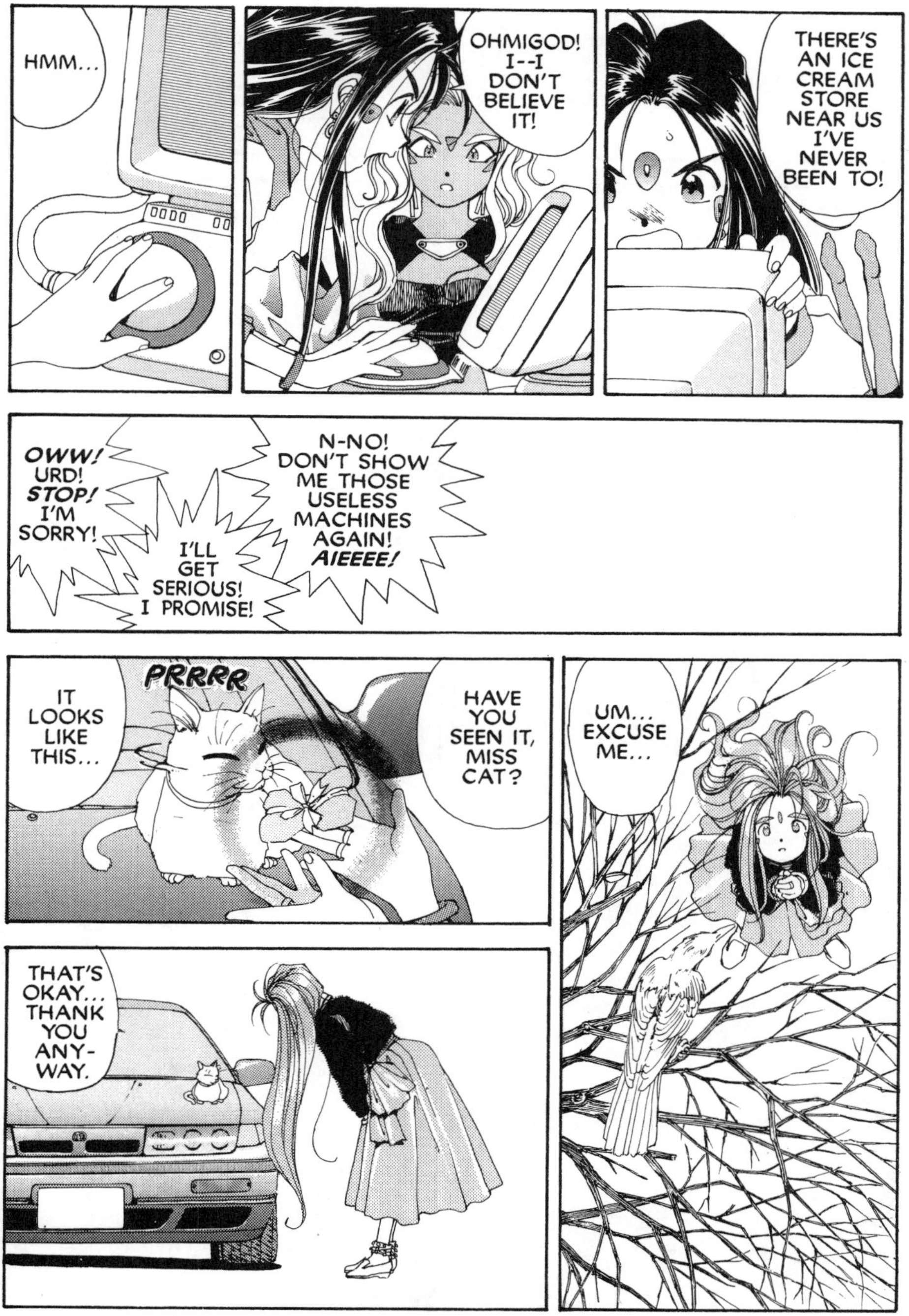
HMM...
OHMIGOD! I--I DON'T BELIEVE IT!
THERE'S AN ICE CREAM STORE NEAR US I'VE NEVER BEEN TO!
OWW! URD! STOP! I'M SORRY!
N-NO! DON'T SHOW ME THOSE USELESS MACHINES AGAIN! AIEEEE!
I'LL GET SERIOUS! I PROMISE!
PRRRR
IT LOOKS LIKE THIS...
HAVE YOU SEEN IT, MISS CAT?
THAT'S OKAY... THANK YOU ANY-WAY.
UM... EXCUSE ME...

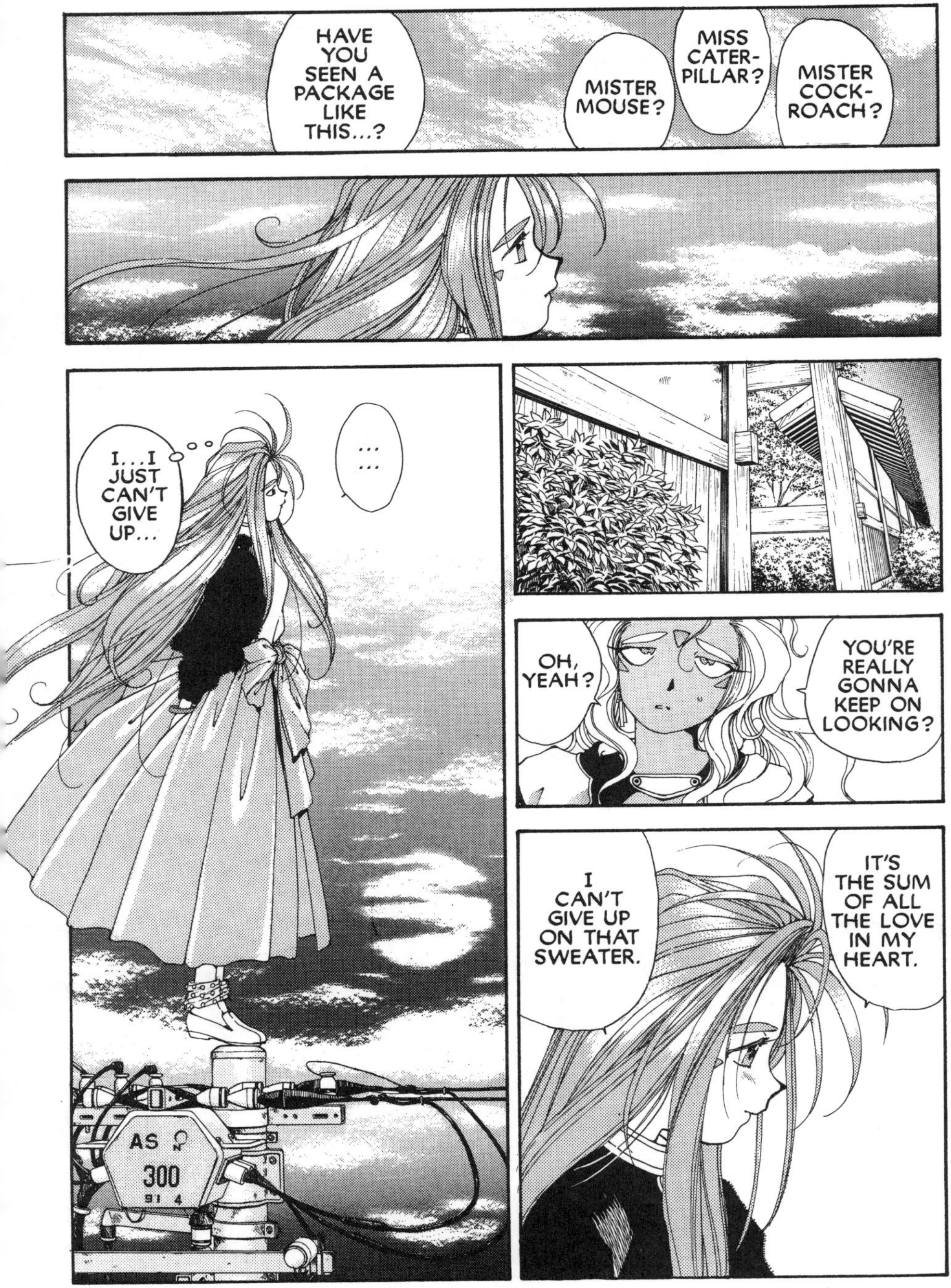
HAVE YOU SEEN A PACKAGE LIKE THIS...?
MISTER MOUSE?
MISS CATER-PILLAR?
MISTER COCK-ROACH?
I...I JUST CAN'T GIVE UP...
......
AS
300
91 4
OH, YEAH?
YOU'RE REALLY GONNA KEEP ON LOOKING?
I CAN'T GIVE UP ON THAT SWEATER.
IT'S THE SUM OF ALL THE LOVE IN MY HEART.

HUH...

I GUESS I UNDER-STAND.

EVEN ME, ONCE I START SOME-THING...

...IT KINDA PISSES ME OFF TO GIVE UP!

BEHOLD! URD'S DIRECT CONNECT EIGHT RING FULL POWER INCANTA-TION!

Sweat-er... Come to Me!

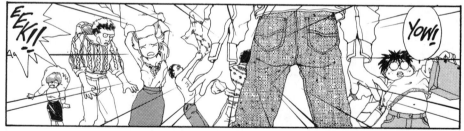

EEK!!

YOW!

MMPH?!

THAT'S OUR URD.

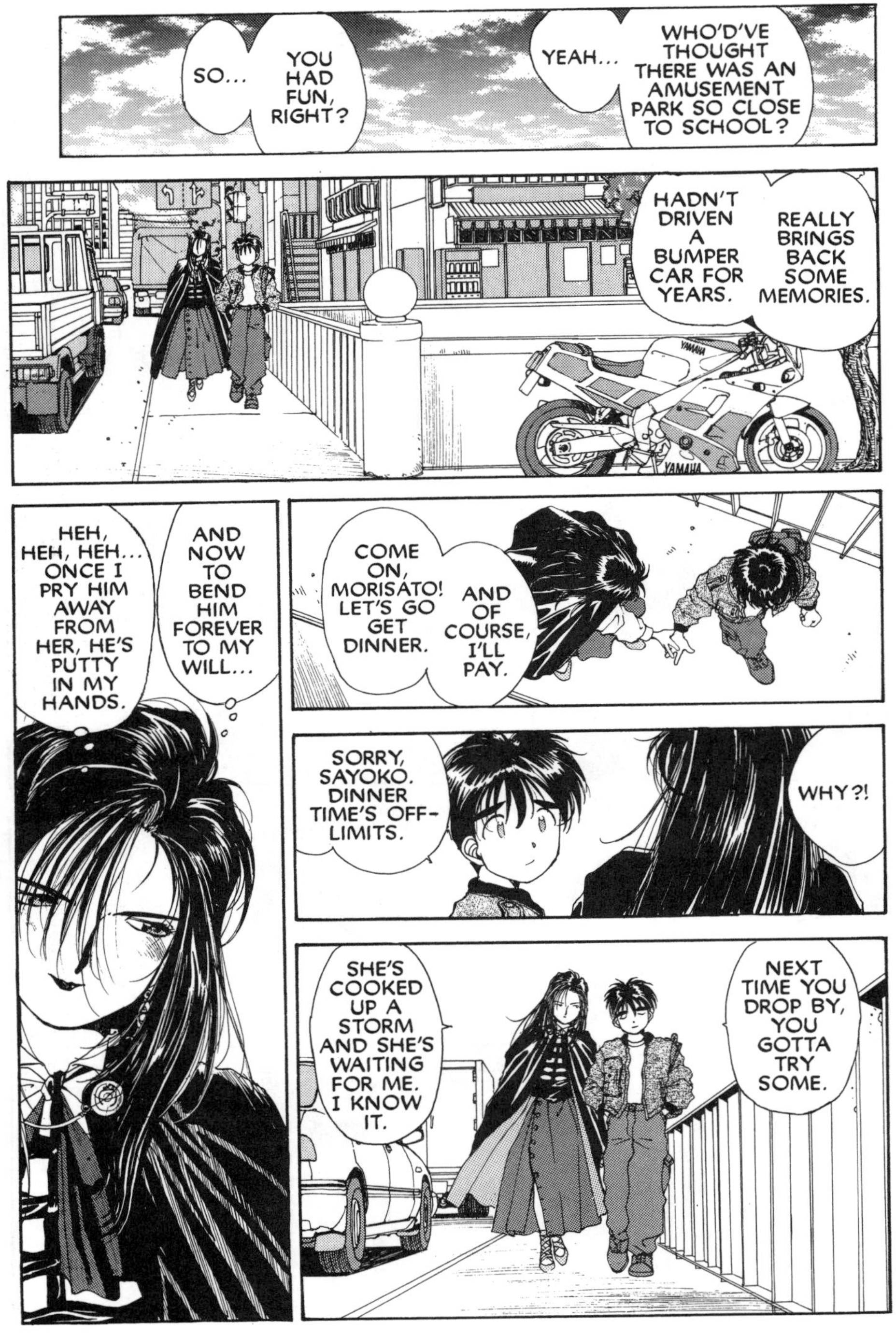
SO...
YOU HAD FUN, RIGHT?
YEAH...
WHO'D'VE THOUGHT THERE WAS AN AMUSEMENT PARK SO CLOSE TO SCHOOL?
HADN'T DRIVEN A BUMPER CAR FOR YEARS.
REALLY BRINGS BACK SOME MEMORIES.
HEH, HEH, HEH... ONCE I PRY HIM AWAY FROM HER, HE'S PUTTY IN MY HANDS.
AND NOW TO BEND HIM FOREVER TO MY WILL...
COME ON, MORISATO! LET'S GO GET DINNER.
AND OF COURSE, I'LL PAY.
SORRY, SAYOKO. DINNER TIME'S OFF-LIMITS.
WHY?!
SHE'S COOKED UP A STORM AND SHE'S WAITING FOR ME. I KNOW IT.
NEXT TIME YOU DROP BY, YOU GOTTA TRY SOME.

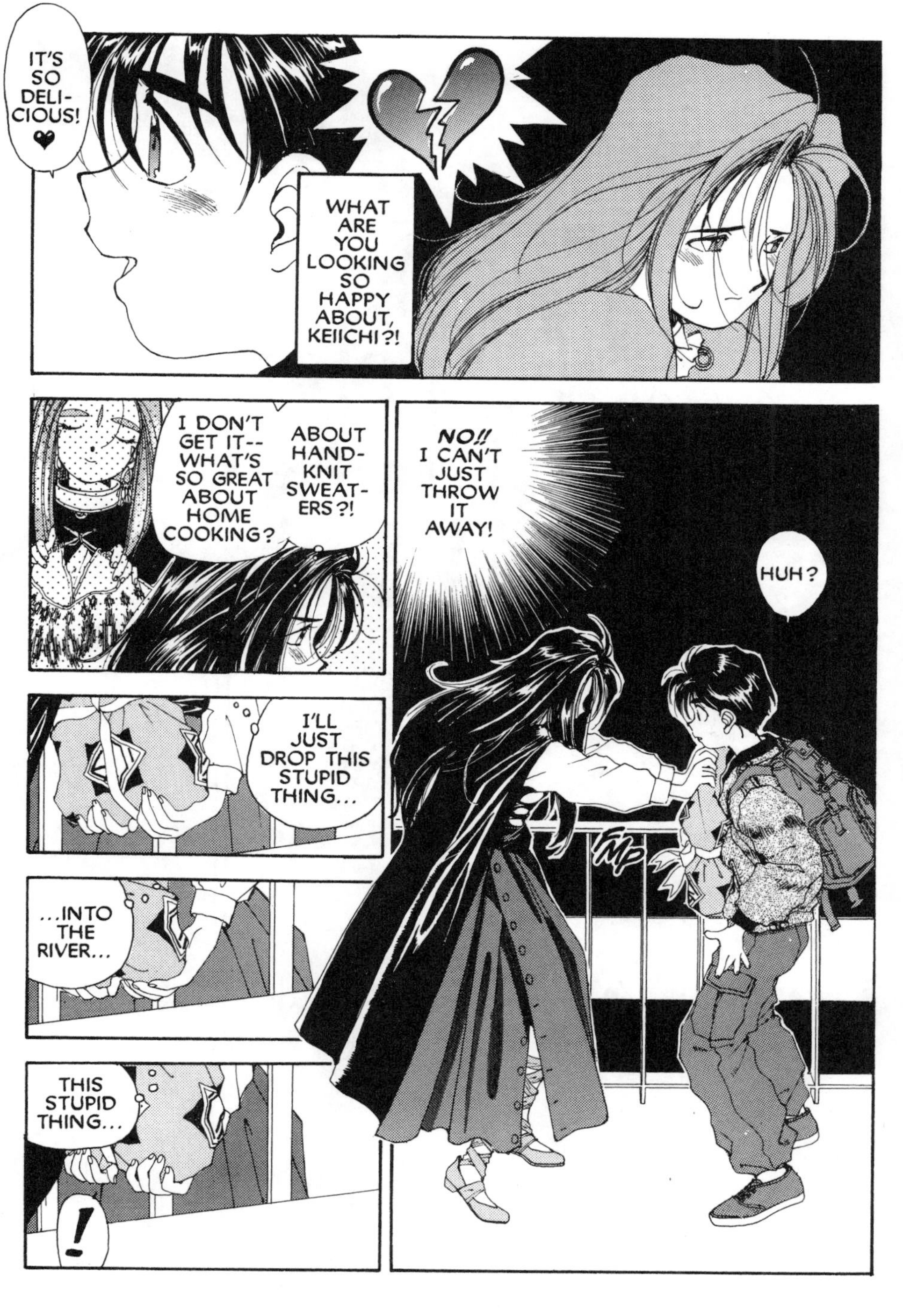
IT'S SO DELI-CIOUS! ❤
WHAT ARE YOU LOOKING SO HAPPY ABOUT, KEIICHI?!
I DON'T GET IT-- WHAT'S SO GREAT ABOUT HOME COOKING?
ABOUT HAND-KNIT SWEAT-ERS?!
I'LL JUST DROP THIS STUPID THING...
...INTO THE RIVER...
THIS STUPID THING...
!
NO!! I CAN'T JUST THROW IT AWAY!
HUH?
FMP

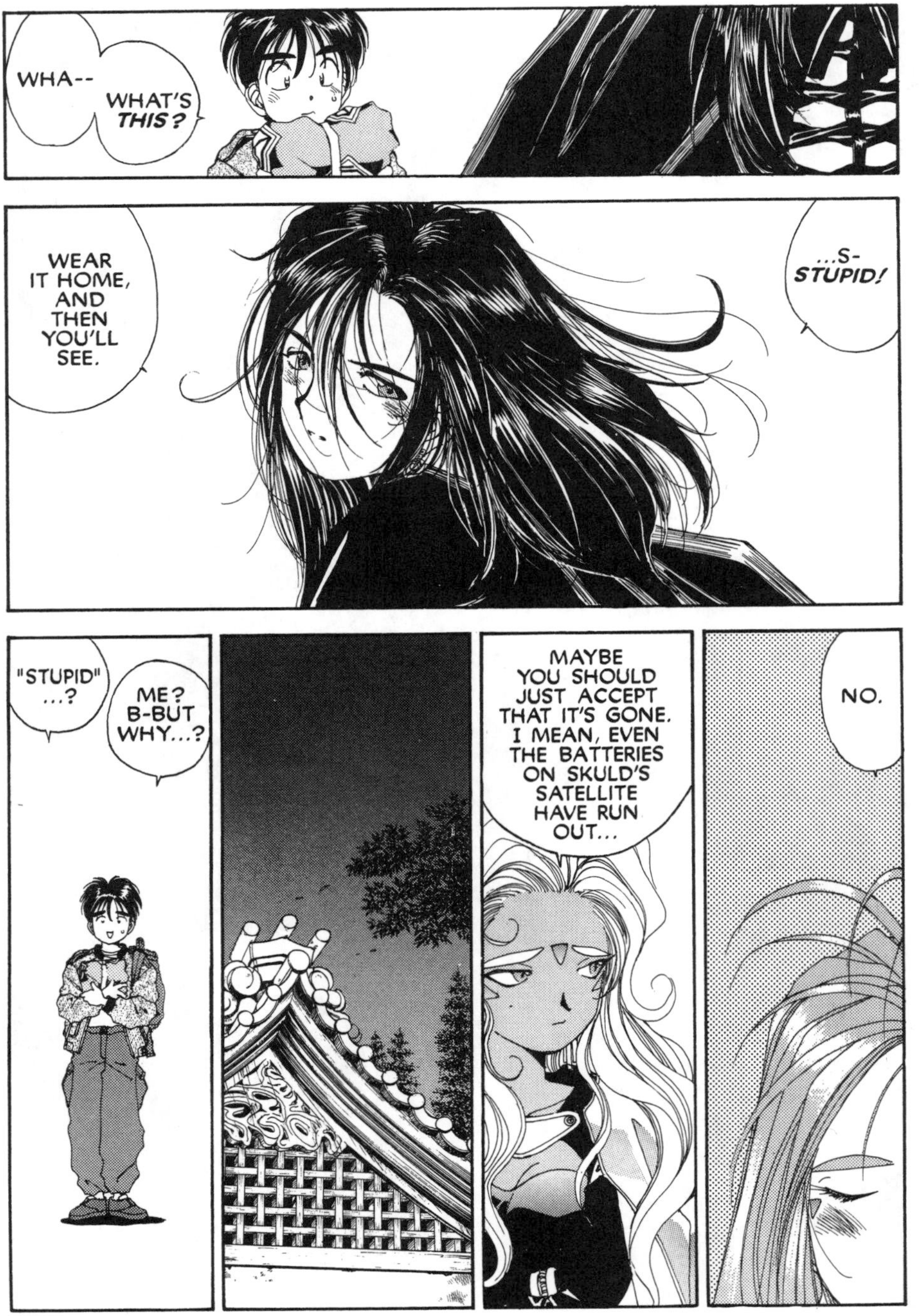
WHA--
WHAT'S *THIS?*
WEAR IT HOME, AND THEN YOU'LL SEE.
...S-*STUPID!*
"STUPID" ...?
ME? B-BUT WHY...?
MAYBE YOU SHOULD JUST ACCEPT THAT IT'S GONE. I MEAN, EVEN THE BATTERIES ON SKULD'S SATELLITE HAVE RUN OUT...
NO.

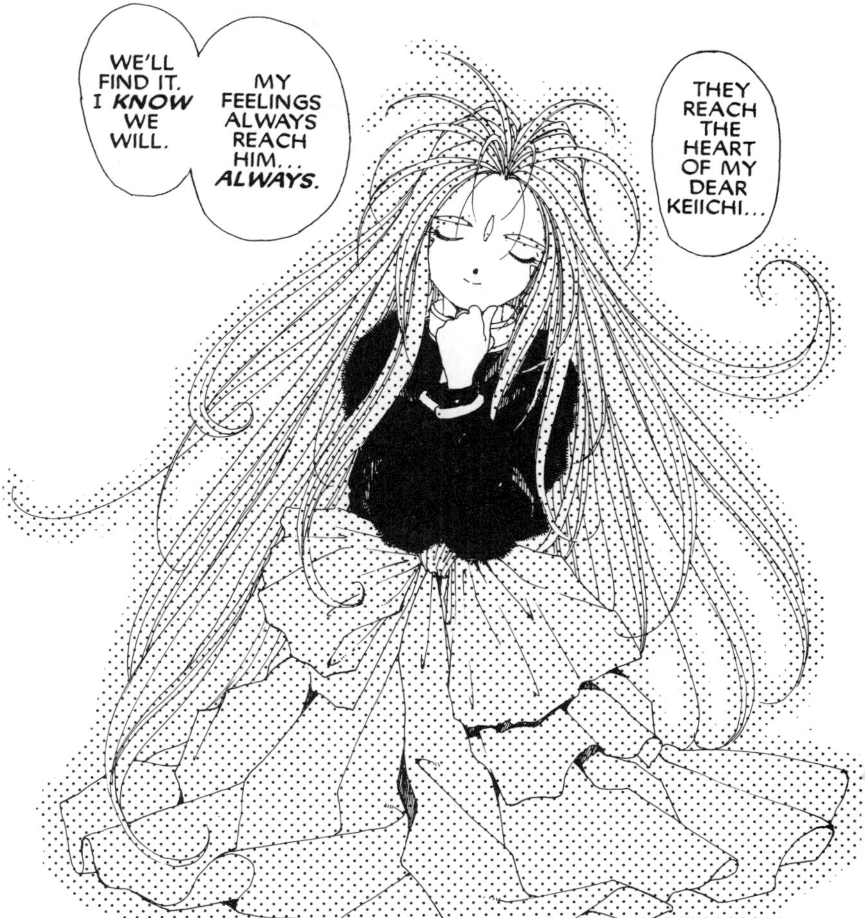
WE'LL FIND IT. I **KNOW** WE WILL.
MY FEELINGS ALWAYS REACH HIM... ***ALWAYS.***
THEY REACH THE HEART OF MY DEAR KEIICHI...

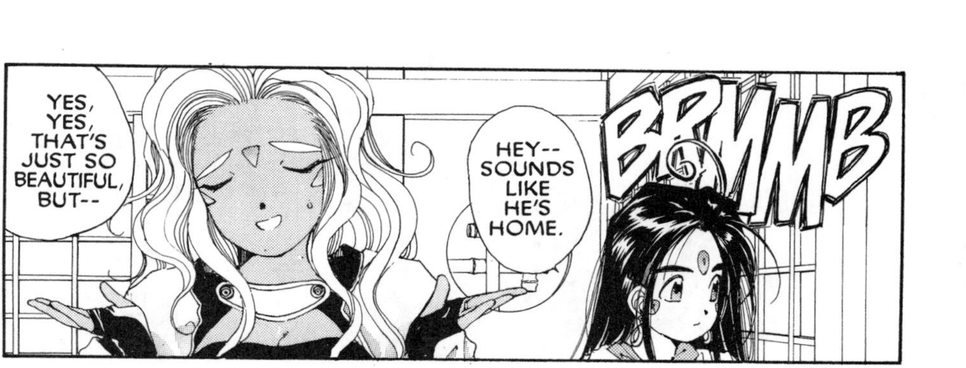
YES, YES, THAT'S JUST SO BEAUTIFUL, BUT--
HEY-- SOUNDS LIKE HE'S HOME.
BRMMB

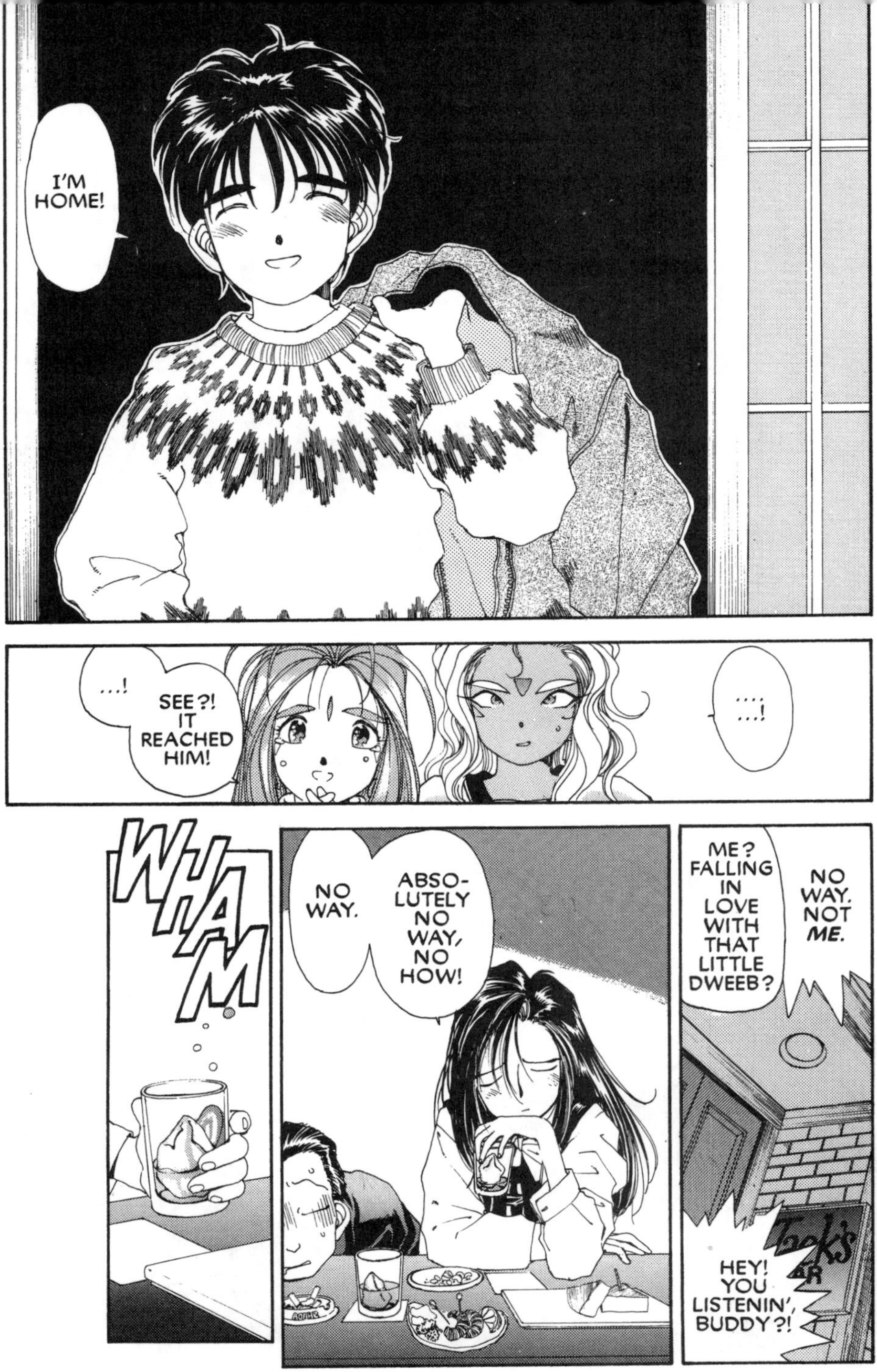
I'M HOME!
...!
SEE?! IT REACHED HIM!
... ...!
WHAM
NO WAY.
ABSOLUTELY NO WAY, NO HOW!
ME? FALLING IN LOVE WITH THAT LITTLE DWEEB?
NO WAY. NOT *ME.*
HEY! YOU LISTENIN', BUDDY?!

Oh My Goddess!

ああっ女神さまっ **The Queen of Vengeance**

Cover Gallery

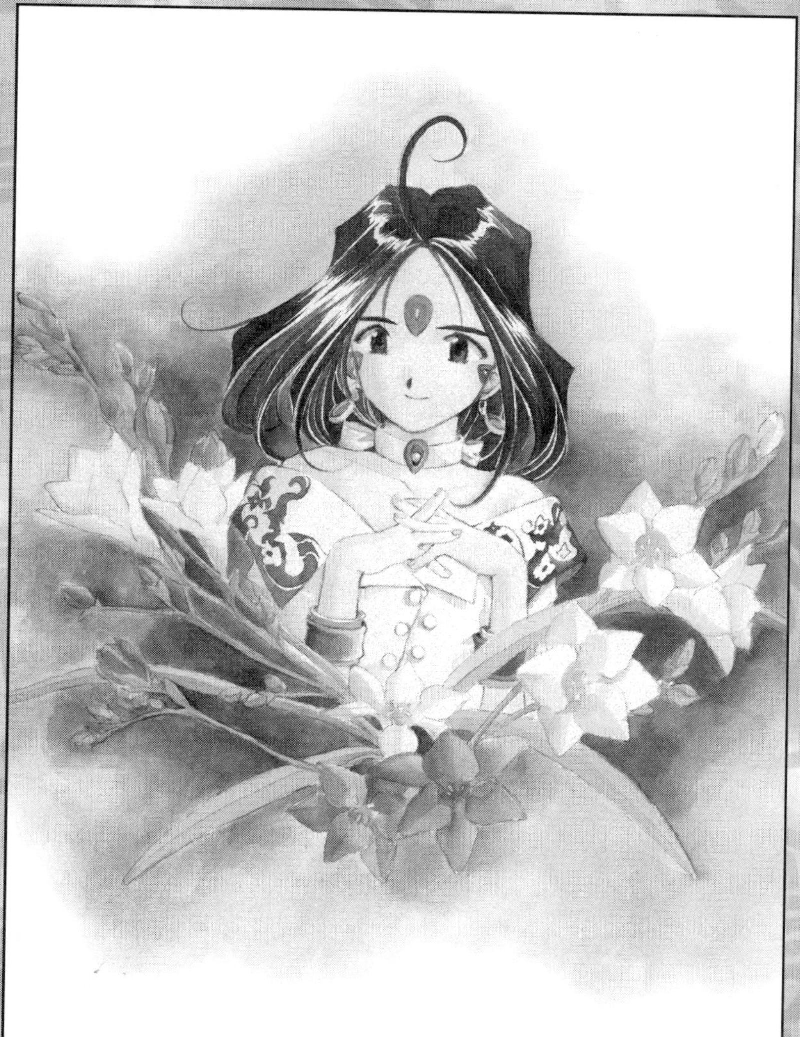

Oh My Goddess! Part IV issue 1

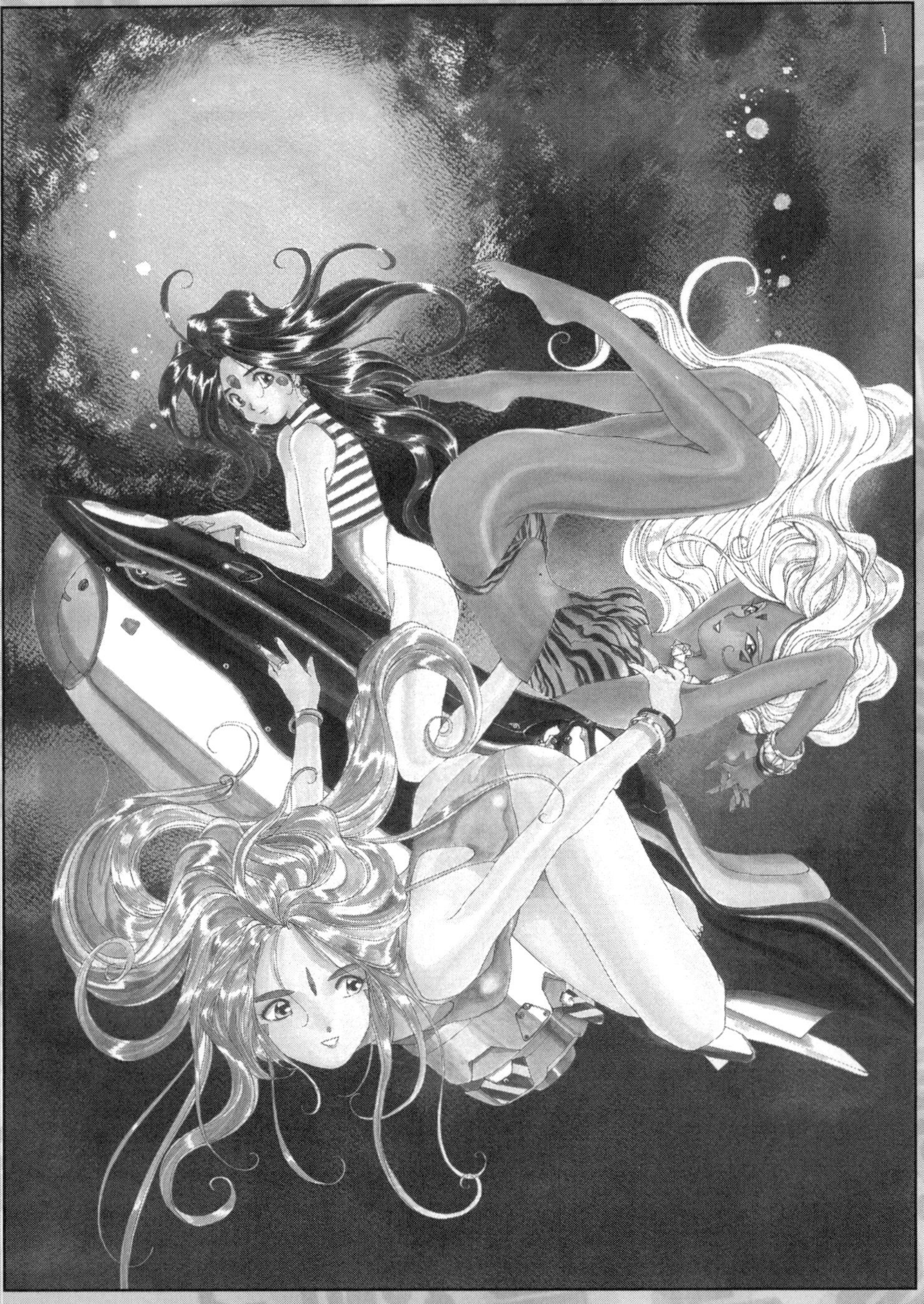

Oh My Goddess! Part IV issue 2

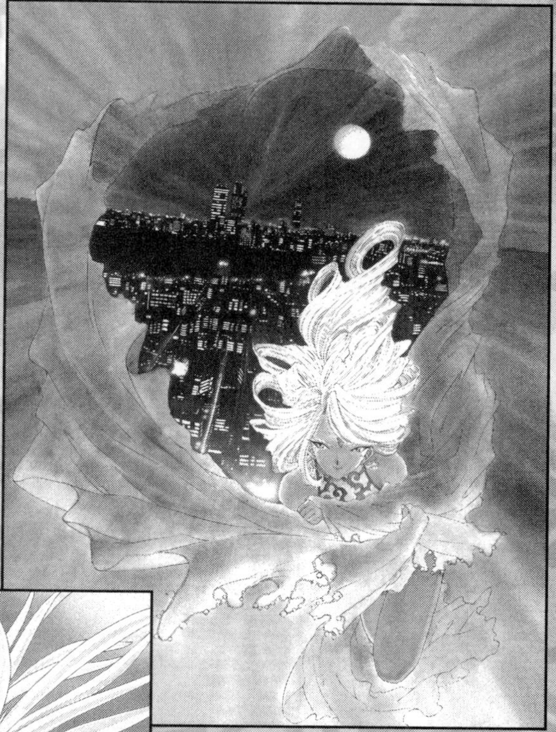

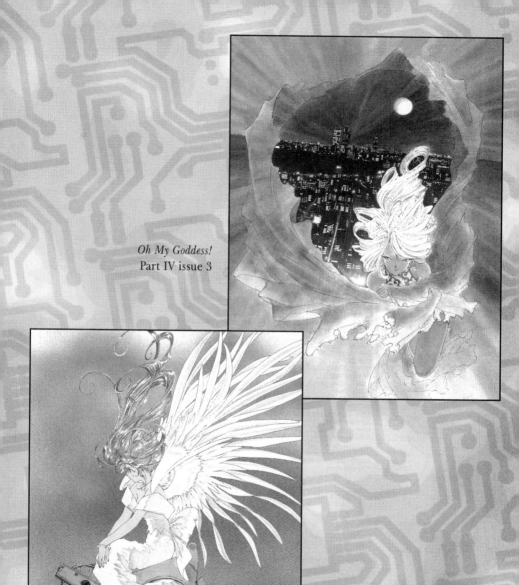

Oh My Goddess!
Part IV issue 3

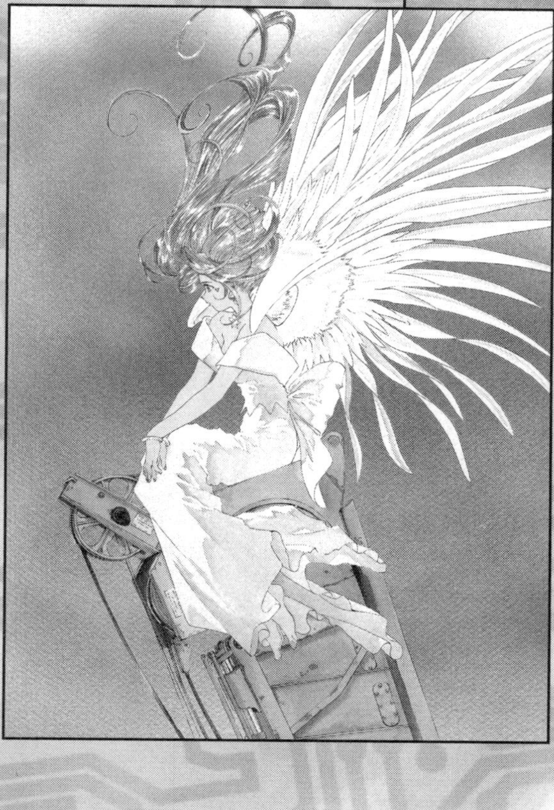

Oh My Goddess!
Part IV issue 4